Cultural Awareness for Children

Cultural Awareness for Children

Judy Allen
Teacher, Administrator, and Co-founder,
Learning Tree School

Earldene McNeill
Co-founder, Learning Tree School
Instructor of Child Development
Eastfield College, Mesquite, Texas

Velma Schmidt, Ed.D.
Professor of Early Childhood Education
University of North Texas, Denton, Texas

Addison-Wesley Publishing Company

Menlo Park, California ¤ Reading, Massachusetts ¤ New York
Don Mills, Ontario ¤ Wokingham, England ¤ Amsterdam ¤ Bonn
Sydney ¤ Singapore ¤ Tokyo ¤ Madrid ¤ San Juan ¤ Paris
Seoul, Korea ¤ Milan ¤ Mexico City ¤ Taipei, Taiwan

A Publication of the Alternative
Publishing Group

Managing Editor: Diane Silver
Project Editor: Lois Fowkes
Design Manager: Jeff Kelly

Illustrations:
  Barbara McNeill Brierton
  Learning Tree children

Design: Seventeenth Street Studios

Printed in the
United States of America.

ISBN 0-201-28731-5

8 9 10 - ML - 95 94

In Fond Memory

"What are you doing? What will you do this week to foster an appreciation for diversity? Will you put into practice what you have learned?" Dr.Schmidt's benediction rang in our ears as we left her "Teaching Children of Diverse Cultures" class. Our teacher's interest in others challenged us to do more than we were doing. She accepted all cultural backgrounds; she loved diversity and the study of it.

On May 21, 1991, as **Cultural Awareness for Children** *was in production, Velma Schmidt died very suddenly of a stroke. She was our friend, at times our colleague, but most important to us, she was our teacher and mentor. For almost twenty years the three of us studied cultures, ethnicity, and children. We wrote together, presented workshops, participated in seminars, and traveled together. We debated on some subjects and agreed on most.*

Velma visited our school on numerous occasions. "I have come to learn," she would say. She delighted in observing children making their own bread, using water in the classroom, dictating stories, or acting out a drama. She often joined in the dancing, dressing in full skirt and dancing with a determined step.

Dr. Schmidt never failed to dot an i or cross a t, and we learned a great deal from writing with her. She has touched each word in this book. We hope that its message will be a challenge to you, and that when you hear the words, "What are you doing?" you will have an answer.

—*Judy Allen*
Earldene McNeill

CONTENTS

Preface, ix

Introduction, xi

African and African-American Cultures, 3

American Indian Cultures, 35

Chinese and Chinese-American Cultures, 71

Japanese and Japanese-American Cultures, 107

Korean and Korean-American Cultures, 143

Mexican and Mexican-American Cultures, 171

Thai Culture, 199

Southeast Asian Cultures, 229

Multicultural Resources, 247

PREFACE

In 1970, several families in Dallas came together to share their ideas on awareness and understanding of the cultures found in Texas and in the United States. The idea for a school for young children developed out of this discussion—one that would integrate cultural awareness into the curriculum. Hence, The Learning Tree was established.

In the beginning, the families created the curriculum; they contributed materials and ideas from their family backgrounds. Japanese families shared child-sized kimonos, kites, and hanetsuki (a badminton game); a Sioux friend brought clothing for children to model and taught them to round dance; others brought recipes to try, games to play, and songs to learn. Families appreciated being encouraged to share their culture with the school family, and we learned that when a school is enriched with numerous cultures, the curriculum is enriched.

In addition to knowledge gained from the parents, we searched for accurate information in books and films and talked to people from different cultural backgrounds in the community. The creative activities and information in this book outline the program for cultural awareness. As the children experience each culture every year, we revise and expand the program. The approach in this book demonstrates one way young children can become culturally aware.

Our major concern is that many citizens fail to accept the diversity of traditional customs and lifestyles practiced in this country. For many years, a predominant goal in the United States was to achieve a melting pot, based on the philosophy that all cultures should be recast to form a new American society. Because of the strength of each individual's heritage, the melting pot idea did not work. By helping children and families develop an appreciation for all cultures and backgrounds while retaining their own customs and ethnic identity, some progress toward harmony can be made.

To foster an acceptance of diversity, adults working with young children need to be aware of their stereotyped views of various cultures and present correct information about each one. Racist attitudes need to be changed to positive feelings toward others. Parents must inform their children about the contributions and strengths of the many cultures in our society. Enhanced cultural appreciation by others can encourage pride in one's own ethnic heritage and build self esteem.

We recommend that you use this book in the context of a cultural experience. Combine the information in this book with the activities so that the children begin to understand something about the total life of the culture. Help children see ethnic groups as part of the modern world, separating how different peoples lived in the past from the way they live today. Provide additional authentic, accurate information about ethnic groups, and invite members of each culture to your classroom.

The background information helps to organize experiences and activities according to the children's age group and developmental level. Adapt this information to your children's level of understanding. Some of the experiences will be appropriate even for eleven year olds. Some will be above preschoolers' level of understanding, but most can be adapted. Be selective. Children who remain in the same school for several years have the advantage of building on information as they mature.

Evaluate pictures, books, and other materials before you use them. Many of the publications written twenty or more years ago may not be accurate or may give a stereotyped view of the culture; materials published in the last decade may give more authentic information and a more positive image of cultures. One reason for these changes is that authors from each culture are now writing the books.

Keep abreast of the current happenings among the cultures in your community and in the country. Inform yourself about the variations within each culture and about the differences in customs across the United States. Be aware of the continuing changes in customs and traditions.

We hope that the information and activities in this book influence the acceptance of diversity and pluralism. If people can keep their individual cultural identity while working and living in harmony, we shall all move forward. As cultural understanding for each other increases, our country and all its citizens will be enriched.

ACKNOWLEDGMENTS

We are grateful to the Learning Tree staff for their enthusiasm and hard work in making a cultural awareness program work. We would like to express special thanks to Cindy Page, Chris Kretchun, Peggy Fredrickson, and Dandi Weiss. Thank you to Joanna Streiff for her ability to capture on film those special moments.

We are also grateful to the many families and friends who have shared their cultures and their experiences with us, thereby enriching our school and lives.

Special thanks to Solina Kasten-Marquis, Learning Tree parent, for starting a Spanish program for young children and sharing her knowledge of the Hispanic culture with us. Her exceptional skills in typing and editing this manuscript make us forever indebted to her.

We would also like to mention Pat Carter, Doris Serrell, Mikki Floeter-Jenson, Elisa Lara, and Yolanda Guerra, past teachers at The Learning Tree, and thank them for adding their enthusiasm to the creation of an exceptional school.

To Betty Pryor, we express our appreciation for sharing her knowledge of good literature for children, which helped us in our search for books and materials.

INTRODUCTION

INFORMAL EDUCATION

The philosophy of The Learning Tree is that learning is effective when children work at individual levels of success in an atmosphere that encourages learning without pressure. Pressure leads to frustration. In the Learning Tree classrooms, many levels of learning are happening at the same time. Teaching plans are flexible enough to turn children's interests and questions into activities. The atmosphere is informal, with all or most of the learning centers in use at the same time.

The importance of establishing an informal atmosphere is based on the belief that children can learn to work actively with a minimum of limits or rules. Children who can move about freely in their active learning can accomplish their own goals without interfering with the activities of others. They may choose to work alone or in small groups.

The informal atmosphere of The Learning Tree is achieved through individualization, independent learning, and the arrangement of the environment into learning centers. An effective program must include these three factors and be supported by your understanding of the developmental growth of young children.

CHILD DEVELOPMENT

An informal program requires that learning experiences be based on children's developmental characteristics. The Learning Tree program can be adapted to the abilities of children from 4 to 10 years.

A basic principle of child development is that each child is a unique human being. Each child has a developmental timetable, bringing to school an individual level of functioning and growing and learning at an individual rate.

Each child also has individual interests. The program must be flexible enough to help each child be a successful learner and it must allow for a wide range of learning levels and rates of development.

Young children are very active—their muscles develop through activity, and they want to see, touch, taste, smell, and listen to everything in their environment. They learn through activity and through their senses, resting when they are tired and working when their energy is renewed through relaxation and nutritious snacks.

Since the young child is very active and often acts without thinking, socializing may be physical rather than verbal. With your suggestions and help, children begin to learn to be successful with language and to enjoy being with other children and engaging in activities using language. When experiences with other children are pleasant, many social interactions occur each day.

Social interactions necessitate language. Language is also an important key to learning throughout life. For the young child, verbal development is essential. No child should be expected to learn to read words that are not in his spoken vocabulary. The Learning Tree provides opportunities for children to extend their language by talking to each other, by hearing and creating stories and poems, and by experiencing the variety of activities planned throughout the year. Each new activity adds words to the child's spoken vocabulary. The Learning Tree environment provides many objects and materials that children can discuss and manipulate, as well as activities that give them an opportunity to experience the real thing or to role-play a point of view.

The concepts of "long ago" and "far away" require maturation and experience in order to be understood by young students. We have often found that continuity of experiences sparks interest and enthusiasm for a creative and child-centered study of diversity. For example, the developmental stages of providing a means of shelter, a basic need in all cultures, are experienced by the three-year old, crawling in and out of a child-built longhouse; the four-year old is actively involved in painting tribal symbols. At about five years of age, the child wants to dramatize stories like Little Runner of the Longhouse; the six-year old adds bold pictures of longhouses to landscape drawings and constructs models of longhouses after learning more about American Indians' diverse styles of homes. The seven-year old writes plays, stories, and poems embellished with American Indian names and symbols, and delights in visits to the American Indian display at the museum.

Young children have difficulty visualizing information and thinking abstractly, so it is essential that a program for them provides real experiences and concrete materials. Children engaged in art, numbers, science, or the letters of the alphabet must first manipulate and experiment with materials in the environment. After many hands-on experiences, they will gradually connect this understanding to letter and word symbols. For many children, success and understanding at the symbolic level occur after the age of six or seven.

The first school experience for young children provides the opportunity to live and work with others who are of a similar age. Placing children from several age groups together sets the stage for cooperative learning and for interdependence.

Younger children tend to be egocentric, or self-centered. As they live with other children and adults in the give-and-take world of school, they are able to consider how their actions affect others. Gradually, their thinking matures so that they can understand how other children feel.

INDEPENDENT LEARNING

When children begin school, they are very dependent on adults, but learning the routines and mastering basic skills encourage independence. For young children, learning is a continual process of receiving help as needed so that they develop into children who are able to learn by working independently.

Independence implies the ability to solve one's own problems, knowing that adult help is always available. Problems may include settling disagreements with others, deciding which materials to use for a project, or sharing equipment with other children. To solve a problem, different solutions are considered and a choice is made. If the result proves to be unsatisfactory, another solution must be tried. The more problem-solving experiences children have, the better they are able to judge the appropriateness of a given response. The creative activities and the opportunity to make choices at The Learning Tree give children practice in learning to solve problems and make decisions.

INDIVIDUALIZATION

Acknowledgment of individual differences is fundamental to an individualized program. Children at The Learning Tree begin at their own level, learn at their own rate, and remain with one activity for as long as they are able to benefit from it. No two children are alike in developmental level, learning rate, or the amount of time they spend on one activity.

In an individualized approach, children work at personal levels of success, so that they feel successful and are generally motivated to try new activities. Success indicates to children that learning is a satisfying activity and that they have the ability to learn. The one-to-one relationship between children and adults provides the emotional support and security young children need. The adult responds to the level, style of learning, and interests of each child.

Individualization is not confined to a one-to-one teaching/learning situation. It can take place when children with similar interests, needs, or goals meet in a small group. At times the activity of the small group may be interesting to all children. Large group activities may include making plans for the day, sharing stories, playing games, listening to music, dancing, and discussing special concerns of the school family. Problems are solved together as they come up. Children and adults meet when they need each other—when there is a common interest, a celebration, or a visitor.

The adult has many roles in the informal classroom. The adult may function as a director or teacher working with aides, parents, or volunteers. The adult is an observer, listener, facilitator, and director.

As an observer, the adult learns to know the personality, strengths, and interests of each child. On the basis of this information, equipment and materials are placed in the environment to extend individual interests. Records are made of the progress and activities of each child. The observer sees how children solve their own problems and how they help each other.

As a listener, the adult listens patiently to children's interactions, ideas and concepts the children are trying to under-

stand, levels of language development, and concerns that affect a child's emotions. The adult asks questions that lead to ways of finding answers.

As a facilitator, the adult determines when to help children solve their problems and when to let them solve problems themselves, when to encourage children into an activity

and when to let them think or rest, when to ask a child a question to extend thinking and when not to interrupt concentration, when to add materials to the environment to encourage learning and when to remove them.

As a director, the adult plans the environment so that learning can take place, keeps parents informed of the development and growth of their children, plans field trips, invites resource people to visit the classroom, encourages the growth and education of parents and others who help in the classroom, plans daily activities that interest some of the children, and introduces new ideas with concrete materials.

The adult supports children through periods of sensitivity in which they awaken as individuals with the curiosity that motivates them to explore and investigate their world. Learning centers permit such investigation to take place.

LEARNING CENTERS

The indoor and outdoor environments are arranged into learning centers. Equipment and materials that relate to one area of interest are organized in a learning center. The adults help children learn how to use the equipment, how to take care of it, and how to put it away. The learning centers help children develop:

• Social skills in the give-and-take of getting along with each other;

- Coordination and large and small muscles;
- Creativity and imagination in the use of a variety of materials;
- Emotional stability through guidance and the experience of living in a group;
- Language through conversing, planning, sharing, and problem solving;
- Reading readiness through symbolizing their own language;
- An understanding of the world around them as they dramatize adult roles and as they reconstruct the world with raw materials;
- Problem-solving skills of living and learning;
- Concepts of color, size, shape, and space.

The learning centers are:

Family Living
Music/Dance
Art
Books/Pictures
Discovery Table
Manipulatives and Games
Woodworking
Nature/Science
Outdoor
Blocks

CREATIVITY

One important goal of The Learning Tree is to keep creativity alive and spontaneous. Young children will create often if they have the freedom to do so. Important elements in nurturing creativity are a variety of materials, time, and acceptance of ideas. Set up a corner supplied with many different kinds of materials.

Children are not told what to make or which materials to use. They may or may not make an item that has been introduced or discussed. If they decide to create something, allow them to select from the available resources. Some children may find materials outdoors, or bring items to school from home. Large blocks of time enable children to work out an idea, completing a project or adding to a work in progress. The final product is not so important as the process the child uses in thinking, planning, trying out different methods and finally creating something to his or her satisfaction. Always be on hand to brainstorm, assist, encourage, support, and praise.

Children create in many ways. They make their own rules for games; they dictate or print their own stories, plays, and poems; they make their own books; they invent their own dances and new verses to songs; they create masks, models, and pictures; they build with tools, blocks, damp sand, and mud.

The photographs, drawings, and ideas in this book illustrate the many ways children create at The Learning Tree, and the emphasis on creativity is especially desirable when children participate in cultural awareness.

PARENT PARTICIPATION

An important part of a program for young children is open communication and close relationships with parents. Parents must be a part of their children's experiences in school. Parental participation in the classroom and on field trips and in the sharing of talents, hobbies, and interests helps to build a close relationship, and an active but informal parent group is a tremendous asset to a program. Monthly meetings, where parents feel comfortable and free to express themselves and where they are kept informed of the school's activities, are social as well as educational events. Informal gatherings fulfill the needs of parents and give them opportunities to discuss problems and topics of interest and to share ideas with other parents and adults. Periodic parent-teacher conferences help parents understand the growth and development of their child. Parents and teachers can work as partners through participation, meetings, and conferences.

Parents help in the classroom one day a month, teaching traditional crafts and helping children prepare ethnic foods. They also accompany children on field trips. A study group of mothers from The Learning Tree began as an informal social coffee hour, meeting regularly to study topics of their choice and to help the school. A food cooperative developed out of these discussions.

Some Learning Tree activities include the entire family. For example, parents and children enjoy Mexican and other cultural dinners as part of the experiences of these cultures. The Culture Fest, involving all of the families, is an annual event marking the end of the school year. Dinners and other cultural experiences are ways to help parents and children develop cultural awareness.

A group of very committed parents at The Learning Tree

decided that the community should know what cultural awareness means. They wanted to share with the community what their children were sharing with them—and the Culture Fest was born! The group decided to focus on a number of cultures. Research was done on the authentic foods, games, crafts, and traditions of each. These became a part of the Fest in the form of Mexican and American Indian villages, models of African homes, a papier-mache replica of Mt. Fuji, and other cultural hallmarks. Entertainers from some of the cultures performed traditional dances and music. The Culture Fest has become an annual event and fund raiser for the school.

CULTURAL AWARENESS

This book documents the portion of the program of The Learning Tree that develops cultural awareness. Many other goals and themes incorporated into the program have been omitted from this publication.

The school was designed to bring together families from many ethnic backgrounds. One goal of The Learning Tree is that children learn to appreciate and accept all people as a result of their daily experiences with children from diverse backgrounds and their families.

Some young children today have opportunities to associate with children of other cultures in their neighborhoods, schools, churches, and communities. The cultural themes in the Learning Tree program form the nucleus of a lifetime of cultural awareness and an appreciation for the richness other cultures

add to our society. Cultures may be introduced separately with an ongoing comparison of similarities and differences as each new culture is presented, or similar cross-cultural themes may be presented, beginning with the lives of the children in the classroom. Use family experiences as well as those of the community by being aware of cultural events.

The seeds of awareness are sown in this program. The lifestyles, foods, and customs of various cultures are shared. The hands-on approach is used in all

activities. Artifacts, pictures, and many other items are used to create an atmosphere representing a particular culture. Children role-play the customs and lifestyles they learn about, using clothing, household items, and tools to add reality to the dramatization. Through participation in the suggested activities and meeting families from different cultures, children will begin to appreciate the rich diversity of customs and contributions from the many cultures in America and will add to this understanding year by year. These experiences will be the beginning of a lifetime of appreciation of all cultures.

Children can decide how involved they will become in the cultural themes. Some children involve themselves completely; others participate in selected activities that capture their interest. Occasionally, a

child will not be interested in some part of the study and will consequently choose not to participate. Other materials and activities are always available for these children. The flexibility of the program allows for individual interests and different skill levels.

It is important, too, to afford children of different cultural backgrounds and orientations their privacy. Children may be unwilling to share insights into their own cultural heritage until a relationship of trust has been established with other classmates. Do not push children to participate in activities and do not put children on the spot to validate information. Let them decide how and when they wish to express their ethnicity.

A first cultural event for parents and children at The Learning Tree is a social evening with a dinner. The parents share information about their own cultural backgrounds. They discuss how the customs and lifestyles of their present family compare with that of their families when they were children. The discussions help parents to realize the cultural influences of their parents and the cultural changes they have made as parents. The parents share food they enjoyed as children and talk about how the present American culture affects their children. When children learn to love and respect each other, the attitudes of the parents are also influenced. A related goal of cultural awareness is that through studying the contributions of all cultures, children will develop an appreciation and understanding of their own culture.

Cultural Awareness for Children

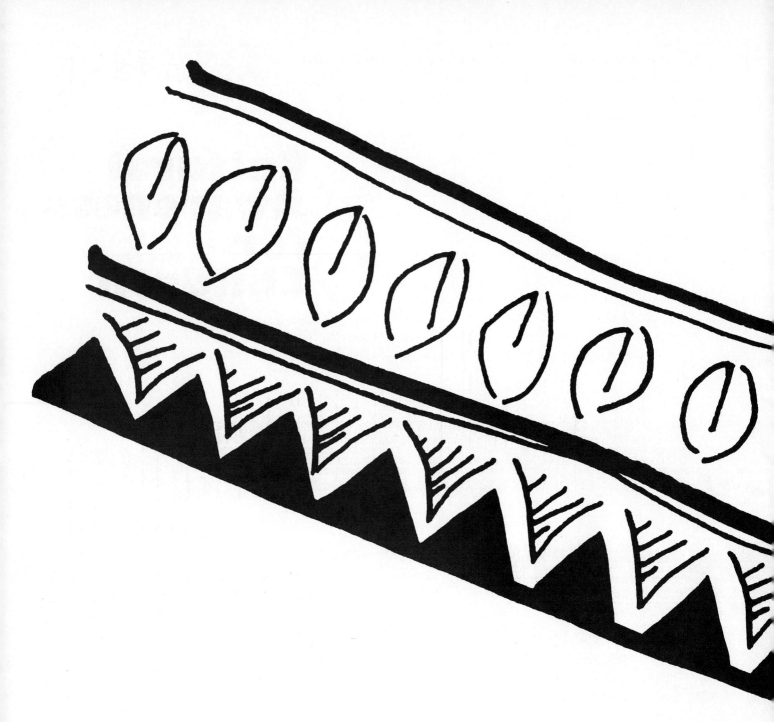

AFRICAN AND AFRICAN-AMERICAN CULTURES

Africa is a vast continent of varied regions and many cultures. Children learn that modern technology has brought high-rise apartment buildings, supermarkets, and fast food to many areas, but it is the traditional lifestyle of the countryside that sparks excitement for dressing in Ashanti kente cloth, gathering items to sell in an Ouadia marketplace, or creating a Basonga face mask.

Experiences with food, folktales, African languages, and family customs bring to life a rich African heritage. Many African-American families explore African customs and history in an effort to understand their beginnings. All people may benefit from an enhanced awareness of African influence on literature and the arts worldwide.

The diversity of Africa and its people promotes an investigation of similarities and differences within a culture and an appreciation for cultural values.

Mary Lois Sweatt, our consultant for this unit, is an artist and an expert in African movement and dance. She has worked with African-American children and adults to foster an appreciation of their culture and heritage through dance and movement.Having also traveled extensively in African countries, she has been a valuable resource person to The Learning Tree from its beginning.

FAMILY LIVING

HOMES

Although major population centers have public buildings and apartments and homes that resemble those in other cities, traditional dwellings are found throughout Africa. Corrugated iron roofs now replace many of the thatched variety. The way people live depends upon the region in which they live. The climate affects the way people dress and the kinds of houses they build. Along the coast in West Africa, houses may be built on stilts; in Chad and other West African countries, rural homes are made with grass and mud walls and thatched roofs; the Dogon group build their houses with woven straw and mud walls on the sides of mountains.

In the classroom, the Family Living Center provides the foundation for cultural awareness of African experiences. How families live, what they eat, what they wear, and how they care for their babies are explored in this center. Children expand the ideas they develop in the center with activities from other learning centers in the room.

When the environment is changed into an African village,

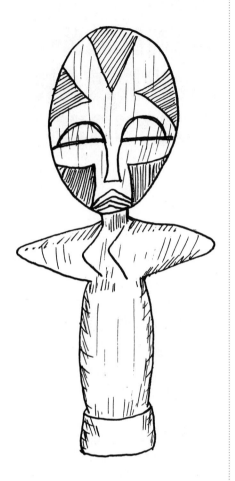

young children role-play the life of the village. They try on African clothes, play African musical instruments, wear authentic wooden masks, examine carved wooden statues and other works of art, and listen to African music and folktales from many of the countries on the continent.

Benin Tree House

A loft area can become a tree house on stilts providing a model of an African home, like those built along the coast of Dahomey, now known as Benin. Place green bamboo sticks that are long enough to wedge between the floor and ceiling around the loft to resemble the tall native grasses. Attach straw mats to the sides of the loft to resemble the straw-covered houses of the Dogon.

Nigerian Thatched Hut

A large cardboard carton may be used to make a mud home such as those found in Nigeria. Windows and doors are cut out and children paint the sides in earth tones and pile dried grass on the top to resemble a thatched roof.

Chad Round House

The round houses of Chad and the Cameroons may be constructed using two cardboard pattern boards, available at fabric stores. Unfold them and attach them together to form a cylinder. Cut a door in the front. Large circles of brown butcher paper may be used for the roof; fringe the edges to resemble a thatched roof.

A descriptive book to read to children about the lifestyles of West African groups is *The Village of Round and Square Houses* by Ann Grifalconi. Other excellent resources are *Ashanti to Zulu*, by Margaret Musgrove, and *Who's in Rabbit's House?* by Verna Aardema.

DRAMATIC PLAY

The following items may be provided or made to encourage role-playing and dramatization of folktales as well as to help children become familiar with the artifacts of these cultures.

—baskets made of woven straw to be carried on the head or used to serve food.
—bead necklaces, bracelets, earrings, and other jewelry made by children.
—bowls made of wood or gourds.
—carved wooden Akuaba dolls.
—carved wooden animals.
—carved wooden masks, available at import stores.
—drinking vessels, bowls, rattles, and other items made from calabash gourds.
—straw mats for the floor.

CLOTHING

Traditional clothing varies according to region and group. Only a few examples are included here. Today, many African families also wear Western-style clothing.

—A *dashiki* (De-SHE-ke) is an East African ceremonial shirt worn by men.
— *Kente* (KEN-te) cloth is brightly colored cloth that is draped around the body and knotted on one shoulder; it is worn by both men and women.
— Ceremonial headdresses are worn in dances by many different groups.
— A kerchief or *gele* is a cloth head covering that may be worn by African women of many different groups and by many African Americans.
— Dance skirts made of raffia are worn in ceremonial dances by the Dogon, Masai, and Zulu tribes.
— An *oja* is a Nigerian baby carrier made from a wide sash that is wrapped around the mother's body to form a secure sling; babies are carried, rocked, and nursed as their mothers go about their daily work.
See Creative Art Expression in this unit.

Ji-Nongo-Nongo Means Riddles by Verna Aardema and *The Cow-Tail Switch: A Folktale of Africa* (filmstrip from Coronet Film and Video) are two excellent resources.

FOOD

Although foods differ from region to region, some are common throughout most of the continent; corn (mealie is a common mush), cassava (tapioca), yams, and bananas are typical.

(Safety Note: Be sure to obtain parental permission before allowing children to eat anything, in case of allergies or diet restrictions.)

Fou-fou

Fou-fou is a dish served in many African countries. It has the consistency of pudding and is usually served with the main course. In the West African countries of Ga and Ghana, fou-fou is made from cassava or white yams; the Hausa tribe makes it out of cornmeal; Nigerians make it out of rice. Fou-fou is eaten by scooping up a small amount with three fingers and then dipping it into a stew.

Prepare fou-fou by cooking tapioca pudding without sugar or substitute cornmeal mush using the following recipe.

Boil 2 C water. Add 1 t salt and 1 C cornmeal. Cook, stirring constantly, until the mixture thickens. Serve with a pat of butter.

Tapioca Fruit Soup

2 T quick-cooking tapioca
1 1/2 C water
1 T sugar
Dash of salt
1/2 C orange juice concentrate
1/2 C diced orange sections
1 sliced banana

Combine the tapioca and water in a saucepan. Cook and stir over medium heat until mixture comes to a boil. Remove from heat.

Add sugar, salt, and orange juice. Stir to blend. Cool. Stir again after 15 minutes. Cover and chill. Fold in orange sections and sliced bananas. Other fruits may be substituted.

Tapioca Pudding

Have a child or adult read the recipe from a package of tapioca. Children can measure and stir the pudding. Discuss how tapioca comes from the cassava root. Some children may wish to write or dictate the steps they followed.

Boiled Yams

Yams, or sweet potatoes, are grown in many sections of Africa and are a staple for many African families.

Let children peel the raw yams, put them in a pan, and cover them with water. Add a small amount of salt to the water and bring it to a boil. Cook until tender. Drain. Then add sugar and butter and let children mash the yams before eating them.   Yams may also be cooked with the peel on. Place them in a pan, cover with water, add salt, and boil until tender. Drain, cool, and peel. Then slice and serve. Have butter, sugar, salt, pepper, and cinnamon available so that children can experiment with different flavors.

Fried Yams

Fried yams are eaten like french fries. In Nigeria, a fried yam snack food is called "small chop". To prepare it, children peel the yams, allowing about one half per child. Adults cut them into thin slices and drop the slices into hot oil to deep-fry them. Drain and serve in small cups or paper cones.

Groundnuts

Peanuts are called groundnuts in Africa. They are grown in Ghana, Nigeria, and many other West African countries. Groundnut stew is eaten by many families.

African Groundnut Stew

2 lbs beef stew meat or chicken
1 C chopped onion
1 C peanut butter
3 T curry powder
3 T flour
2 cans beef or chicken stock
1/2 C chopped celery
1 box frozen cut okra
4 chopped carrots
2 squash, sliced
2 C roasted peanuts

Brown the meat in oil. Add the chopped onion. Gradually mix in the peanut butter, curry powder, and flour. Add the stock, celery, okra, carrots, squash, and peanuts. Simmer until the vegetables are tender.

Peanut Stew

Peanut stew can be made from raw or roasted peanuts. Roasted peanuts give a better flavor. Children enjoy shelling the peanuts.

1 C roasted, shelled peanuts
4 C water
5 beef bouillon cubes

Combine all ingredients. Bring to a boil and simmer for 15 minutes. Add salt to taste. Serve hot or cold.

Cocoa/Chocolate

One of the most valuable trees in the tropical rain forests of Africa is the cacao. Seeds from the cacao trees are used to make cocoa and chocolate. Brilliant pictures depict the gathering of cocoa in Africa in the book *The Drums Speak*, by Marcan and Evelyn Bernheim.

Provide several different forms of chocolate for tasting: powdered cocoa, unsweetened chocolate, chocolate candy bars, instant chocolate pudding, and white chocolate. Some children are surprised that sugar has to be added to chocolate to sweeten it. Extend the tasting experience by having children prepare their own servings of hot chocolate or chocolate pudding using the following recipes.

Hot Chocolate

Mix together 1 t cocoa, 3 t sugar, and 1/3 C powdered milk in a cup. Fill the cup with hot water and stir.

Chocolate Pudding

Mix 2 T instant chocolate pudding and 1/3 C cold milk in a cup. Stir until thick.

Milk and Honey

An African custom is to prepare a beverage of milk and honey in a large trough made from a hollowed-out log. Everyone drinks from the trough using long straws made from reeds. In the classroom children can drink their milk and honey from individual bowls.

Mix 1 C honey and 1/2 gallon cold milk. Pour into a large wooden salad bowl to resemble a trough. Then dip individual portions into small bowls. Drink with drinking straws in the African style.

Peanut Butter

Put 1 1/2 C salted roasted peanuts, 1 T oil, and 1 t honey into a blender and blend to the desired consistency. Let children spread it on crackers or bread.

Fried Bananas

Bananas are grown in many countries in the rain forest region of Africa. To fry bananas, slice them lengthwise and sprinkle with lemon juice, brown sugar, and cinnamon. Fry in a small amount of butter. *The Little Cooks: Recipes from Around the World for Boys and Girls*, adapted by Eve Tharlet, describes this recipe.

African Market

The markets of many countries of East and West Africa are colorful places, full of exciting sounds and varied smells. People from far and near bring their wares to sell or trade at a central location. Many kinds of food—oranges, tomatoes, cassava, yams, coconuts, dates, groundnuts—are available. Meat and prepared foods, such as groundnut stew, may also be purchased. Baskets, pottery, wood carvings, jewelry, and clothing are displayed on straw mats on the ground. Musicians with drums, flutes, and kundis may stroll through the crowds, playing and adding to the excitement.

Market day is a special day in many villages because the marketplace is where people meet to exchange news and see friends.

More information on the African market may be found in the Special Events section.

Count on Your Fingers African Style, by Claudia Zaslarksy, gives a splendid view of a market.

CREATIVE ART EXPRESSION

CLOTHING

One of the first things young children want to do when exploring a culture is to try on traditional clothing. Have clothing available for children to examine or let them make their own by adding a creative touch to an existing garment or using a pattern and starting from scratch. Involve the children in measuring for size, deciding where to cut, determining what tools are needed, and selecting materials. Foster creativity by asking questions, supervising the project and providing reinforcement.

Headdresses

A headdress made of banana-leaf fiber is an important part of a dance costume when a successor to the chief of the Watusi tribe of East Central Africa is selected. It is also worn during the dance performed by a young prince who is preparing to become a royal page. In the past, headdresses made of lion's manes were worn by Masai dancers of Kenya. Today headdresses made from banana leaves and ostrich feathers are worn by Zulu men of West Africa.

To make a ceremonial headdress, children may decorate 12-by-18-inch sheets of colored construction paper. Cut fringe along one 18-inch side, leaving a two-inch headband, and staple the band to form a crown. Colored feathers, yarn, and colored paper glued to the headdress give a special effect.

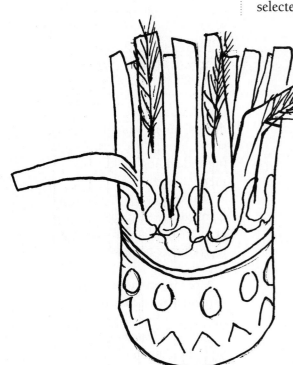

Ashanti Kente Cloth

Kente cloth is a brilliantly colored, intricately woven fabric that was first worn by the kings of the Ashanti nation in Ghana, West Africa. Nyame the Sky God, a character in the folktale *A Story, A Story* by Gail E. Haley, wears a kente cloth robe.

Kente cloth was originally made of silk and was used to make robes that were draped around the body and tied on one shoulder. It was also used to make sashes and turban-like head coverings. It has become very popular with many African Americans, providing a vivid link to their African heritage.

Fabric resembling the intricate designs of kente cloth is sold in many fabric stores. Make kente cloth robes for children to wear in the classroom by cutting pieces measuring about one by two yards. Wrap the fabric around the child's body and knot it on one shoulder.

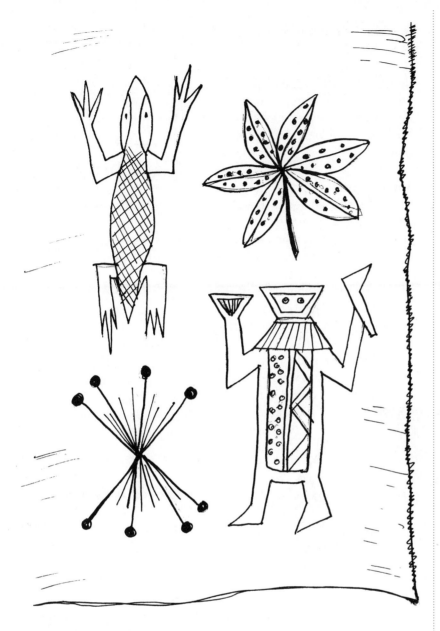

Ashanti Printed Cloth

The Ashanti people of Ghana painted and stamped patterns on fabrics used for garments. To make Ashanti cloth, you need fabric and items that can be used for printing designs, such as spools, bottle caps, small cookie cutters, and vegetables cut into shapes.

To make printing pads, place folded wet paper towels in a shallow dish. Sprinkle about 1 tablespoon of dry tempera paint onto each wet towel. Let it set until paint is moist. Let the children press various items on the pad and then use them to print designs on the fabric.

Tie Dyeing (*Adire)*

In Nigeria, the people of the Baulé tribe use a special method to create beautiful designs on fabric. There it is known as *adire,* but in the U.S. it is known as tie dyeing.

To create tie-dyed designs on fabric you will need white fabric cut in 18-inch squares (old sheets are suitable); a dowel rod, one inch in diameter and about 12 inches long; string; a four-color package of food coloring; four bottles of alcohol (one bottle per color used); and paint brushes.

Place the end of the dowel rod in the center of the cloth. Wrap the cloth over the dowel, tying it tightly with string at two-inch intervals. Pour one bottle of food coloring into each bottle of alcohol and mix to make the dyes. Let children paint the cloth between the strings with dye, using several different colors. When the cloth is dry, unwind the string, remove the dowel, and watch children's faces as they discover the wonderful designs they have created!

Dance Skirt

Raffia or grass dance skirts are worn by Dogon and Zulu tribesmen of East and West Africa in ceremonial dances. Children enjoy wearing these skirts as they play drums and listen to authentic African music.

To make a dance skirt, use a large, tan-colored plastic trash bag. Fold the bag lengthwise over a strip of fabric. Cut fringes on the bag in long slits to within one inch of the fold. Gather the bag on the fabric strip and tie it around the child's waist. Two bags may be stapled together end to end for larger children. Brown butcher paper may also be used for making dance skirts.

Kerchief and *Gele*

African women of numerous tribes wear head coverings to market and as part of formal festive dress. These styles are popular and are worn by many African American women today.

The kerchief is a triangle-shaped scarf that is worn tied around the head and knotted either at the nape of the neck or in front. The *gele* is a scarf several yards long that is wrapped around and around the head turban-style. Both of these head coverings are decorated with elaborate designs.

Children make kerchiefs and geles using the Ashanti cloth they have printed. They decorate a 16-by-28-by-16-inch triangle of fabric to make a kerchief, and a 72-by-12-inch rectangle to make a gele.

Dashiki

A *dashiki* is a ceremonial shirt made from colorful patterned fabric.

It is worn by Nigerian men. Women in many West African countries also wear long dashiki-type dresses. The dashiki has become fashionable in America for men, women, and children.

Fold a 12-by-36-inch piece of fabric. Cut a neck opening that is large enough to fit over the child's head. The sides are left open. Let the child use crayons and marking pens to decorate the dashiki. It can be worn with or without a sash.

Fabric printed with African designs and colors can be purchased at fabric stores. You may use it to make several dashikis for children to wear during role-playing.

Money Bags

In Ghana and Nigeria, men and women wear money bags around their necks when going to market. The decorated bags are made of leather. The Yoruba of Nigeria have elaborately beaded money bags; other groups decorate their bags with feathers.

Children can make money bags to wear at their own African Market.

Cut heavy fabric or natural-colored vinyl wall covering into 21-by-8-inch pieces. Fold the length of fabric up 8 inches to form a pocket and staple or sew it together on each side. Fold the other end down to make a flap for the bag. Attach a 25-inch strap to the bag so that it may be carried around the neck. Children can use beads, feathers, and marking pens to decorate the bags.

Excellent resources are *Africa's Living Arts,* by Anthony Marshall, *Ashanti to Zulu: African Traditions,* by Margaret Musgrove, and *Count Your Way through Africa,* by Jim Haskins.

JEWELRY

The creativity of some Africans is demonstrated in the way they use bone, shell, stone, and metal to make the bracelets, necklaces, earrings, and rings that they wear on their arms, legs, fingers, and necks. Provide materials, books, and pictures so that children are able to create all kinds of jewelry.

Rings

Rings may be made by forming multiple loops of fine silver- or gold-colored wire. A small stone may be attached to the ring by wrapping wire around it several times and giving the ends a twist.

Necklaces and Bracelets

Necklaces and bracelets may be made by stringing seashells, animal bones, beads, shells, seeds, pods, and nuts. Children use yarn, inexpensive leather strips, string, or colored cord or electrical wire for stringing. Hardware stores sell small drill bits that can be used for making holes, and colored wire is available from the installation department of telephone companies. Leather strips may be found in quantity at sporting goods stores. Gold cording may be purchased at a fabric store.

Bones from turkey necks make beautiful jewelry! Ask parents to save the bones. Boil the neck in water until all the meat falls off. Then wash the bones with soap, drain, and dry in a sunny window.

Bones may then painted with brightly colored or metallic gold or copper tempera paint. Add a small amount of white glue to the paint to prevent it from rubbing off. After the paint is dry, let children string the bones with beads and other materials.

Earrings

To make large, dangling earrings, children string bones, metal disks, or beads on colored telephone-cable wire, fasten the ends of wire together, and hang them over their ears.

Masai Collar Necklaces

Masai women wear circles of metal wire that hang from the neck and cover the entire chest. The necklaces are so heavy that special leaves are used as padding to protect the skin.

To make a Masai necklace, cut the center out of a large paper plate. Let children deco-

rate the rim of the plate with designs and punch holes in the outer edge. They may hang shells and clay beads from the outer edge of the rim with wire. Cut the rim in one place to fit it around the child's neck.

Clay Beads

To make clay beads, mix together 1 C cornstarch, 2 1/2 C baking soda, and 1 1/2 C cold water. Cook the mixture, stirring frequently, until thick, or until the mixture pulls away from the sides of the pan. Let the mixture cool and have children form small, marble-sized beads from the clay. Use a drinking straw to make a hole in each bead. Bake 45 minutes at 300°.

Darkness and the Butterfly, by Ann Grifalconi, and *Mufaro's Beautiful Daughters,* by John Steptoe, are stories children enjoy.

DECORATIVE ART

Charcoal Drawings

Some Africans use charcoal as a drawing tool. Children can break pieces off of a burned log and use the charcoal to create designs on paper. Show children the work of Nathan Jones, an African-American artist who is famous for his charcoal drawings.

Masks

African tribes combine the use of elaborately decorated masks with movement and music to celebrate life. Many cultures in Africa use masks in their dances and ceremonies. A collection of authentic carved masks from Africa is useful in a classroom. Children can use them to dramatize, to create other masks, and to study design.

Have cardboard, construction paper, and poster board avail-

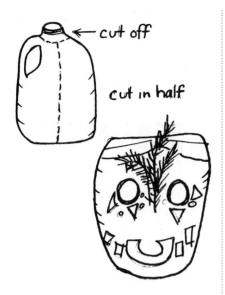

able. After children become familiar with different styles of masks, they cut the cardboard to desired sizes and shapes. Using a variety of materials such as feathers, yarn, shells, clay, paint, and metal disks, children may decorate the masks, adding other features with paint, crayons, and marking pens. Attach a string or piece of elastic to the sides of the mask to hold it in place.

Basonga Masks

Masks resembling the ones worn by the Basonga tribe of the Congo River region may be made from gallon milk jugs (one jug makes two masks). Cut the jug in half and cut holes for eyes, as shown in the illustration. Children can decorate the mask with dried beans, seeds, colored macaroni, feathers, yarn, wire, metal disks, or scraps of shiny paper.

Wonderful books to read to children when making masks are *Why the Sun and the Moon Live in the Sky,* by Elphinstone Daynell; *Who's in Rabbit's House?* by Verna Aardema; *Aio the Rainmaker,* by Fiona French; and *Lord of the Dance,* by Veronique Tadjo.

Shields

Dazzling shields covered with animal fur were once a part of a Zulu warrior's tribal costume. Shields were also used by the Masai, as well as by tribes in the Cameroons. Some were made from a hippopotamus hide painted with designs. Today, Africans use shields in dances and ceremonies to act out the victories won by warriors in the past.

Provide materials, including marking pens, crayons, leather strips, paints, fabric, and brad fasteners. Encourage children to study pictures of shields and discuss design ideas with one another. Cut 12-by-18-inch pieces of cardboard in the desired shapes. Let children use the materials provided to decorate their shields. They should decide where to attach the strap, depending on how the shield is to be carried.

You may also have children tie sticks together to make a frame; willow sticks work well. Cut a sheet of paper to match the shape of the frame. Children can decorate it and attach it to the frame, then add a strap for carrying.

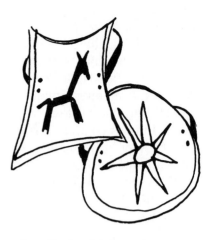

Fly Whisks (Ilukeres)

Ilukeres were carried by rulers of the village. They were used by the Ashanti kings of Ghana to denote royalty and also to fan away flying insects. They were usually made from the tail of an elephant or lion and had engraved gold handles. Today an authentic ilukere is a prized art object.

To make an ilukere, cut 1-by-10 strips of crepe paper. Gather twelve strips of the paper at one end and tape them to the end of a 5-inch length of cardboard tube. Attach a loop of cord to the other end of the tube for carrying on the wrist. Decorate the handle of the ilukere using marking pens, colored tape, or colored paper.

These make a pleasing swishing sound. An excellent example of an ilukere is one owned by Nyame the Sky God in the folktale *A Story, A Story,* by Gail Haley.

CLAY, POTTERY, AND BASKETS

Clay

Children are able to manipulate clay according to their developmental stages. Children make clay ropes, snakes, and pound clay into many shapes, moving on to create figures and specific items. Encourage children to combine symbols and objects together to create miniature scenes, toys, or dioramas.

Pottery

Throughout the centuries, like many other cultures worldwide, Africans have used local clay to make tools, utensils, dishes, and ornaments. Today, some Africans still make pottery by hand, using ancient methods and incorporating traditional designs.

To make clay pottery pieces, use natural red clay or potter's clay. See the Creative Art Expression section in the American Indian Cultures unit for directions.

Dogon and Zulu Houses

A small replica of a Dogon or Zulu mud-and-thatch home can be made using paper and clay. Have children form a circular wall of clay. To make the thatched roof, cut straws from an old broom or use dry grass. Gather it into a bunch and tie it together at one end. Fan the other ends of the bundle into a cone shape to set on the top of the wall. Use a sharp tool to make a door on one side of the wall.

Barotse Coil Baskets

The Barotse tribe in Zambia uses woven grass fiber to make a coiled basket. To copy this method of basket making, you will need styrofoam soup bowls, cotton rope cut in two-foot lengths, and white glue. Show children how to dip the rope in glue and coil it inside the bowl, starting in the center of the bowl and working around to build up the sides. When the rope reaches the top of the bowl, squirt more glue between the rope layers and let the basket dry. When completely dry, carefully remove the basket from the bowl. Let children paint the basket with bright colors; mix approximately one part paint to one part white glue.

African-American Artists

Many noted artists have been inspired and influenced by African art. Have books, paintings, sculpture, and pottery available for children to examine to gain an appreciation for the contributions of African-American artists. Include the work of Vivian Browne, Jean Lacy, Paul Keene, Franklin White, Russ Thompson, Raymond Saunders, Frank Frazier, Charles Searles, and David Philpot.

NATURE AND SCIENCE

ANIMALS

East Africa is the home of the largest number of big mammals in the world. In Kenya there are elephants, lions, cheetahs, giraffes, rhinoceroses, crocodiles, and hippopotamus. (Tigers *do not* live in Africa.)

Wildlife refuges and game preserves are found throughout countries in Africa to protect these national treasures. Many of these animals have been designated as endangered species. Discuss the importance of protecting these animals and the meaning of "threatened" or "endangered" species.

Display large pictures and posters of African animals and make picture books available. An excellent periodical with a wealth of detailed information can be obtained from *Zoo Books*, P.O. Box 85271, San Diego, CA 92138. Other resources are *African Animal Giants and Safari!*, from the National Geographic Society.

Sets of plastic zoo animals are fun for children to play with in a sand table. Encourage children to create natural habitats for the animals, using rocks, plants, grasses, and painted backdrops.

Snakes (Da Ga)

Da Ga is the Nigerian word for snake. Children can create paper snakes, using shades of brown, green, and orange construction paper. Cut strips of paper measuring 1 by 8 inches.and let children put the strips together to form chains, flattening each link. Cut out heads on the fold so that they are a double thickness of paper. Attach the head to the flattened chain with a brad so that it can swivel.

Why Mosquitoes Buzz in People's Ears, by Verna Aardema, provides an inspiring beginning for this creative venture.

PLANTS

Coconuts

Coconut palm trees grow in East Africa. The meat of the coconut is used for food and the milk is used for drink. The tree's fronds or branches are used to make thatched roofs. The oil from the dried coconut meat, called copra, is used in making soap and cosmetics.

Coconuts provide many learning experiences for young children. They enjoy examining the coconut, feeling its surface, and shaking it to hear the milk splash inside. The activity also encourages many questions that often lead the child to resources outside the classroom.

One way to open a coconut is to hammer a nail into one of its eyes. Children are eager to make this hole themselves. Some may want to taste the milk. After the hole is made, pour all of the milk out of the coconut. Then place the coconut on newspapers spread on the floor and have children take turns hitting it with a hammer until it splits. As the children taste the meat of the coconut, encourage them to

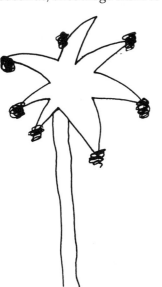

suggest appropriate words to describe the taste. Provide packaged coconut for children to compare with fresh coconut.

Gourds

In some parts of Africa, gourds grow wild, and the bottle-shaped fruits are dried and used to hold water and other liquids. One kind of gourd, the calabash, has a hard enough shell to be used as a cooking pot over a fire. Other types of African gourds are used as cups, bowls, and musical instruments.

Children can do many things with gourds. Display a variety for close examination. They will shake them and guess what is inside. Cut one open to show them the inside. A cleaned out gourd can be used as a cup or bowl. Save the seeds for planting in the spring, allowing gourds to mature on the vine. In some locations, this may take several months. Seeds may also be used for making jewelry or decorating masks.

Groundnuts

Groundnuts in Africa are the same as peanuts in America. Provide a basket of groundnuts for children to count, crack, and eat. Discuss how they grow and how they are harvested, using pictures and other resource materials. If possible, take a trip to a peanut field. Share information about George Washington Carver and his development of the many uses of peanuts.

LANGUAGE DEVELOPMENT

Use language development to help children become aware of African cultures. Hands-on experiences involve talking with other children and adults, listening to stories and new ideas, and learning new vocabulary. Real experiences give meaning to new words. Using the new words may be the beginning of learning a second language. The African environment in the classroom encourages thinking, exploring, and asking questions as children begin to understand the new culture.

Vocabulary

The following words may be used in labeling pictures and objects in the room.

Terms

Swahili (swa-HE-le)—the language spoken throughout East Africa

Bantu (BAN-tu)—a tribe in South Africa

Masai (MA-si)—an East African tribe that raises cattle

Dogon (DOH-gohn)—a tribe of cliff dwellers in West Africa

Anansi (ah-NAN-see)—a character in a group of African folktales; Anansi is part spider and part man

Basonga (ba-SON-ga)—tribe of people in Congo River region

Barotse (ba-ROH-tsee)—Zambian tribe

Swahili Words

axatse (ox-AHT see)—shaker made from a gourd

baba (BAH-bah)—father

chakula (cha-KOO-la)—food
fagio (fah-GEE-o)—broom
gudulia (goo-DOO-lee-ah)—clay jar
jambo (JAM-bo)—hello
karibu (ca-REE-bu)—welcome
mama (MAH-mah)—mother
mbira (m-BEER-a)—thumb piano
ngoma (na-GO-mah)—drum and dance
punda (POON-dah)—donkey
rafiki (rah-FEE-kee)—friend
shekere (SHEK-er-ee)—another name for *axatse*
tembo (TEM-bo)—elephant
uzuri (u-ZOO-ree)—beauty
watoto (wah-TOE-toe)—children

Print words on cards for children who are ready to write. Children will use some of these words in the stories they create.

Africa
Atlantic
calabash
cassava
Congo
dashiki
desert
dialect
equator
grassland
ground-nut
kente
tattoo

Pictures and books about African cultures help children learn new words as they become aware of the different lifestyles. As children seek labels for their activities, tell stories, and engage in dramatic play, encourage them to use their new words. Additional words and terms may be found in the various sections of the unit.

Folktales

Folktales reflect the fundamental beliefs of a culture. Young children do not understand all the history, folklore, and symbolism of an original folktale, but many tales have been adapted for their enjoyment. Early exposure to folktales provides a foundation that enables children to understand them more fully in later years. Young children appreciate hearing about and dramatizing the interesting characters, the predictable pattern of the story, the adventure, and the anthropomorphic animals. These are some examples of folktales young children enjoy hearing and dramatizing:

Anansi, the Spider: A Tale from the Ashanti, by Gerald McDermott;
A Story, A Story, by Gail E. Haley;
Why the Sun and Moon Live in the Sky, by Elphinstone Daynell;
Why the Sun Was Late, by Benjamin Elkin;
The Clever Turtle, by A. K. Roche;
Bringing the Rain to Kapiti Plain, by Verna Aardema.

African Toe Puppets

The African toe puppet originated in the regions of the Ivory Coast and Mozambique in the 1940s and 1950s. Authentic toe puppets are made from bamboo, with lion fur for hair and strings made of vegetable twine. There are two figures of different sizes; the taller one is the male, and the shorter is the female. The puppets are attached to the big toes of each foot, freeing the hands for clapping or playing a drum.

Children can make toe puppets using small cardboard tubes from bathroom tissue rolls. Have them draw facial features on the tubes and glue on a tuft of fake fur for hair. Cut arms and legs from tagboard and punch holes in each end. Attach them to the tubes with brads or pipe cleaners. Thread 12-inch strings through the holes on the ends of the arms and tie them together. The legs of the puppet should wiggle when the strings are hooked over the child's big toes.

Children can make their toe puppets dance to traditional music while clapping their hands.

MUSIC AND DANCE

Much of the traditional African music is not written down; it is passed from person to person. A musician spends a lifetime perfecting his mastery of native instruments, embellishing the traditional rhythmic pattern that he has been taught. Many Africans have a unique way of making music with their bodies, such as clapping their hands; slapping their shoulders, sides, and thighs; clicking their tongues; and stomping their feet. Children will enjoy improvising as they imitate rhythms.

Present an African rhythm and have children imitate the pattern first without music. Then add authentic African music. Children are able to learn the rhythm very quickly and soon create their own patterns, and children and adults can imitate each other's rhythm patterns.

In many African countries, people use their natural resources to make musical instruments. If possible, instruments similar to those used in Africa should be available for the children's use.

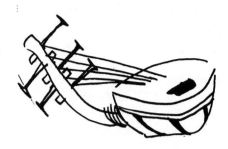

African String Instruments

A *kundi* is a type of wire-stringed guitar made from a goat skin stretched over a wooden frame. Arabic people introduced stringed instruments including the *oud* (ood), which is a form of lute, the lyre, and simple harps and fiddles.

Kundis and other African instruments are available at import stores. Other valuable sources for instruments include

— Caribee Percussion, 207 Clinton St., Santa Cruz, CA 95062
— Music for Little People, Box 1460, Redway, CA 95560. A source for gourd pianos, the balafon and the mbira, this company also carries a wide selection of other instruments, records, and multicultural videos, and allows you to listen to records or musical instruments before buying them.

Wooden Xylophone (*Balafon*)

The *balafon* is a xylophone-type of instrument used by tribes in West Africa. It is made of different lengths of wood tied onto a wooden frame with leather thongs. Gourds are placed under the wooden frame to give resonance to the tones as the balafon is struck with wooden mallets.

Children make their own balafon from eight boards 1/2 inch thick and two inches wide. The

longest board is 12 inches long. Assist children as they measure, mark, and saw boards. Give each child a board and a square of medium sandpaper. After the boards are sanded smooth, have children place them, in order of length, on 2-by-16-inch strips of carpet. The boards are then struck with a wooden mallet to produce an unusual musical tone.

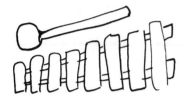

Drums

The drum is the most important instrument of Africa, and there are many different kinds of drums, made from a variety of materials—tree trunks, elephant tusks, tortoise shells, and clay. Drums carved from wood, with thin slits cut in the top, are called slit drums. They have a deep, resonant sound when struck with a wooden stick. The *gangan* is a drum used by the Yoruba tribe; it is made from a hollow log that has an animal hide stretched over the top and tied down with leather drawstrings.

A drum for the classroom can be made from a large, solid, plastic leaf basket turned upside down. The sound is beautiful. Several children can play the drum at the same time, striking it with their hands. Tall plastic waste baskets make a different sound. Experiment with different kinds of containers. Children can also make drums from cans and large ice cream cartons.

The arm drum used by some tribes is carried under the arm and played as the musician dances. Arm drums can be constructed from oatmeal boxes. Children cover a can or box with brown butcher paper and decorate it with beautiful designs, using marking pens, paint, crayons, or pieces of construction paper.

Authentic drums are available at import stores and from the resources listed above. They are a delightful addition to a classroom.

Flutes

In Africa, flutes are made of bamboo, clay, ivory, seashells, and antelope horn, depending on the region. Flutes are made of different lengths. Each length makes a different tone.

Flutes can be made out of cardboard tubes from bathroom tissue, paper towels, or wrapping paper. Cut a circle of tissue paper and place it over one end of the tube. Attach it with a rubber band. Show children how to hum into the other end of the tube to make flute-like sounds. Cut two or three small holes on the side of the flute and show children how to place their fingers on the holes to change the sound.

Shakers (Ishakas)

Shakers made of woven straw or cane are a type of instrument used in Nigeria. Ishakas are three or four feet long and have seeds, beans, or small pebbles inside. They make a special sound and are used when dancing. Shakers can be made from long wrapping paper tubes. Put a few beans or pebbles inside the tubes. Cover both ends with a circle of brown paper and tape securely. Let children decorate the shaker with designs. Small shakers may be made in the same way using tin cans or cardboard juice cans.

Another kind of African shaker with a very unusual sound is an *axatse*. This instrument is made form a large calabash gourd that is

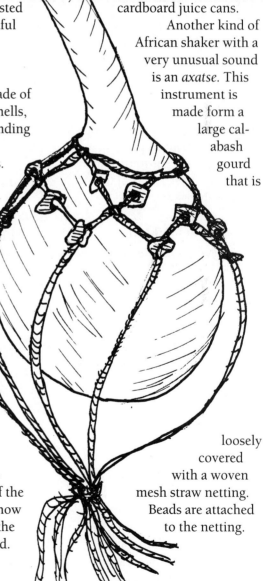

loosely covered with a woven mesh straw netting. Beads are attached to the netting.

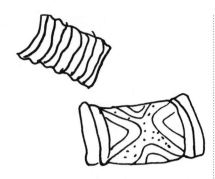

In Nigeria these shakers are called *aqbe,* and in the Congo they are called *lilolo.* The instrument is known as a *shekere* to many musicians in the U.S.

To make an African axatse, use a liter-size, plastic soft drink container with the cap on it. Cover it with a plastic mesh bag (the kind that is used to package turkeys, lemons, limes, or garlic in many grocery stores). Children can attach pea-size colored glass beads to the netting using short pieces of telephone-cable wire.

Thumb Piano (*Mbira*)

The *mbira* is an instrument that comes from the tribes of West Africa. This instrument, sometimes called a *kalimba,* is plucked with the thumbs to create an unusual sound. Children feel very competent playing the mbira because it makes music. It is helpful to have several available for them to use.

Songs—Jazz

In most African music, a leader sings a solo line and a chorus of singers answers. It is this kind of response singing, brought to America from Africa, that led to the call-and-answer type of singing in American Negro spirituals and later in jazz. American jazz is popular throughout much of Africa.

Aretha Franklin and Stevie Wonder are just two African-American musicians who express basic African rhythms in their music.

Songs—Traditional

Suggest that school families contribute words and music, in both English and African languages, of favorite songs and lullabies they sing at home. These can be recorded either at home or in the classroom.

At the Learning Tree, children listened to a recording taped by one of the parents, of moms singing to their sick children in a Kenyan hospital. This listening experience generated questions about the ages of the "babies," how old is "too old" to have mother sing, and meanings of words.

Recordings

Call and Response by Ella Jenkins. Folkway Records. Children enjoy singing the repetitious words and using instruments to accompany this collection of chants and songs from West Africa.

Jambo and Other Call-and-Response Songs and Chants by Ella Jenkins.

Induku Zethu-Zulu by Ladysmith Black Mambaso Zulu. These a cappella African harmonies are beautiful and soothing.

Dance Afro Beat by Orlando Julius Ekemonde. This is an example of mixing the old and the new, using the talking drum from Nigeria.

Little Johnny Brown by Ella Jenkins. A collection of songs that have been passed down for generations in African-American communities throughout the United States, including songs, chants, and civil rights freedom songs.

Rhythms of Childhood—African Impressions by Ella Jenkins. This collection of authentic African chants and folk songs encourages interpretive dance.

A Ram Sam Sam—Making Your Own, An African folk song that children enjoy dancing to.

Children enjoy the poetry of Langston Hughes. They create interpretive dance to "Danse Africaine" and "My People" from his book *Selected Poems.*

Additional recordings are listed in Resources at the end of the unit.

GAMES AND MANIPULATIVES

African and American children play similar games, including hopscotch, marbles, soccer, jacks, one potato-two potato, jump rope, and duck-duck-goose.

Sails in the Wind

Tie two corners of a 3-by-3-foot scarf around a child's waist as if you were making a skirt. The child holds the other two corners out in back and creates a sail by running in the wind.

African Jump Rope

A popular game in Ghana is played with a bag of small rocks tied to the end of a rope. The children form a circle. One player stands in the center and swings the rope around, close to the ground. Children jump over it. The player who misses is out of the game.

This game is adapted for younger children to play outside. Tie a beanbag securely to the end of a jump rope. The children form a line. The teacher swings the rope in a circle and children count the number of times they jump over it. If the rope hits a child's foot, he or she has to go to the " lion's den" and wait until another child misses.

Marbles

A game similar to marbles can be played by shooting nuts, pecans, hickory nuts, or acorns with the thumb. The target is other nuts, which are placed in a line on the floor or outdoors on the ground.

Basket Balancing

Some Africans carry heavy loads on their heads. Encourage children to try to master this skill by balancing small straw baskets on their heads and walking across the room. Children who have mastered this skill can try it in a relay race.

Anansi the Spider Flannel Board Game

Ask a parent to make the characters from *Anansi the Spider,* by Gerald McDermott. The characters can easily be made out of felt. Children love to tell and retell this story, using the characters on a flannel board. Other folktales may be portrayed, such as *The Clever Turtle,* by A. C. Roche, and *The Magic Tree,* by Gerald McDermott.

By Melissa

Wild Animal Lotto Game

A game with real photos of animals, this lotto game also gives information about each animal on the back of the cards.

Cards

Many different games are created using a deck of playing cards that have beautiful and colorful pictures of African tribal leaders. The cards are distributed by Identity Toys. See Resources.

Counting and Sorting

Use plastic and wooden African animals for counting and sorting.

Mankala

Mankala is a counting board game played by young and old throughout Africa and the middle East. There are many variations, and it is known by many different names. In Nigeria it is called *Ayo,* in Liberia it is known as *Wari,* and in Mali it is called *Oware.* All of these names mean "transferring." The game is played on a board that has two rows of six cups. Seeds or pebbles are transferred from cup to cup.

In an adaptation of this game, twenty small, smooth stones (aquarium stones about the size of an almond) are placed in a long, wooden bread bowl. Stones are transferred into four small wooden bowls (egg cups) using wooden tongs. Children try placing the same number of stones in each cup. Encourage children to suggest variations of the game.

Toys

In the classroom children might enjoy using a View Master to see reels of Africa, puzzles of African wild animals, and Black dolls, which are available from Shindana Toys, 4161 South Central, Los Angeles, CA 90011. See Resources for other ideas.

SPECIAL EVENTS

African-American Artists

Have local African American dancers, painters, sculptors, and musicians come to school to share their culture through their art forms, communicating to the children through music, dance, and creative handcrafts. African-American dancers can demonstrate dances from African and African-American cultures and explain basic movement.

Take a trip to the art museum to see African art exhibits.

African Market

After studying African culture for two weeks, children and teachers may organize their own African Market outdoors. Children can make signs for the different stalls. Use straw mats on the ground outdoors for displaying various wares. Designate a special area for music and dancing. Invite parents to shop for handmade jewelry, Basonga masks, paintings, Ashanti cloth, and coiled baskets; sample authentic foods; and listen to African music.

Send the following note to the parents before the big event:

Dear Parents,
On Wednesday, February 24, you are invited to our African Market!
Shops will open at 11 o'clock.
There will be art objects, pottery, sculpture, batik, jewelry, Ashanti cloth, clothing, and food for sale.
Come by and shop!

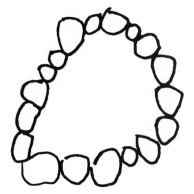

CELEBRATIONS

Emancipation Day—September 22

This is the anniversary of the day that Lincoln read the Emancipation Proclamation in 1862.

Harambee Day—Last week in October

During the week prior to Halloween, some communities observe Harambee Day, which means "Let's all pull together."

Kwanzaa—December 26-January 1

Kwanzaa is a cultural holiday celebrated by African-American families. As described by its creator, Dr. Maulana Karenga, "It is a time for the gathering of our peoples, celebration of ourselves and our achievements, and rededication to greater achievements."

Emancipation Proclamation—January 1

This is the anniversary of the signing of the Emancipation Proclamation by President Lincoln, freeing the slaves in all areas "still in rebellion."

Martin Luther King's Birthday—January 15

National Freedom Day—February 1

This day is set aside to commemorate the signing by President Abraham Lincoln of the proclamation abolishing of slavery in 1863.

National Black History Month—February

Famous African-Americans to learn about during February include Langston Hughes (poet), Daniel Hale Williams (surgeon), Thurgood Marshall (Supreme Court Justice), Barbara Jordan (member of Congress), and Leontyne Price (opera singer).

RESOURCES

N Nursery
K Kindergarten
P Primary
I Intermediate
A Adult

Books for Children

Aardema, Verna. *Bringing the Rain to Kapiti Plain.* Dial Press, 1981. NK
Colorful photographs accompany this poetic text about much-needed rain and "the feather that helped to change the weather."

Aardema, Verna. *Ji-nongo-Nongo Means Riddles.* Four Winds Press, 1979. P
Both the author and the illustrator, Jerry Pinkney, are famous for their contributions to the world of children's literature. Riddles are enjoyed mainly by school-age children, but all can appreciate the earth-tone sketches featuring clothing, designs, animals, and people of Africa.

_____. *Who's in Rabbit's House?* Dial Books for Young Readers, 1977. NKP
Children enjoy this popular folktale.

_____. *Why Mosquitoes Buzz in People's Ears.* Dial Books for Young Readers, 1975. NKP
This West African tale about a disaster caused when Mosquito tells Iguana a tall tale is cleverly retold by Aardema. The story is ideal for dramatizing, and the drawings by Leo and Diane Dillon show inspired designs that reveal numerous shapes, images, and color blends.

Adler, David A. *A Picture Book of Martin Luther King, Jr.* Scholastic, Inc., 1989. KP
This fine biography tells the story of a man and his times; he was protester, leader, minister, Nobel Peace Prize winner, and student. A wonderful choice to read at any time, including African American History Month.

Bang, Molly. *Ten Nine Eight.* Greenwillow Books, 1983. NK
Father and daughter lovingly share a quiet moment in this bedtime counting rhyme. Molly Bang's glowing illustrations capture the eyes of young children.

Barrett, Joyce Durham. *Willie's Not the Hugging Kind.* Harper & Row Publishers, Inc., 1989. P
Poor Willie! He was convinced that hugging was silly. A loving family allows him to work out his dilemma in his own way.

Buffett, Jimmy, and Savannah Jane Buffett. *The Jolly Mon.* Harcourt Brace Jovanovich, 1988. NK

A tale of high Caribbean adventure about islands, dolphins, and a mystical singer of songs, the Jolly Mon.

Caines, Jeannette. *Just Us Women.* Harper & Row Publishers, Inc., 1982. NKP
The importance of family ties is presented in this brief adventure about Aunt Martha and her favorite niece. The recreation of the two women as they "mosey about" enables children to see the varied interests of black people rather than the stereotyped ones so often portrayed in literature.

Carlstrom, Nancy W. *Wild Wild Sunflower Child Anna.* MacMillan Publishing Company, 1987. NKP
Sunflower child is an appealing black child with a creative flair. African-American illustrator Jerry Pinkney presents Anna and her world of nature through bright watercolors.

Carue, Jan. *Children of the Sun.* Little, Brown and Company, 1980. P
Illustrations depict a folktale about twin brothers on a quest to explore "greatness and goodness." Captivates all ages.

Craft, Ruth. *The Day of the Rainbow.* Puffin Books, 1991. NKP
Vignettes of city dwellers' interactions introduce children to a variety of characters and occupations.

Crews, Donald. *Parade.* Greenwillow Books, 1983. NK
Bold illustrations and brief text present a joyous view of a parade highlighting diverse cultures. Other favorites by this talented African-American author/illustrator are *Truck, Freight Train, School Bus,* and *Carousel.*

Dale, Penny. *Bet You Can't.* J. B. Lippincott, 1987. NK
The creative play between brother and sister is, on one level, the essence of this book. However, the reader cannot overlook the excellent illustrations of these African-American children.

Daly, Niki. *Not So Fast, Songololo.* Atheneum Publishers, 1986. NK
Lively text tells the story of a South Afrcan child and his granny on a shopping trip to the city that ends in a surprise for him. Royalties from the sale of this book will be donated to establish school libraries in South Africa.

Dragonwagon, Crescent. *Half a Moon and One Whole Star.* Aladdin Books, 1990. NKP
Splendid visions and poetry make this book a literary lullaby.

Flournoy, Valerie. *The Patchwork Quilt.* Dial Books for Young Readers, 1985. KP
Brightly detailed paintings illustrate the warm family relationship centering on the creation of a patchwork quilt. The memory quilt, lovingly constructed by Grandma, Mama, and Tanya, contains bits of fabric from articles belonging to each family member.

French, Fiona. *Aio, the Rain-Maker.* Oxford University Press, 1975. NK

With ideas for dramatizing, this picture book captures children's attention with full-page illustrations of masks, designs, and animals. The brief text is written in a poetic style.

Fulton, Eleanor, and Pat Smith. *Let's Slice the Ice: A Collection of Black Children's Ring Games and Chants.* Magnamusic-Baton, 1978. NK
Rhymes, songs, and chants have always been a favorite activity of young children. This collection is well illustrated and contains music and directions for more than thirty verses.

Greaves, Nick. *When Hippo Was Hairy and Other Tales from Africa.* Barrons, 1988. I
Children enjoy facts about lions, leopards, cheetahs, wild dogs, hyenas, and other animals with interesting backgrounds. The illustrations are in color, and some fill the entire page. Stories from African mythology are included to add a literary touch.

Greenfield, Eloise. *African Dream.* Thomas E. Crowell, 1977. NK
The poetic approach and charcoal illustrations take the reader to Africa, a continent with mangoes, drums, and villages of long ago, and reflect this African-American author and artist's love of African culture.

_____. *Grandpa's Face.* Philomel Books, 1988. KP
Knowing that feelings never change and that love can be depended upon strike a strong emotional impact in this story about a young girl and her grandfather.

Grifalconi, Ann. *Darkness and the Butterfly*. Little, Brown and Company, 1987. NK
A book for "scaredy cats"! Young children can learn to understand their fear of darkness as a wise woman and a butterfly help Osa become fearless.

_____. *The Village of Round and Square Houses*. Little, Brown and Company, 1986. KP
Beautifully illustrated by the author, this book tells about life in a village that she visited and is told through the eyes of a round house occupant in the Cameroons.

Haley, Gail. *A Story—A Story*. Atheneum, 1970. NKP
The adventures of Anansi, as he outwits others, are told here in bold color and geometric illustrations.

Havill, Juanita. *Jamaica's Find*. Houghton Mifflin Company, 1986. NK
The lesson of honesty that is taught in this short book impresses children. Anne O'Brien's watercolors make subtle suggestions about the characters' feelings.

_____. *Jamaica-Tag-Along*. Houghton Mifflin Company, 1989. NK
The bright watercolors add to this portrayal of how a little sister learns from being left out of things, a positive solution to a common problem.

Hayes, Sarah. *Happy Christmas, Gemma*. William Morrow, 1986. NK
A traditional celebration, dramatized by an African-American

family, gives a positive view of minorities.

Hudson, Wade, and Valarie Wilson Wesley. *Book of Black Heroes: From A to Z*. Just Us Books, 1988. PIA
The focus of this book is to increase understanding of the many contributions that African-American men and women have made to American society. Modern-day and earlier heroes that are reviewed include Marian Anderson, concert singer; Matthew Henson, arctic explorer; Lorraine Hansberry, playwright; Langston Hughes, poet; Benjamin Quarles, historian; Paul Robeson, actor and humanitarian; Edmonia Lewis, sculptor; Marcus Garvey, activist; Benjamin Banneker, astronomer and inventor; and Ira Aldridge, actor.

Humphrey, Margo. *The River that Gave Gifts*. Children's Book Press, 1987. KP
Respect for elders is a major theme in this colorful book about children who created gifts of love for Neema.

Isadora, Rachel. *Ben's Trumpet*. Greenwillow Books, 1979. KP
An imaginary trumpet reacts to music from the Zig Zag Jazz Club, and Ben finally gets a break from a benevolent trumpeter.

Johnson, Angela. *Tell Me a Story, Mama*. Orchard Books, 1989. NK
This book has the love and warmth of an extended family, of stories about "when you were little."

Keats, Ezra Jack. *John Henry— An American Legend*. Alfred A. Knopf, 1965. NKP
John Henry, "that steel-driving man," comes to life in a vividly illustrated story of strength, duty, and dedication.

Kerwen, Rosalind. *Legends of the Animal World*. Cambridge University Press, 1986. P
Animal stories from eleven different cultures examine strong relationships felt between people and the animal kingdom. One of a collection of six legend books.

Lessac, Frané. *Caribbean Canvas*. J. B. Lippincott, 1987. NK
Mrs. Lessac's paintings reveal her fascination for island life. Proverbs and poems complement this collection.

Lewin, Hugh. *Jafta*. Carolrhoda Books, Inc., 1983. NK
A young African boy can run as fast as a cheetah and dance like a zebra—comparing himself to African animals is a favorite pastime. Other excellent books for young children by the same author are *Jafta's Mama*, *Jafta's Papa*, and *Jafta and the Wedding*.

McCauley, Jane R. *Africa's Animal Giants*. National Geographic Society, 1987. KP
Beautiful, large, color photographs embellish this text that is filled with information about the biggest, tallest, and fastest animals on earth.

McDermott, Gerald. *Anansi the Spider*. Holt, Rinehart, and Winston, 1972. NKP
This story from the long-established culture of Ghana has been passed on orally for many

generations. Kwaku Anansi's adventures are illustrated in a combination of geometric forms and colors.

McKenna, Nancy Durrell. *A Zebra Family*. Lerner Publishing Company, 1986.   P
This book dispels stereotypes about South Africa, with its varied houses, homelands, modes of transportation, and interesting lifestyles, including life on a farm in Ekuvukeni and in Cape Town, the country's capital.

McKissack, Patricia C. *Flossie and the Fox*. Dial Books for the Young, 1986. NK
Outfoxing the fox is the theme of this magnificently illustrated story. Flossie Finley learns responsibility as she goes about an errand.

Mendy, Phil. *The Black Snowman*. Scholastic, Inc., 1989. KP
The magic of a kente and a loving snowman enable two little boys to believe in themselves.

Michels, Barbara, and Bettye White. *Apples on a Stick*. Coward-McCann, Inc., 1983. KP
This collection of playground poetry by African-American children is offered as an affirmation of their cultural heritage and a joyous addition to play for all children.

Mogel, Linda D. Harriet Tubman: *They Called Me Moses*. Parenting Press, Inc., 1988. P
Harriet Tubman's courageous and bold life is told through a brief text and shaded drawings that capture her adventures from a child's point of view.

Musgrove, Margaret. *Ashanti to Zulu*. Dial Press, 1982. NP
African traditions from various regions of the continent are presented through a picture collage.

Pomerantz, Charlotte. *The Chalk Doll*. J. B. Lippincott, 1989. NKP
Rose enjoys her mother's remembrances of Jamaica and growing up too poor to afford store-bought things. Can Jamaica be so far away and different? Playing in the sticky tar on the streets, waiting for mom to finish that special dress, playing dolls and making clothes for them is a part of growing up for many little girls in the world.

San Souci, Robert D. *A Boy and the Ghost*. Simon and Schuster, 1989. NKP
Courage and a kind nature give Thomas power over a legendary ghost and reward enough to help his family in this a Southern black folktale.

_____. *The Talking Eggs*. Dial Books for Young Readers, 1989. NKP
Adapted from a Creole folktale, this fanciful story of a "mystical ole aunty," her two-headed cow, and flocks of multi-colored laying hens paint a delightful tale for children. Jerry Pinkney's vibrant pictures bring the story to life.

Schroeder, Alan. *Ragtime Tumpie*. Little, Brown and Company, 1989. KP
An intriguing story about the life of a famous entertainer, Josephine Baker. This fine book with its imaginative insight and

touching illustrations is popular with children.

Seeger, Pete. *Abiyoyo*. MacMillan Publishing Company, 1989. KP
Here is an artistic treasury of music, magic, and monsters that children will ask for again and again.

Serfozo, Mary. *Rain Talk*. Margaret K. McElderry Books, 1990. NK
This entertaining, easy-to-read book is illustrated in vivid watercolors.

Smith, Kathie Billingslea. *Martin Luther King*. Simon and Schuster, 1987.   P
This biography of the famous freedom fighter interests children as they begin to learn about civil rights. Photographs and colorful illustrations of the minister, orator, and crusader embellish the text.

Steptoe, John. *Baby Says*. Lothrop, Lee, & Shepard Books, 1988. NK
Being a big brother may mean setting aside one's own plans for play. This famous African-American author and illustrator depicts a loving relationship between brothers through a text for toddlers illustrated in crayon.

_____. *Mufaro's Beautiful Daughters*. Lothrop, Lee & Shepard Books, 1987. NKP
This African fable delights children.

Stuart, Gene S. *Safari*. National Geographic Society, 1982. P
Safaris in Southern Africa are included in this book about cus-

toms, animals, and plant life. Fascinating, large-as-life photographs are informative, as well as aesthetic.

Tadjo, Veronique. *Lord of the Dance.* J. B. Lippincott, 1988. KP
The author and illustrator uses bright colors to tell the story of the Senufo people. This book will delight mask lovers.

Tusa, Tricia. *Maebelle's Suitcase.* MacMillian Publishing Company, 1987. NK
Illustrations in pencil and watercolors help to portray the story of love between an aged woman and a bird. Children cannot resist this funny tale about a one-hundred-and-eight-year-old woman who lives in a tree.

Walter, Mildred Pitts. *Ty's One-Man Band.* Scholastic, Inc., 1980. NKP
Ty discovers Andro, the mysterious originator of a fanciful one-man band. Text is dotted with ear-catching rhythmic sounds that children love. Supply children with their own combs and wooden spoons and add an old-fashioned washboard for a living- language experience.

Ward, Leila. *I Am Eyes. Ni Macbo.* Greenwillow Books, 1978. NK
Elands, starlings, and moon-flowers are new words for children to wrap their tongues around as they hear about Kenya and a clever girl who lives there.

Williams, Vera B. *Cherries and Cherry Pits.* Greenwillow Books, 1986. NK

This author and artist presents a clever tale about Bedimmi, a talented illustrator. "As she draws she tells the story of what she is drawing." This young black girl spins yarns about "the man whose skin is dark brown" and "the boy in the purple and white shoe."

Zaslavsky, Claudia. *Count on Your Fingers African Style.* Thomas Y. Crowell Junior Books, 1980. NK
The author, a math teacher, teams with artist Jerry Pinkney to produce this clever book describing how finger counting is used for communication of price and quantity in an East African marketplace.

Children will also enjoy the following books. Look for them in your library.
Bernheim, Marc and Evelyn. *The Drums Speak.*
Dayrell, Elphinstone. *Why the Sun and the Moon Live in the Sky.*
Dietz, Betty, and A. and M. Babatunde. *Musical Instruments of Africa.*
Feelings, Muriel. *Moja Means One: Swahili Counting Book*, and *Jambo Means Hello.*
Glubok, Shirley. *The Art of Africa.*
Haskins, Jim. *Count Your Way Through Africa.*
Roche, A. K. *The Clever Turtle.*

Books and Periodicals for Adults

Black Issues in Higher Education. Cox, Matthews, and Associates, Inc., 10520 Warwick Avenue, Suite B-8, Fairfax, VA 22030. This bi-monthly publication, with its distinguished list of guest writers, features excellent articles, reports on many topics

concerning African-Americans, and position statements.

Child Health Talk.
This newsletter is produced quarterly by the National Black Child Development Institute. NBCDI's membership is made up of people who are committed to the positive development of black children and youth. It includes hints about nutrition and safety, developmental guidelines, and a "Doctor's Column."

Comer, J. P. *Maggie's American Dream: The Life and Times of a Black Family.* Penguin, 1988. The mother is the main protagonist in this book by a professor of psychiatry at Yale Child Study Center.

Hale-Benson, Janice E. *Black Children: Their Roots, Culture, and Learning Styles.* The Johns Hopkins University Press, 1982. This is an important book for educators who search for ways to improve schools and programs. Information about how black children learn and the effects of black culture on black children is presented, along with a helpful section about how culture shapes cognition.

Madhubuti, Haki R. *Kwanzaa: A Progressive and Uplifting African-American Holiday.* Third World Press, 1987 (revised). This booklet describes the purpose and African roots of the holiday. It includes symbols, decorations, and gifts at the feast, Karamu, along with a helpful Swahili pronunciation guide.

Reynolds, Barbara. *And Still We Rise*. USA Today Books, 1988. A collection of interviews with fifty black men and women. Children benefit from the strong role models they provide. USA Books, P.O. Box 450, Washington, D.C. 20044.

Films, Filmstrips, and Videos

Aardema, Verna. *Who's in Rabbit's House?* Distributed by Weston Woods.   NKP
Children find pleasure in viewing this filmstrip that relates the folktale made popular by the book. Leo and Diana Dillon join Aardema in creating a visual language lesson. Also available in 16mm and video.

_____. *Why Mosquitoes Buzz in People's Ears*. Distributed by Weston Woods.   NKP
This West African tale retold by Aardema in her popular book is available as filmstrip, 16mm film, and video.

Bang, Molly. *Ten Nine Eight*. Distributed by Educational Record Center, Inc.   NKP
This favorite story is now on filmstrip and cassette.

Haley, Gail. *A Story—A Story*. Weston Woods.   NKP
This adventure is available in 16mm and video.

Haseley, Dennis. *The Old Banjo*. Distributed by Educational Record Center, Inc.   NK
An American Library Association "Notable Children's Filmstrip" selection.

Isadora, Rachel. *Ben's Trumpet*. Distributed by Educational Record Center, Inc.   NKP

Ben's trumpet comes alive with color and special effects to present an outstanding rendition of this popular story.

Keats, Ezra Jack. *A Letter to Amy*. Distributed by Weston Woods.   NK
This favorite story, along with other popular Keats books, is available as a filmstrip, 16 mm film, and video. Addtional stories are *Peter's Chair, Whistle for Willie*, and *The Snowy Day*.

Kwanzaa: A New Afro-American Holiday. Distributed by Society for Visual Education, Inc., 1986. This filmstrip provides information about this new African-American holiday. It describes some of the activities that take place during the holiday, using colorful photographs and simple narration to show how Kwanzaa is celebrated.

McDermott, Gerald. *Anansi the Spider*. Distributed by Weston Woods.   NKP
This traditional story is available as filmstrim, video, and 16mm film.

McKissack, Patricia C. *Flossie and the Fox*. Distributed by Weston Woods.   NK
A filmstrip version of this magnificently illustrated story.

Steptoe, John. *Mufaro's Beautiful Daughters*. Distributed by Weston Woods.   NKP
The dramatic enactment of an African fable delights children with its splendid musical score and glowing artistic embellishments. Also available as video and 16mm film.

Sub-Saharan Africa: The Land. Distributed by Society for Visual Education, 1989. Four filmstrip and cassette sets with guide that are a must for the teacher's library.
Program 1: Africa's Geography and Climate. 15.07 min. This program is to present the major regions of Africa. The portions that show the humpbacked cattle, camels, sheep, and goats interest children.
Program 2: The African People: Past and Present. 15 min. You can use this strip to counteract stereotypes and give children a better understanding of ethnic diversity. This filmstrip also enables you to understand the value of retaining one's own cultural traditions, whether in an urban or rural setting—important information to share with children.
Program 3: Africa's Natural Resources. 12:30 min. Learning about resources is often dull for children, but this strip provides information about cloves, cassava, gold, plantains, cotton, and other items. Some of the sections show tea pickers, coffee growers on the Ivory Coast, and cotton baggers. You provide the narration, so you can adjust the text to the group's developmental level. Numerous extended activities are presented in the guide.
Program 4: Africa's Changing Occupations.. 11:20 min. This program presents information about job opportunities and problems of Africa's urban areas, and women's roles are explored. The guide suggests use with intermediate and junior high age. We suggest that you use the information to prepare a presen-

tation that is suitable for younger children.

Children of Wax: A Folktale from Zimbabwe. Distributed by Churchill Films. 5-1/2 min. KP
A different type of family is presented in this tale from Zimbabwe. The adventure of the older brother, Ngwabe, turns from a sad tale into a happy one.

The Cow-Tail Switch: A Folktale of Africa. Distributed by Coronet Film/Video, 1981. KP
Excellent for dramatization, this animated Liberian folktale interests children with its shields, magic, and brightly colored clothes.

Goggles. Learning Corporation of America. Distributed by Coronet/MTI Film and Video, 1989. NK
Ezra Jack Keats' book comes to life through this 12-minute dramatization. Tricking older boys turns out nicely for Peter, Archie, and Willie, the dog. Young children appreciate what friendship means when one is up against the bad guys. A discussion guide is included.

Martin Luther King, Jr.: A Peaceful Warrior. 15 min. Society for Visual Education, Inc., 1986. PIA
This brief explanation of the civil rights movement is interesting to older children, third grade and up, and the printed information for teachers is useful for extended activities. The subject matter—slavery and deprivation of civil-rights—is not suitable for young children.

The Rug Maker: A Folktale of Africa. Distributed by Coronet Films, 1981. KP
This animated folktale of East Africa encourages children to learn a useful craft. It is set in a village. Children enjoy the bright designs of West Africa and the excellent opportunity for dramatization.

Materials and Experiences

The ABC Head Start Doll. ABC School Supply. No. 278-305-92.
Life-sized (24-inch) doll with movable eyes and rooted hair.

Baby Whitney. Lomel Enterprises, Inc., P.O. Box 2452, Washington D.C. 20013.
You may choose clothing for this "warm skin-tone doll."

Bendable Families. Distributed by Afro-American Company.
Set of four bendable people that includes an Anglo, African, Hispanic, and Asian. Suitable for cognitive and manipulative play.

Black Boy and Girl. ABC School Supply, No. 448-701-92.
Figures may be purchased separately. Also available: Black Family, No. 513-705-92.

Black Career Workers. ABC School Supply, No. 513-803-92.
A firefigher, police officer, school patrol, construction worker, grocer, letter carrier, and street worker.

Brother and Sister Dolls—Black Boy and Black Girl. ABC School Supply, No. 487-240-92, No. 487-241-92.
Baby dolls that are a nice size.

Christopher and Christine. ABC School Supply Co., No. 404-844-92.
Set of two 19-inch dolls with black ethnic features, including Afro hairstyles.

Community Dolls. Community Playthings, No. D27, 28, 29 and D35, 36.
These appealing dolls are made for easy dressing by small fingers. Black girl, black boy, black baby and black dolls in western dress are choices.

Dramatic Play Puppetry. ABC School Supply.
Order from the "Black Family Group," "Community Workers," "Occupational Group," and "Family Puppets." "Community Worker Puppets" include non-white and white. Features are similar, but colors vary among these nontoxic, flame-resistant, hand-washable puppets.

Duplo Ethnic World People. ABC School Supply, No. 479-159-92.
Set consists of eighteen, including African, Asian, Anglo, and "workers."

Family Group. Kaplan, No. 1X2921.
An eight-piece set with grandmother, grandfather, and baby, among others. Black family is on heavy board and aids in imaginative play.

Family Puppets. Educational Teaching Aids.
Each family includes father, mother, sister, brother, and baby. Hispanic, African, and Anglo are represented.

Godina. ABC School Supply, 632-399-92.
Vinyl 14-inch doll with Afro hairstyle.

Life-Size Newborns—Black Boy and Black Girl. ABC School Supply, No. 487-348-92, 487-385-92.
Realistic 19-inch dolls come with accessories.

Professional Careers. Kaplan, No 1X0697.
Black nurses, doctors, and business people that encourage cultural appreciation.

Realistic Flexible Doll Sets—Black Family. ABC School Supply, No. 512-751-92.
Family set includes father, mother, brother, sister, and baby.

Safari Wild Animal Set. ABC School Supply, No. 305-234-92.
Set of twelve animals.

Wooden Family Figures. Child Craft, No. 151050.
Black family with six members aids in imaginative play.

Instruments
Mbira. Music for Little People. P.O. Box 1460, Redway, California 95560.
A West African melodic instrument that can be managed by school-agers.

Drum. Music for Little People.
A west African telegraph system.

Balafon. Music for Little People.
This original xylophone is constructed of gourds, sticks, and hardwood keys.

Posters and Pictures

Black America Multicultural Study Prints. Educational Teaching Aids, No. 2985D-E9.
Traces black history in America. For older children.

Black Images Book Bazaar, 142 Wynnewood Village, Dallas, TX 75224.
Specializing in books, games, greeting cards, cultural prints, and artifacts from the black perspective. Catalog available.

Contemporary Black Biographies. Distributed by Cole.
Fourteen easy-to-read biographies with brightly colored photographs describe personalities from the African-American community.

Contemporary Blacks and Twentieth Century Blacks. Social studies posters distributed by Shack Industries, 3300 W. Cermak Rd., Chicago, IL 60623.
Fourteen portraits in each set of brightly colored prints, with an explanation of each famous contributor.

Famous Black People in American History. Distributed by Educards.
School-age children can gain an understanding of the contributions of African Americans from these cards that are designed with a picture and factual statement on each person's role in our nation's history.

Forty Famous Americans. Kaplan, No. 1X2980.
Each display card has suggested activities and games about prominent African Americans in U.S. history. For older children.

Puzzles

Black ABC's: Alphabet Puzzle. Distributed by Afro-American Distributing Company.
A twenty-six-piece puzzle with upper and lower-case letters that are recognized by children as they manipulate the inlay pieces.
Martin Luther King. Distributed by Judy/Instructo.
This twelve-piece woodboard inlay puzzle is used by young children to learn about the prominence of this civil rights leader.

One, Two, Three Africa: Numbers Puzzle. Distributed by Afro-American Distributing Company.
Inlay extra-thick cardboard puzzle with 25 pieces; illustrates the outline of Africa.

Records and Audiocassettes

Broonzy, Bill. *Bill Broonzy Sings Folk Songs.* Distributed by Smithsonian/Folkways Records.
Children and adults enjoy these gospel and folk songs.

Dance Afro Beat. Distributed by Music for Little People.
Reggae music performed by a drummer.

Induku Zether-Zulu. Distributed by Music for Little People.
NKPI
Authentic African folk music performed a cappella. Available in album and cassette.

Jackson, Franz. *Play Your Instruments and Make a Pretty Sound.* With Franz Jackson and His Original Jazz All-Stars.
Dixieland jazz introduces musical instruments to children.

Jenkins, Ella. *A Long Time Ago.* Ella Jenkins with Brother John Sellers. Distributed by Smithsonian/Folkways. African-American music.

_____. *Counting in Swahili* with Ella Jenkins. Distributed by Kimbo Educational, LP record FC7661. Response songs and chants performed as only Ella Jenkins can.

_____. *Ella Jenkins Collection.* Educational Teaching Aids, No. 92524-E9. Set of fourteen records that may be bought separately.

_____. *Jambo and Other Call-Response Songs and Chants.* Claudia's Caravan, No. 214. "On Safari" and "Counting in Swahili" are sung again and again by children.

_____. *Little Johnny Brown.* Produced by Folkways Records, distributed by Scholastic Records, No. SC7631. A collection of traditional songs from black communities. Includes favorites such as "He's Got the Whole World in His Hands" and "Hammer, Hammer, Hammer."

_____. *My Street Begins at My House.* Distributed by Smithsonian/Folkways. These call-and-response favorites engage all in a cultural experience.

_____. *This-A-Way, That-A-Way.* Distributed by Smithsonian/Folkways. Children and educators still enjoy this 1973 album of "cheerful songs and chants." "Miss Mary Mack" and "Do You Know Your Country?" are favorite cultural selections.

_____. *You'll Sing a Song and I'll Sing a Song.* Distributed by Smithsonian/Folkways. These songs from around the world are favorites in schools everywhere.

Jones, Bessie. *Bessie Jones Step It Down.* Distributed by Rounder Records, One Camp St., Cambridge, MA 02140. This leading performer of traditional music from the Georgia Sea Islands has contributed to an understanding of rhythm and movement, games, and songs. Also enjoy the book with the same name.

Leadbelly. *Leadbelly Sings Folk Songs.* Distributed by Smithsonian/Folkways. Fifteen-song collection can be used for listening experience or sing-along with older children.

Mattox, Cheryl Warren, collected by. *Shake It to the One That You Love the Best.* JTG of Nashville, 1989. NKP Cassette and scores for African-American game songs, line game songs, clapping rhymes, and lullabies. Vivid illustrations complement the musical scores.

Moore, Thomas. *Sleepy Time.* Thomas Moore Records "Thomas Moore and his music help children feel good." This record, with best-loved lullabies like "Kum Bah Yah," can do just that. Other records by this humanitarian are *My Magic World* and *The Family.* "Don't Worry" helps children to feel OK about their families.

Sorveto Never Sleeps. Distributed by Music for Little People. The Zulu jive, a powerful, rhythmic sound, features women singers.

Catalogs and Supply Houses

Afro-Am Distributing Company, 819 S. Wabash Dr., Chicago, IL 60605. "Afro-Am Educational Materials for Pre-Kindergarten through High School" catalog lists a variety of excellent materials, including the items they produce, such as excellent posters (Jesse Jackson among others), clever growth charts with life-size African-American children, and books for adults. They distribute Ella Jenkins records, collections of children's books, and much more.

Alternative Videos, Beverly Debase, P.O. Box 2707, Dallas, TX 75227. (214) 388-2407. This supplier specializes in non-traditional videos, particularly Black videos. Videos entitled "Black Artists" and "Malcolm X" head the list of culturally significant audiovisuals.

Identity Toys, Inc., 2821 N. 4th St., Milwaukee, WI 53212. Board games for all ages, puzzles, card games, stuffed black dolls, and books (including a Nubian baby book) that aim at developing pride and self-esteem.

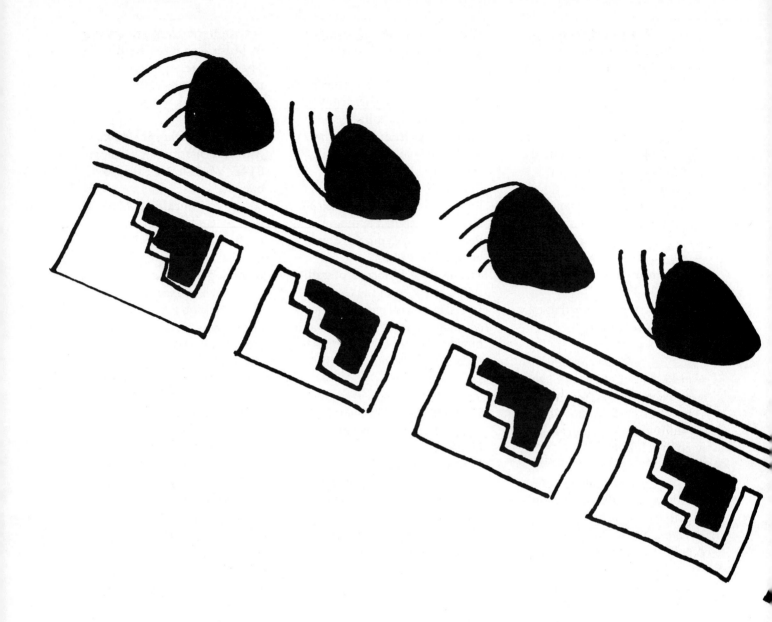

AMERICAN INDIAN CULTURES

Young children learn that there are many different American Indian groups in the United States and that each group has different customs. Their way of cooking, style of dress, and social structure depend on the tribal group to which they belong. Traditional beliefs vary in the practice of religion and ceremony, and groups have different attitudes toward nature. Language may be the single most important distinguishing factor; there are many languages and dialects among the tribes.

Children learn to use the terms "Sioux," "Hopi," and "Iroquois" as easily as "Native American" and "Indian." They learn that American Indian people today live in all fifty states, some in cities, some in towns, and some on reservations. Some American Indians choose to follow the traditional way of life for their nation, while others choose not to do so.

An effort has been made in this unit to explain how some groups lived long ago and how they experience the world today. Children learn that American Indians are an important part of America's past, present, and future.

We are grateful to Gregory Gomez, who served as a consultant, adding information to the historical content and to the preface of this section. Mr. Gomez, a Lipan-Mescalero Apache, has been adopted into the Southern Cheyenne-Arapaho Starhawk Warrior Societies and the Kiowa Tia-Piah Warrior Society and is a Sun Dancer with the Lakota Sioux. Mr. Gomez is presently employed by the United States Department of Health and Welfare with Headstart and is a curriculum writer for "A World of Difference," a public awareness program sponsored by the Anti-Defamation League.

FAMILY LIVING

HOMES

Talk with children about their own families and homes. Ask who cleans their house, who takes care of them when they're sick, who makes the rules, and who tells the stories. Invite an American Indian leader in your area to your school to explain how the various Indian families live. Encourage children to compare the roles of family members in various cultures.

Today, most American Indians live in modern houses, whether they live on or off a reservation. In the Southwest, some traditional types of homes are still used, including the Navajo hogan and the Hopi pueblo, which are described in this section.

In the past, Indian dwellings always varied according to the environment, which influenced the differences in tribal lifestyles. Long ago, tribal customs and ways of life dictated the architecture, size, and location of the villages. Climate and available materials were also factors in the construction of homes.

In order to identify the natural environment of long ago, four houses from the many types of permanent and temporary dwellings have been chosen. *Where Indians Live: American Indian Houses*, by Nashone, is an excellent resource.

Plains Indians—Sioux Tipi (Tepee)

The Sioux nation is comprised of fourteen tribes and is considered a Northern Plains

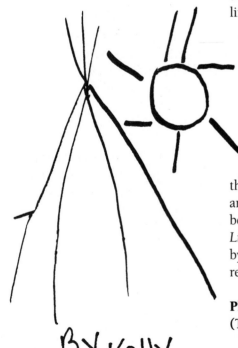

By Kelly

culture. Today most of the Sioux people live in modern homes. Some are clustered communities, with homes closely spaced, while others are sparsely located on communal tribal lands.

Tipis are used for religious and cultural ceremonies. Often the tipi is erected for special occasions, such as powwows. In the past, most Sioux Indians lived in permanent villages in cabins made of poles and bark, with floor mats indoors and porches added for comfort. For a part of the year they carried the portable tipi with them as they moved to hunt. Each family or tribe decorated its tipi with symbols of brave deeds or other family or group experiences.

Children can make a tipi by stretching fabric over a frame after they have determined the location, size, and structure for the frame. For example, a sheet may be draped over a card table or spread over an outdoor climbing gym.

Study the designs of one tribe to decide how to decorate the sides of the tipi. The Yankton are Sioux, with habits, beliefs, and designs similar to those of other Sioux peoples both east and west. Children can use some of their popular flower designs, zigzags, stars, and geometric shapes, and traditional symbols to convey stories about life experiences as the Sioux hunters did long ago. Paul Goble's books, *Gift of the Sacred Dog* and *Buffalo Woman*, have beautiful illustrations of tipis.

Southwest—Hopi Pueblo

Today many Hopi live and work outside the reservation in Arizona, which is completely surrounded by the large Navajo reservation. Others live on the reservation in modern housing or in traditional adobe-style pueblos.

The Pueblo groups made the first multi-storied buildings similar to apartments. In the past, most of the pueblos or houses were built in a stair-step design, with each floor set back by the depth of one room from the front of the floor below it. Built from stones and mud, these clusters of box-shaped houses fronted open spaces where community events such as dances and ceremonies took place. The style of the pueblo provided protection and comfort. Ladders were used to reach the different stories. As new housing was built, changes were made in hatchways, windows, doors, and other traditional features. Study the remodeling that has taken place over time, and share these facts with the children.

To construct a Hopi pueblo for role-playing, use different-sized boxes, including a refrigerator box and several smaller ones. Paint the boxes brown and stack them to make the pueblo several stories high. Children can paint ladders and windows on the sides of the boxes.

Children also enjoy making a table-top Pueblo village using several sizes of small boxes, paint, sticks, paper, and glue. Books with pictures of pueblo life can give children ideas.

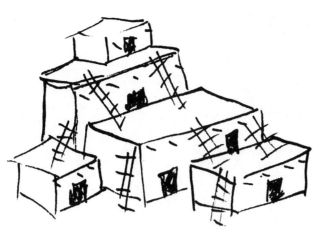

Sand may be sprinkled on the pueblos before the paint dries; ladders may be made by gluing twigs together; figures may be added to the village; sections of egg cartons may be used to make beehive ovens. Encourage children to work cooperatively or separately, depending on their developmental stage, to create an authentic scene.

Southeast—Seminole Chickee

Today, there are five state and federal Seminole reservations in Florida, some with modern houses, and some with model villages. In the model villages, homes with open sides and roofs thatched with palmetto leaves are much like the chickee lived in long ago. The Seminoles built these homes on raised

platforms with little or no room for furniture, except hammocks for sleeping or mats on the floor. It is so warm in the Everglades that many Seminoles prefer to live in a style that is similar to the traditional chickee. They have modified ranch-style cement block homes to include features of the chickee, such as large side-by-side windows to make it cooler.

Children add palmetto leaves made out of construction paper for the roof to an already existing platform or tree house to make a house chickee style.

Northeast—Iroquois Longhouse

It is important to inform children that most Indian people today live in single-family modern styles of housing. Most Iroquois who live on reservations live the same way as their neighbors who are not Indians.

The Six Nations of the Iroquois are the Mohawk, Oneida, Onondaga, Cayuga, Tuscarora, and Seneca. Long ago, the structure of the Iroquois longhouse varied with each of these nations. The typical longhouse was a multi-family residence that had rooms lining the two sides of the central hall. Twenty families might be accommodated within the longhouse, each family with its own fire. Over the doorway, a symbol indicated the family's clan.

Make an Iroquois longhouse out of a large cardboard box. Cut doors and windows and add a painted roof. Children can play in the house, pretending to lie on the bunks and to cook over the fires in the central hall. The construction of the longhouse can be a children's project, or it can be part of the preparation of the environment by the teacher.

A longhouse that will accommodate several children can be made for role-playing the Iroquois lifestyle of the past. Cover two card tables with 36-inchwide brown butcher paper. Attach paper to the tops of the tables with masking tape. Cut and staple two 36-inch-wide pieces of brown paper the length of the tables to use for a roof. Leave one end open. Crumple pieces of newspaper and stuff them inside the stapled roof. Using black tempera, paint designs on the roof to simulate bark. Hang a piece of imitation fur or burlap over the front opening to serve as a door.

Little Runner of the Long House, by Betty Baker, is available from most libraries and is a wonderful story for children because it depicts Iroquois families living in a longhouse and gives children this traditional model to dramatize.

Northwest Coastal—Kwakuitl Community House

In the past, dense forests provided cedar logs for the large wooden homes of the Northwest Coastal tribes. Each tribe created its own style of architecture. Today, homes are built more often for a single family in a modern style. A traditional building still in use is the Community House or Big House. It is not a house for a family, but rather a place for meetings and celebrations. It can be used for a potlatch, a give-away feast with good food and gifts for everyone, and provides a stage for dances that dramatize ancient stories. This large wooden building is decorated with traditional paintings and totem poles carved with symbols identifying the group. It has an opening in the roof for smoke from the open fires.

Ask children to work with you to prepare a model of the Community House for a potlatch. A platform or stage in one corner of the classroom is handy for this purpose. The front of the platform makes a perfect place to set totem poles. Gifts such as child-made jewelry, drawings and paintings of Indian symbols, and boxes with painted symbols are stacked on the stage. Children select favorite stories for dramatizing. *The Angry Moon,* by William Sleator and *Whale in the Sky,* by Ann Siberell, are folktales that describe the totem pole.

DRAMATIC PLAY

Unfortunately, as children begin to role-play family life other than their own, they rely on sterotypes portrayed in movies, books and television programs that they have seen. Help children understand that there are numerous American Indian languages and cultures and be aware of stereotypes they have adopted. Discourage demeaning labels such as "savage," "squaw," "papoose," "brave"; the use of terms such as "sit Indian style;" the singing of "Ten Little Indians"; and so on. Wearing feathered headbands, collecting scalps, and making a whooping war cry are common images to be dispelled.

CLOTHING

One of the first things young children want to do when exploring a culture is to try on traditional clothing. Have clothing available for children to examine, or have them make their own by adding a creative touch to an existing garment or using a pattern and starting from scratch. Involve the children in determining what tools are needed, selecting materials, and deciding where to cut.

Today, many American Indians wear traditional clothing at least some of the time. Traditional clothing may also be worn to ceremonies, and represents the cultural artistic expression of each person. Today, the American Indians' lifestyle is much like that of

other Americans, which includes wearing modern clothes.

As with houses, clothing style was dictated by the environment; according to the area in which they lived, the American Indian people wore clothing suited to their needs, made from materials available to them. Thus, American Indians in different regions differed in their style of dress. You must study variations in climate, geography, resources, and therefore, styles in order to explain these differ-

ences to children. (See Creative Art Expression.)

Have clothing available for children to examine. Contact American Indians native to your area for information about the clothing and hairstyles characteristic of their groups. When traditional clothing is tried on, children will often behave in ways they have seen on television or in books. Describe again American-Indian lifestyles and encourage authentic role-playing.

Most American Indians wore shirts, moccasins, long dresses,

and long, full skirts. Style and materials used to make the following items vary according to the tribal group: shirts; moccasins; long dresses; long, full skirts; beaded bags; jewelry; woven shawls; wrist cuffs; robes; leggings; leg rattles; arm bands; anklets; and headdresses. Have examples from different tribes available.

Paul Goble's books, such as *The Gift of the Sacred Pony* and *Star Boy,* reveal beautiful designs on clothing. *The Seminole,* by Emilie Lepthien, has a section about crafts.

Sioux Cradle Boards

Cradle boards for infants were sometimes very elaborate—some were lined with soft fur or moss and decorated with beads. Instructions for making them are in Creative Art Expression.

FOOD
● ● ● ● ● ● ● ● ●

Any experience that includes the sense of taste adds more meaning to the development of that concept for the young child.

Some traditional tribal foods are no longer served on a daily basis; some are prepared only for special days. Many American Indians regularly eat traditional foods.

Some traditional foods of the Hopi include parched corn, blue fry bread, blue marbles, blue cornmeal pudding, and roasted piki. In the past, piki bread was made by mixing boiling water and blue cornmeal with cooking ashes. This mixture was spread over a hot stone, then rolled tissue thin and served crisp. Today piki bread is baked only for special occasions, using methods handed down for generations.

Yankton Sioux foods include wild rice, coffee, fish, birds, prairie turnips, fruits and vegetables, small game, buffalo, and corn. Today, some of the traditional vegetables are still grown by American-Indian farmers. Wahanpi (a soup of meat and vegetables) and wojapi (fruit pudding) are served today for special occasions. Fry bread and peppermint and herbal teas are also enjoyed.

Seminole favorites include turkey, beef, corn, rice, turtle stew, fruits, and fish. Sofkee is a broth of maize (flour boiled in water).

Iroquois people often mixed corn and beans. Other favorites were mushrooms, sassafras, turkey, deer, bear, and duck. Hot maple sap was poured over popcorn and called "snow food" "Snow candy" may also be made by drizzling maple syrup over crushed ice.

Cornbread, corn on the cob, popcorn, peanuts, sweet potatoes, and roasted pumpkin seeds are some common foods enjoyed that were contributed by the American Indian. Many can be prepared in the classroom. Blue cornmeal and blue corn meal chips are available in many gourmet and health food stores.

(Safety Note: Be sure to obtain parental permission before allowing children to eat anything in case of allergies or diet restrictions.)

Hopi Blue Fry Bread (*Sak-wa-wee-oe-qu-vee-kee*)
About 2 1/2 C flour
About 1/3 C blue cornmeal (can be purchased at a health food store)
About 1 T baking soda
Powdered milk (optional)
About 1 t salt
About 2 C. water
Lard or cooking oil

Put flour in a large bowl. Add about a handful of the blue cornmeal, a little salt, and baking powder. Add a small amount of powdered milk if desired (optional). Mix the dry ingredients well. Gradually add water, a little at a time, mixing it in with your hands until you have a soft, pliable dough. Let the dough set for about one hour before frying time. Form a small ball of dough for each piece of fry bread. Roll out the dough balls with a rolling pin to about 1/2 inch thick. Fry the dough in hot oil until the edges are browned on both sides.

Blue fry bread may be eaten with salt or honey on it. It is usually served with beans or stew.

The corn on the Hopi reservation comes in many colors. The dark blue corn is ground and someviki (*soe-me-vee-kee*) is made by adding ashes (*qoots-vee*) that are made by burning dry corn cobs, dried leaves, stems, and pods of bean plants.

We adapted the Hopi recipe for fry bread and make it the following way:

Fry Bread
1 C flour
2 t baking powder
1/2 t salt
3/4 C milk
Cooking oil

Mix ingredients together, adding more flour if necessary to make a stiff dough. Roll out on a floured board until it is very thin. Cut into strips, about 2 to 3 inches long and 1 inch wide. Drop into hot oil. Brown on both sides. Serve hot with butter or sprinkle with sugar. This recipe makes about 10 servings.

TRANS-PORTATION

Boats
Today, Seminoles use air boats rather than the dugout canoes they relied on in the past. The art of building birchbark canoes by hand is practiced today by only a few craftsmen; most boats are made by machines. Used long ago for transportation and trade, the canoe is used today for sports, recreation, and travel.

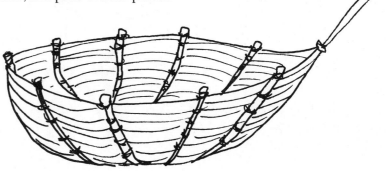

Mandan

Sioux sometimes traveled in bullboats, round, tub-shaped boats made of woven willows lashed together with rawhide and covered with buffalo hides, then sealed with resin. In the past, Iroquois people made boats from hollowed tree logs. Children can use a large box to make a canoe. They paint the canoe and select a design to put on the outside. Groups decorated their boats with special symbols that were important to the culture. A canoe makes an enjoyable prop for role playing in the Family Living Center.

racket. Strong twine was woven inside the frame, and thongs held shoes on their foot. Today, a modern version is used for sport and travel in snowbound areas.

Children can make snowshoes using the lids of shoe boxes. Have them place one foot inside the center of the upside down lid. Draw around the foot and punch holes on either side of the outline. Lace a strip of cloth or leather through the holes and over the foot and tie the ends around the ankle.

Travois

Iravois, pulled by dogs, horses, or people, were used by some Plains groups for carrying their possessions when they traveled. They were also used to carry old, young, or sick family members.

Children can make a travois by stretching canvas or other strong cloth between two poles, each about five feet long. The poles cross or come together at the top and the treasures are piled on the travois.

Snowshoes

Iroquois made snowshoes by bending a strip of wood and bringing the ends together to make an oval frame that looks something like a large tennis

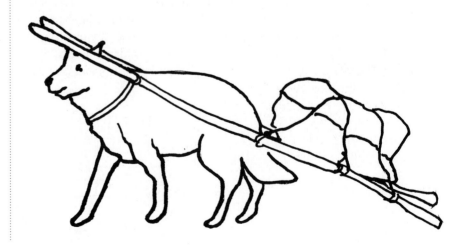

CREATIVE ART EXPRESSION

Creativity means beginning with ideas generated by children. The role of the adult is to foster creativity by asking questions, supervising the projects and providing reinforcement. Provide many choices of materials.

CLOTHING

Headdresses

Today, headdresses are worn at tribal ceremonies. The headdress of the Plains cultures is familiar to children because it is often the stereotype. Children should be taught that headdresses were different for each tribe and some did not wear them at all. Traditionally, headdresses are worn only by men.

Iroquois men wore a cap with a band, its crown covered with feathers. One feather stood straight up from the center. Provide feathers and paper for children so that they may construct their own headdress.

When showing children a picture of Osceola, a Seminole, point out the headdress designed with an ostrich plume tucked in the folds of a turban-like cap. Books with a picture of

Osceola include *Osceola,* by R. P. Johnson, and *The Seminole,* by Emilie Lepthien. Show children how to wrap 36-inch lengths of soft fabric around their heads turban style and help them tuck feathers in the folds.

A length of red fabric tied on the side and knotted is one headdress worn by Hopi men and boys. The western hat is also popular today.

Sioux chiefs often wore a band with just a single feather, which can be made from a strip of corrugated cardboard. Children can decorate the band and use a real feather. War bonnets can be purchased and shown to children, explaining that each feather represents a story. Sioux feathers were often notched or trimmed to give them a specific meaning, making each headdress highly stylized.

With imagination and materials, children can make headdresses in several ways to represent different tribes and nations.

Cradle Boards

Sioux babies were carried in cradle boards made of wood and animal

hides and lined with soft moss. Often boards were lavishly decorated. Lizard or turtle charms were attached to some, wishing long life for the infant.

Iroquois cradle boards have a supportive strap fitting across the forehead called a tumpline; it is woven from the inner fibers of the elm, basswood, or cedar.

Make cradle boards by cutting a piece of cardboard into a 12-by-18-inch rectangle—about the size of a baby doll. Punch holes on each side of the cardboard, about three holes on each side. Place the doll on the cardboard. Lace strips of cloth through the holes and crisscross them over the doll to hold it onto the board. Tie the ends of the strips to make the tumpline, or tie the strips into loops that fit over the shoulders.

To furnish the Family Living Center with cradle boards, adults can make them. Children may make additional cradle boards as interest and ability allow. Provide the materials and books with pictures, and children will create interesting models.

Shirts and Skirts

Explain to children that today most American Indian people dress in modern clothing except for special occasions such as powwows, American Indian Month, and special festival days.

In the past, Seminole women wore long patchwork skirts trimmed with braid and cape-like blouses made of net. Seminole men wore knee-length shirts to protect them from mosquitoes. Children can decorate circles of loosely woven fabric to make Seminole capes. Cut fabric in 36-inch circles. Cut a hole for the neck and then let children use fabric markers to draw symbols on their capes.

In early times, Iroquois women wore buckskin dresses; later, they wore blue and red broadcloth skirts. Iroquois men wore a breechcloth and a short skirt. Leggings and a long fringed shirt were added in the winter. A Sioux explained that the clothing was fringed to allow rainwater to run off instead of soaking in.

Sioux women wore buckskin dresses decorated with fine-quill

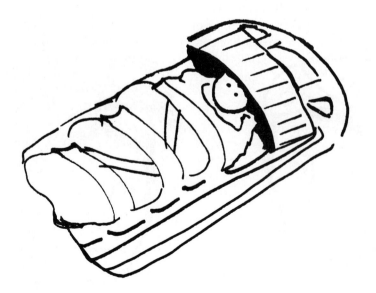

embroidery and beadwork. Sioux men wore vests, robes, buckskin shirts, and leggings decorated with porcupine quills.

Haida people of the Northwest wore rain ponchos of cedar bark and fur capes from sea otter hides. Decorative, wide-brimmed hats from bark added protection from the sun and rain. They resemble farmers' hats from China (see Creative Expression in the Chinese/Chinese-American unit). Beautiful designs were woven into blankets used as robes. Provide large squares of fabric, about 36 by 36 inches, for children to use to make these Haida robes. They can paint designs on the fabric.

Leather Pouches

Many American Indian tribes made pouches from soft animal skins. These were used for carrying a variety of objects, such as bear claws, magical stones, or medicines. The pouches were elaborately decorated. The Iroquois used dyed moose hair to embroider designs on their pouches. Other tribes used colored beads to decorate the pouches.

Children can make pouches using soft cotton knit fabric. Draw 12-inch circles on the fabric and then let children cut them out. Punch an even number of small holes around the edge of the circle, about two inches apart. Let children decorate the pouches using marking pens and colored beads, and then weave a leather string in and out of the holes for a drawstring. They can string a few beads on the ends of the drawstring. Encourage the children to find all kinds of treasures to carry in their pouches.

DECORATIVE ART
●●●●●●

Jewelry

American Indian jewelry is identified by unique characteristics of a tribe's style. Iroquois brooches, bracelets, and earrings are made from silver coins and ingots hammered into sheets and decorated by stamping and perforating with traditional designs. The Seminole Indians string small glass beads to wear around the neck like a collar. Sioux men and women wear medallions made of beads in symbolic colors, trimmed with more beads and shells. Several Pueblo groups—the Hopi, the Navajo and the Zuni—create beautiful silver and turquoise jewelry. To preserve this craft, the Hopi have established an artisan cooperative on their reservation to teach the art to the young people of the tribe. Provide an assortment of jewelry made by American Indians for children to examine and try on.

Children can make bracelets and necklaces by stringing shells, metal disks, bones from meat (such as ham, round steak, and neck bones), and different shapes of colored paper with holes punched in the middle. Items may be strung on leather strips or yarn. For easier stringing, wrap one end of yarn with masking tape.

To make a medallion, children can draw symbols on a cardboard shape, then glue beads to the face of the medallion, and string it on yarn. To make jewelry with a roulette (dots) effect, children can hammer a blunt nail like a spike into the surface of metal disks.

Different shapes and sizes of pasta with holes for stringing can be dyed in brilliant colors to make beautiful beads. Blue becomes an attractive turquoise color. Let children string them on silver cord (available from fabric stores) to make striking Navajo turquoise jewelry.

Dyed Macaroni Beads

1 quart jar with lid
4 bottles of alcohol (1 bottle per color used)
4 bottles food coloring (red, yellow, blue, green)
Pasta in all sizes and shapes suitable for stringing
Stacks of newspaper

Pour one bottle of coloring into each bottle of alcohol and mix well. Fill the quart jar to the top with the pasta. Pour the alcohol-food color mixture over the pasta. Place the lid on the jar and tighten securely. Shake the jar up and down for about 5 minutes or until the pasta is a brilliant color. Open and drain off the liquid into another container. (Save dye for another batch.) Pour pasta onto newspapers spread on a table and let dry.

Armbands and Leg Rattles

Armbands and leg rattles were used as a part of some tribal groups' dress in ceremonial dances. The Creek women wore leg rattles made of conch shells when dancing the Green Corn Dance. Some groups wore leg rattles made from cocoons. Many dancers at powwows wear leg rattles with bells attached.

Children can make armbands (worn on the upper arm) and leg rattles (worn just below the knee) using numerous materials—leather pieces, fabric, beads, markers, sequins, feathers, and small bells. Supply the materials, along with authentic armbands and leg rattles and books and pictures for children to examine before designing their own. Bags of leather strips and strings are available at craft stores.

Boats

Talk about the kinds of boats that were used long ago by different American Indian groups in different regions. Display pictures for children to study. Discuss the kinds of trees, tools, and designs used. Identify the skills needed to build a boat (see Transportation).

Experiment with "sink and float" by having children make small boats. Provide egg cartons, wood scraps, pipe cleaners, crayons, glue, sticks, paper, and cardboard. Suggest that children create boats that will float. Provide a basin, bucket, or pan for experiments.

Bows and Arrows and Quivers

Discuss with children how bows and arrows were used as tools to provide food and protection for families.

For the Iroquois, bows and arrows were the major hunting equipment. They made bows of yew and other hard woods and often decorated them. Demonstrate the use of a bow and arrow for children, and display a collection of arrowheads for them to examine. Cases for carrying arrows are called quivers.

Some quivers were made of buffalo hide, others from deerskin.

Owner Sticks

Owner sticks were staffs used by some Plains and Eastern groups to show possession of property. The sticks were decorated with objects and designs that identified an individual. Many American Indians have descriptive names, such as Yellow Feather, White Dove, Strong Thunder, and Black Horse. Children can choose descriptive names for themselves and decorate an owner stick to represent the name.

Ask children to bring two sticks from home, one as tall as their bodies and one the length of their arm. Have extra sticks available. Lash the sticks together with a leather thong to form a cross. Let children paint markings on these sticks with tempera paint mixed with white glue. They can choose from an assortment of large and small feathers, shells, fur scraps, seeds, beads, colored yarn, and other objects to decorate their sticks. Children can use their sticks to designate seating for their families at Harvest Feast.

Totem Poles

The Kwakuitl (North Coastal) people are famous for their totem poles and house posts. Long ago, they displayed decorated poles with carved crests outside their homes. The totem pole is a symbol, a coat of arms, and a genetic identifier that tells a family's story and origin.

Provide cardboard boxes and paint for children to use to make totem poles. Suggest that they draw on the side of the boxes to decorate them. The finished totem poles add a cultural spirit to the classroom.

Victoria, British Columbia, has a collection of totem poles in the main square and at the Provincial Museum. Stanley Park in Vancouver also has interesting totem poles. The University of British Columbia at Vancouver has a museum on its campus that features an elaborate display of Northwest Coastal Indian posts, poles, and a community house.

Pottery

The Pueblo groups are known for their pottery. Groups can be identified by the designs they use, including the owl (Acoma) and the turtle (Hopi). Pueblo artists make pottery into very beautiful shapes, both for utilitarian items and for toys.

Many Pueblo potters dig their own clay and boil plants to extract color. A yucca stem may be used as a brush to make pattern and designs on the finished piece.

Natural clay can be dug from a creek bed. Children enjoy the outings to dig for clay and the process of drying, pounding, and removing debris from it. Let children add water to the prepared clay and knead it.

When the clay can easily be worked, show children how to shape storage jars, canteens, bowls, and cooking pots out of it, adding traditional or original designs. Preparing the clay is an important activity for motor development and sensory experiences, and it helps children understand how the American Indians made pottery from clay.

The work of the following artists may be of interest to children:

Michael Naranjo is a Pueblo sculptor who works with several museums; Maria Montoya is a master Pueblo artisan from San Ildefonso, New Mexico; Santana Antonio, an Acoma Indian, is known for beautiful pottery; Paul Speckled Rock, a Santa Clara Indian, is a potter, painter, and sculptor.

Arts of Clay, by Christine Price, and *Our Voices, Our Land,* by the Indian Peoples of the Southwest, are good references.

Feather Painting

Children can use feathers as paintbrushes for an unusual effect. Materials from nature are recycled and used creatively in this activity.

Picture-Skin Story—Sioux

In the past, the Sioux did not write their language; instead, they painted pictures on rawhide to depict important events in the lives of the individual painter and the tribe. This was called a "winter count" because it was completed during that season. People used the winter count to pass on the history of the tribe.

Let children cut brown or white wrapping paper into the shape of animal skins and then crush the paper to soften it and give it an animal-skin look. Then they can draw symbols on the crushed paper to make a picture-skin story, showing the important events of the school year or creating an original story.

Legend of the Indian Paintbrush, by Tomie de Paola, is an excellent resource. *The Seminole,* by Alice Opinski, describes hide painting.

Weaving

Hopi men and women weave traditional designs into their ceremonial garments. Yucca leaves and various grasses may be used.

Some Navajo Indians set up a large loom in front of their hogan and weave their highly valued rugs. Provide wool sheared from a sheep for children to examine. Discuss how some Navajo people raise their own sheep.

Children may weave using small looms made from an 8-by-10-inch piece of sturdy cardboard. String yarn from top to bottom around notches. Attach the ends of yarn to the backside of the loom with tape. Provide an assortment of brightly colored fabric strips, feathers, fur scraps, and heavy yarn for children to use to weave rugs.

Apache Burden Basket

Baskets for gathering seeds, berries and nuts were woven and carried by Apache women of the Southwest. Leather strips with small pieces of metal or flint attached to the ends were hung around the sides and in the bottom of these cone-shaped baskets. The metal pieces clanged together and made a noise to scare away snakes hiding in the tall grass.

To make a burden basket, children can weave leather strings through holes in inexpensive baskets. Hammer holes in the center of metal disks. Attach the disks to the ends of the leather strings and bend the disks in half.

Children enjoy taking their baskets outdoors for seed gathering.

Coup Sticks—A Plains Indian Custom

In the past, coup sticks were trophies or symbols of bravery. Each feather on the coup stick represented a brave

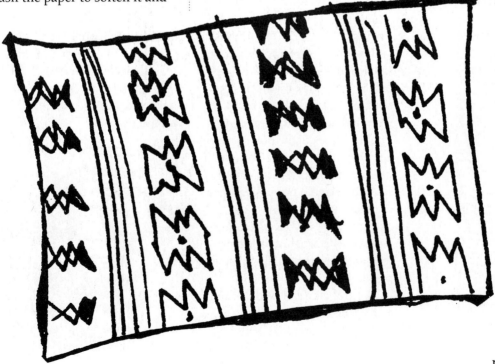

deed. Children can make coup sticks by attaching 1-by-24-inch leather strips to the end of a 36-inch stick. Feathers may be placed in slits cut in the leather strips.

Ojibwa Dream Catcher

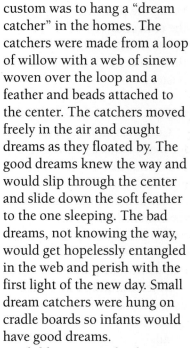

According to an Ojibwa legend, the night air is filled with dreams, good and bad. The custom was to hang a "dream catcher" in the homes. The catchers were made from a loop of willow with a web of sinew woven over the loop and a feather and beads attached to the center. The catchers moved freely in the air and caught dreams as they floated by. The good dreams knew the way and would slip through the center and slide down the soft feather to the one sleeping. The bad dreams, not knowing the way, would get hopelessly entangled in the web and perish with the first light of the new day. Small dream catchers were hung on cradle boards so infants would have good dreams.

Children can make dream catchers by forming a small willow branch into a circle and securing it with a leather string. The string is woven in and out and across the circle to form a web. Waxed dental floss works well for the web. Attach a feather and several glass beads to the center of the catcher. A leather string is attached to the top for hanging.

Rock Painting

The Pueblo groups drew murals on cliffs and canyon walls throughout New Mexico and Arizona. Explain how pictures and symbols are used to convey ideas.

Children like to copy pictographs, using tempera paint on different sizes of rocks. Collecting the rocks can be an interesting part of the activity.

Murals

Murals can be used to illustrate the different types of places where American Indians live. Picture books containing information about the homes and environment of different American Indian groups can be used for reference.

Let children draw and paint mountains, trees, rocks, rivers, animals, homes, buildings, and other things to suggest the environment of a particular group

on large pieces of butcher paper and use them as backdrops for related activities.

Famous American Indian painters include R. C. Gorman, a Navajo; Amado Maurilio Peña, Jr., a Mexican/Yaqui; Jaune Quick-To-See Smith, a French-Cree and Shoshone; and Emmi Whitehorse, a Navajo.

Sand Painting

Although some American Indians believe that a circle painted in sand "spirits illnesses away" from them, present sand painting solely as an art form.

Traditions having to do with religion should not be taught in the classroom. When children view pictures of sand paintings, encourage them to talk about how they are created.

Kachina Dolls

The kachina dolls are beautiful to children, but carving dolls and using them to imitate the kachina dance is offensive to many Hopi families. Instead, have pictures of kachina dolls or authentic examples available and discuss their uniqueness.

NATURE AND SCIENCE

Many American Indians are ecologists, preserving the natural environment and using the resources of the land wisely. They care about keeping the balance in nature and show an understanding for the relationship between themselves and their surroundings. Many American Indians adapt to their environment instead of trying to change it.

Display

A display of natural materials shows the resourcefulness of some American Indians. Talk with children about trees, plants, and animals that live in the mountains, valleys, and deserts, and about the climate of these areas. Include the children in organizing a display area. Encourage them to bring artifacts.

Children enjoy examining materials from nature, such as rocks, bones, animal skins, deer and antelope antlers, dried Indian corn, gourds, feathers, arrowheads, pictures of local natural resources, and even live animals.

The more items you can put into your collection, the more interest and excitement you will be able to generate as children explore the objects and form questions. Encourage families to contribute to the Nature and Science center.

Appropriate books, posters, and pictures provide children with the resources to ask questions and discover answers. The Forest Service of the U.S. Department of Agriculture has a complete set of wildlife posters, including an excellent poster of animal tracks to use when examining different animal feet. Using the real animal feet from the collection, children make prints in wet sand and match them with the tracks on the poster.

Corn

Corn was an important food for many American Indians. Provide a variety of corn for children's examination and experimentation: fresh corn on the cob, dried corn on the cob, Indian blue and red corn, white corn, popcorn, cracked corn, and white and yellow cornmeal.

American Indians long ago used a metate and mano to grind corn. Provide a metate (available at some import and Mexican grocery stores) for children to use. Two stones may be used for grinding. Let children remove kernels of dried corn from cobs. Put corn in a bowl and cover it with water to soak overnight. Then let children take turns grinding the corn.

An excellent resource for these activities is *Corn Is Maize, the Gift of the Indian,* by Aliki.

Dyeing

Berries, fruits, vegetables, and earth are used by American Indians for dyeing cloth.

Vegetables and fruits cut into pieces may be rubbed or pounded into cloth. Let children experiment with a variety of plants, fruits and vegetables, including berries, beets, and flower petals or leaves. The liquid from boiled onion skins makes a yellow color. To dye wool yarn or cloth in the onion skin dye, place it in the liquid for about 15 minutes and then hang to dry. Spinach may be used to make green dye; red clay dissolved in water can be used to paint on fabric.

LANGUAGE DEVELOPMENT

Vocabulary

The following words may be used in labeling pictures and objects in the room.

adobe
buffalo
canoe
coup stick
desert
forest
Hopi
Iroquois
Kwakuitl
Navajo
plains
pottery
powwow
Sioux
tipi
totem pole
wampum
wigwam
woodlands

Additional words and terms may be found in the various sections of the unit.

A majority of groups continue to speak a native language in addition to English. Many others use words of their native language when referring to things that are part of their cultural heritage. Encourage correct use of proper American Indian terms. Authentic languages may be heard on some of the recordings listed in the bibliography.

Stories

Ask children to dictate or write stories using words and ideas suggested by their American Indian experiences and activities. Display large posters with American Indian symbols matched with English words.

Symbols may be copied to print a message.

Symbols

tribe

lake

canoe

canoe with people

walking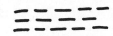

forest

many

lightning

man

woman

cactus

bear track

rattlesnake jaw

mountain

paths crossing

peace

home

time

rain

Include these American Indians in your study: Vine Deloria, Jr., a Sioux writer; Ella Deloria, a Sioux historian and linguist; Charles Eastman, a Dakota Sioux author; and Madge Skelly, an Iroquois communication specialist who invented Indian hand talk.

Folktales

Folktales are more meaningful if one knows the background of the people who originally told them. Stories and tales are still told to children in many American-Indian homes and at school, featuring interesting characters, adventure, and animals who are able to talk and do what people do.

Dramatization

Children usually find props they need for dramatizing stories. Some children need help in deciding on props that satisfy them. Have a variety of materials available for props, which can be used in many ways for many stories.

The following are some favorite stories for dramatization: *The Great Race,* by Paul Goble; *The Angry Moon,* by William Sleator; *Whale in the Sky,* by Ann Siberell.

Navajo Verse

Learn the Navajo verse. Children learn this easily. Motions may be added to the farewell.

Hogooneh (So Be It)
There shall be happiness before us.
(Arms stretched out in front.)

There shall be happiness behind us.
(Arms stretched behind body.)

There shall be happiness above us.
(Arms stretched over head.)

There shall be happiness below us.
(Bend and touch the floor.)

There shall be happiness all around us.
(Turn around with arms spread out.)

Words of happiness shall extend from our mouths.
(Touch lips with both hands and stretch arms outward.)

MUSIC AND DANCE

American Indians have songs to celebrate almost every important event. Their ceremonies feature dances with their songs. The dancers imitate animals and birds and act out stories of their people.

Hoop Dance

The basis for traditional American-Indian dances came from the daily life of the people, and dance continues to play a major role in the lives of many American Indians. When Indian people come together for dance, there is a renewal of acquaintances and an affirmation of traditions.

The formation of a circle in a round dance represents the renewal and rebirth of life; holding hands is a symbol of unity. Some Sioux people hoop dance, using as many as twelve hoops at a time. Let children listen to the songs of the Sioux and practice dancing with a hoop. A small hula hoop may be used; the child holds the hoop and alternates legs in stepping in and out of the hoop.

Celebrations

Powwows are gatherings of many tribes from all parts of the United States and Canada. This reunion of tribal members and extended families is also a revival of American-Indian customs. Music and dancing, games, good food, and crafts are all part of the powwow.

Songs

Recordings of American Indian songs are listed in the bibliography.

Drums

Drums and flutes were some of the instruments used by Indian groups to furnish rhythm for the dancers. Drums are one of the oldest known musical instruments. Many kinds of drums were used by American Indian groups, in ceremonial dances and to announce or celebrate a special event, and they still play an important part in today's powwows and tribal celebrations.

Pueblo drums were made from hollow logs, with animal skins stretched over the open ends. A water drum used by the Chippewa, Seminole, and several Pueblo groups was made from hollow logs or from large clay pots. The log or pot was filled about one third full with water to give a deeper sound that carried for long distances.

Make a community drum for your classroom: A large plastic leaf basket turned upside down makes a nice one—children can produce a great sound by strik-

ing it with a stick that has been padded on one end with a soft cloth, then covered with a piece of sheepskin and tied with a leather thong.

Children are often interested in making a water drum. A large clay pot, metal bucket, or plastic pail can be used, with a chamois for the drum head. Let children use waterproof paint pens to draw designs on the chamois and sides of the drum. Soak the chamois in water so that it can be stretched tightly over the pot. Let children help smooth and hold the skin on the drum as a leather thong is tied around the top. Let the skin dry in the sun to shrink. The drum plays best if the skin is dampened. Discuss with the children their ideas on how to dampen the skin with the water inside. Strike the drum with a stick and listen to the mellow sound.

Children can make individual water drums from three-pound coffee cans, each child

determining the amount of water to use. Put plastic lids on securely. Cover the can with brown butcher paper. Let children draw symbols and designs on the paper. Cut a circle from brown paper, two inches larger than the top of the drum. Crumple the paper to soften it, and tie it on top of the drum with a leather thong.

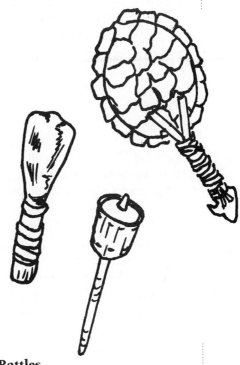

Rattles

Iroquois "singing tools" are birch bark, animal horns, and turtle shells used as rattles. Use small cans as rattles. Let children experiment with different kinds of sounds that can be made. Suggest that they search the yard for stones, sticks, and bottle caps, then fill the cans with their objects, and before sealing them, experiment to find out how many stones it takes to produce the sound they desire. They may then paint designs on the outside of the can.

GAMES AND MANIPULATIVES

American-Indian children play games all children play, but they also have some favorite traditional games.

Lacrosse

Lacrosse, the national game of the Iroquois, is played with a stick that has a net at one end. The object of the game is to throw or scoop the ball into the opposing team's goal. An adaptation of this game, complete with playing instructions, can be purchased at a sporting goods store.

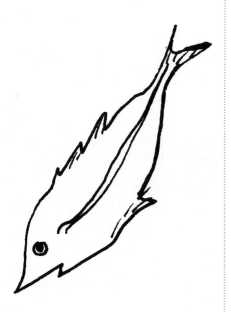

Gigging

In gigging (catching fish by dragging a hook through a school of fish), children imitate Northwestern Indians fishing from a pier. Let them draw and cut out fish, attaching a paper clip to each one. Then they can tie a string to a 36-inch stick to make a fishing pole, tie a washer-shaped magnet to the end of the string, and drag the magnet through the paper fish on the floor.

Stickball

Stickball is a traditional game for Seminole children that is similar to lacrosse.

Cup and Ball

Cup and Ball provides outdoor fun for Sioux children. This game can be made by attaching a cup to one end of a 12-inch leather string and the ball to the other end. The object of the game is to catch the ball in the cup. Begin by swinging the ball above the cup, holding the cup firmly in one hand. Children like knowing that the Inuits made the game from walrus ivory; the Kwakuitl version is called "dzagzegala."

Stone Toss Game

Many American-Indian groups played dice games using a variety of objects for dice. Some tribes used shells and plum or peach stones. The Hopi used small flat stones painted or decorated on one side. The stones or other dice were placed in a flat basket with the decorated sides down. The basket was tossed to make the stones jump. Points depended on how many stones landed decorated-side up. Children may develop their own versions of this game and decide on the point system.

Counting and Sorting

Children may use beads for sorting, stringing, and counting; nuts of different kinds for sorting and describing; unpopped colored popcorn for counting and sorting. Provide small containers and tweezers or small wooden tongs for picking up the items. Children can sort items according to size, shape, or color.

Navajo Weaving

Make a large wooden frame from 36-inch dowels. Cover the frame with burlap. Cut six rows of 2-inch slits vertically across the burlap. Provide a basket of long strips of fabric and yarn for weaving. This can be an ongoing project. Let children sit on the floor and weave. Hang the finished piece on a wall in the classroom.

Puzzles

Provide puzzles depicting authentic American-Indian scenes for children to work.

SPECIAL EVENTS

Interest Trips and Resources

At the beginning of the school year, it is imperative that you find information about the American Indian people who live or have lived in your community, town, or city. If American Indians belonging to nations native to your area still live there, ask them to assist you in collecting appropriate books and authentic artifacts and materials, and in critiquing activities.

Children gain an awareness of the different American Indian groups from resource persons and field trips. Here are some ideas:

• Visit an American-Indian school.

• Invite American-Indian children to visit your school.

• Invite resource persons from American-Indian centers in your community to talk with children and to share authentic artifacts.

• Identify resources for American Indians in your community and inquire about speakers through the public library, Chamber of Commerce, local organizations, heritage centers, and local colleges.

• Visit American-Indian reservations near your community.

• There are many excellent museums displaying American-Indian artifacts along with interpretive centers, archeological sites, and other places of interest throughout the United States. Find out what is available in your area.

Harvest Feast

Celebrate the fall season with a Harvest Feast for the school families. Have children plan and prepare the food for the feast and arrange and set the tables. Families and friends are invited to share in this feast. Traditional foods and dishes that are favorites for the children's families are discussed. Children show a great deal of interest in learning about food preparation methods, such as knowing that, in the past, some American Indians baked beans by burying pots of beans in the ground.

Some of the following traditional favorites can be prepared for the Harvest Feast: turkey, beef, cornbread, corn on the cob, popcorn balls, cranberries, peanuts, sweet potatoes, roasted pumpkin seeds, potatoes, wild onions, tomatoes, carrots, poke (greens), nuts, venison, and blackberries (a Kwakuitl favorite). Selection from this list will depend on the ages of the children who participate.

The Harvest Feast can provide an opportunity to acknowledge the American Indians' respect for the land and harmony with nature. Separate this event from traditional American Thanksgiving, which many American Indians find offensive because of historical injustice.

CELEBRATIONS

The following festivals are celebrated by some American-Indian groups. Many schools have special events about the history of American Indians.

National American-Indian Heritage Month: November

November was officially proclaimed National American-Indian Heritage Month by the President of the United States in 1990.

Indian Day of Glory: June 25

This day commemorates the Battle of the Little Big Horn in 1876, in which the Sioux and Cheyenne defeated Colonel George Custer and the 7th cavalry.

All American Indian Days: the first week of August

During this week, many American-Indian tribes gather in Sheridan, Wyoming, to celebrate.

Gallup Inter-Tribal Indian Ceremonial: Mid-August (dates vary)

Each year Gallup, New Mexico, hosts the Inter-Tribal Ceremonial. This annual pageant of festive traditions features some 500 Indian dancers from many tribes in authentic costumes. A commemorative poster can be ordered from the Inter-Tribal Indian Ceremonial Association, P.O. Box 1, Church Rock, New Mexico 87311. Phone: (505) 863-3895.

Hopi Snake Dance: late August (date varies)

The Snake Dance is the most famous ceremonial of the Hopis. It is usually held in August; the medicine men determine the exact date 16 days before the ceremony.

Red Earth

This is the biggest social-cultural gathering of American and Canadian nations for powwow feasting. It is held the first weekend in June in Oklahoma City. An annual powwow also takes place on Labor Day weekend in Grand Prairie, Texas.

For more information about the times and places of events open to the public, write to the Bureau of Indian Affairs, U.S. Department of the Interior, Washington, DC 20245.

RESOURCES

N Nursery
K Kindergarten
P Primary
I Intermediate
A Adult

Books for Children

Aliki. *Corn Is Maize. The Gift of the Indians.* Harper & Row Publishers, 1976. NKP
All you ever wanted to know about corn! The scientific and historical aspects of corn are described.

Baker, *Betty. And Me, Coyote!* Macmillan Publishing Co., 1982. KP
Linoleum cuts illustrate this American Indian myth about a clever coyote that assists the World Maker. The author's book Little Runner of the Longhouse depicts Iroquois families living in a longhouse.

Baker, Olaf. *Where the Buffaloes Begin.* Frederich Warne and Co., Inc., 1981. P
Stephen Gammell's illustrations add a beautiful note to this sensitive story about Little Wolf, who led the buffalo and saved his people. The text is for older children, but all ages enjoy the tale. It is a helpful resource when constructing a coup stick.

Bash, Barbara. *Desert Giant.* Sierra Club Books/Little, Brown and Co, 1989. KP
The giant saguaro cactus has life-giving properties for the Tohon O'odham Indians as well as for the creatures of the desert.

Baylor, Byrd. *And It Is Still That Way: Legends Told by Arizona Indian Children.* Trails West Publishing, 1989. KP
This famous author, who knows what children love (*Everybody Needs a Rock* and *When Clay Sings),* interviews Navajo, Hopi, Papago, Pima, Apache, Quechuan, and Cocopah children to determine the "best story in the world."

Behrens, June. *Powwow: Festivals and Holidays.* Children's Press, 1983. KP
With the assistance of a number of Hopi and Choctaw people, the author describes an American-Indian celebration when all tribes come together. The colorful photographs enable children to understand that American Indians are contemporary people.

Blood, Charles and Martin Link. *The Goat in the Rug.* Four Winds Press, 1976. NKP
Describes step-by-step process of the weaving of a Navajo rug as told by Geraldine, the goat who furnishes the wool. Useful when constructing a hogan and a loom.

Brown, Virginia Pounds, and Laurella Owens. *The World of the Southern Indians.* Beechwood Books, 1983. P
This excellent book for older readers is also very helpful for teachers who are planning a cultural unit or a study of homes, ceremonies, or famous people. It is a good review for teachers.

Caswell, Helen. *Shadows from the Singing House.* Charles E. Tuttle Company, 1978. P
In the true spirit of this oral culture, the author has gathered a variety of ancient Eskimo folktales for retelling. Our beginnings, the origins and habits of

creatures in nature, and survival of this proud group are examined in these eighteen stories. Eskimo artist Robert Mayokok adds life to the text with his finely detailed drawings of traditional activities and implements of daily use.

Cleaver, Elizabeth. *The Enchanted Caribou.* Distributed by Olive Press, 1985. KP
Children delight in dramatizing this old tale about a young girl who is tricked into doing what she was told not to do.

_____. *The Fire Starter.* Oxford University Press, 1979. KP
Hoping to cheer his grandmother, a boy goes in search of "a fiery torch." Children dramatize this adventure about the colors of fire.

_____. *The Mountain Goats of Temlaham.* Oxford University Press, 1969. KP
A famous legend told with bright splashes of paper collages, this is a favorite for fostering dramatics. The totem poles dominate this story about the mountain goats' revenge on the men of Temlaham.

Cohen, Caron Lee. *The Mud Pony.* Scholastic, Inc., 1988. KP
A Pawnee legend of trust, perseverance, and courage is lovingly illustrated by Native American artist Shonto Bigay.

Damjam, Mischa. *Atuk.* North-South Books, 1990. NK
In this lovely imaginative book, children learn from a theme that teaches that love is stronger than hate.

dePaola, Tomie. *The Legend of the Bluebonnet.* G. P. Putnam's Sons, 1988. KP
The story of how a Comanche tribe is saved by a young girl is illustrated in subtle color.

_____. *The Legend of the Indian Paintbrush.* G.P. Putnam's Sons, 1988. KP
A young American-Indian boy is determined to share the beauty of his Dream-Vision with his people, making a lasting contribution to his culture. Children will be inspired to paint the brilliant sunsets and animal-skin pictures as Little Gopher did in this rich presentation.

Dixon, Sarah, and Peter Dixon. *Children, Families, and the Sea.* Cypress, 1979. KP
The story of thirteen-year-old Dennis Johnson, a Kwakuitl Indian of the Northwest Coastal tribes. Informative text shares the spotlight with meaningful photographs.

Dressman, John. *On the Cliffs of Acoma: A Pueblo Story with a Short History of Acoma.* Sunstone Press, 1984. KP
An accident on an adventure to the mesa top reveals a courageous streak in Christina and Peter.

Eagle Walking Turtle. *Keepers of the Fire.* Bear and Company, 1987. KP
Brilliant paintings interpret the visions of Black Elk, an Oglala Sioux. He explains the spiritual and physical journeys of his people toward peace and harmony with the earth. The colorful simplicity of the drawings attracts the attention and interest of young children; older students can experience the lifestyle and beliefs through the descriptive text.

Esbensen, Barbara Juster. *The Star Maiden.* Little, Brown and Co., 1988. KP
Delicate drawings capture the interest of children as they hear this Ojibway tale.

Fordham, Derek. *Eskimos.* Silver Burdett Co., 1979. NK
Large photographs and illustrations serve as a wonderful guide to teachers and children who want to learn about traditional Eskimo methods.

Garbarino, Merwyn S. *The Seminole.* Chelsea House Publishers, 1989. P
This book, written for older children, can be used by adults as they examine the culture and history of the Seminole. The color section on crafts can be enjoyed by younger children as they decorate or make a patchwork design. This book is useful when constructing the traditional-style Seminole home with a thatched roof of palms.

Gill, Shelley. *Kiana's Iditarod.* Paw Publishing Co., 1987. P
Young children delight in hearing about a race across mountains and tundra and through snow and ice storms. The story is lavishly illustrated with radiant watercolors, clarifying this world-renowned event with pictures of huskies, sleds, maps, a moose, reindeer, and much more.

Goble, Paul. *Beyond the Ridge.* Bradbury Press, 1989. KPI
In attempting to explain death, the author/illustrator selects

from beliefs of the Plains groups, Navajos, and Lakotas.

_____. *Buffalo Women.* Aladdin Books, 1984. KP
In tribute to the tribes of the Great Plains, the followers of the buffalo herds, the author and illustrator dramatically recounts the relationship between the native people and the buffalo. The illustrations of tipis are useful when constructing one.

_____. *Death of the Iron Horse.* Bradbury Press, 1987. KP
The Union Pacific freight train, derailed by the Cheyennes in 1867, is the only train ever wrecked by American-Indian people. This books tells the story of their act of bravery.

_____. *The Gift of the Sacred Dog.* Bradbury Press, 1980. KP
A courageous boy, who is concerned about his hungry broth-ers and sisters, searches for an answer from the Great Spirit. The marvelous characters provide the ingredients for dramatization and allow a glimpse into the lives of the nomadic buffalo hunters who roamed the Great Plains. Beautiful illustrations of tipis.

_____. *Star Boy.* Bradbury Press, 1983. KP
Children enjoy dramatizing legends with the Moon and the Sun as main characters. This traditional tale about the Blackfeet is illustrated in India ink and watercolors. *The Gift of Sacred Pony* by Goble and this book reveal beautiful designs on clothing.

Graymont, Barbara. *The Iroquois.* Chelsea House Publishers, 1988. P
This is another in a series of twelve books on the Indians of North America. "The False Faces" photograph section is enjoyed by all ages. Adults will find this an excellent reference book.

Grie, Shelly. *The Alaska Mother Goose.* Paws IV, 1987. NK
Children delight in repeating these North country nursery rhymes, illustrated with vivid, bold crayon drawings.

Hadley, Eric, and Tess Hadley. *Legends of the Sun and Moon.* Cambridge University Press, 1983. P
Stories from the Blackfeet, Cherokee, Maori, West Africans, Mexicans, and others have similar content, showing the very human elements of these popular characters.

Hall, Geraldine. *Kee's Home—A Beginning Navajo/English Reader.* Northland Press, 1976. KP
Designed as a first reader for Navajo children, this bilingual edition provides a glimpse of Navajo life and language for all young children. Meaningful drawings enhance the text.

Haseley, Dennis. *The Sacred One.* Frederick Warne and Co., Inc., 1983. P
A young boy fears that he can never be brave until an injured bird changes his fate. Deborah Howland, who lived for four years among the Oglala Sioux, provides authentic illustrations.

Highwater, Jamake. *Moonsong Lullaby.* Lothrop, Lee & Shepard Books, 1981. KP
American Indians give children a poetic and photographic presentation of the moon as it moves across the evening sky.

Hoover, Herbert T. *The Yankton Sioux.* Chelsea House Publishers, 1988. PIA
Descriptive text and photographs give details of the past and present of the Yankton Sioux. This is an excellent resource.

Jernigan, Gisela. *Agave Blooms Just Once.* Harbinger House, 1989. NKP
Southwestern art is this author's specialty. Complete with letter forms based on Hohokam design and a phonetic pronunciation key, this alphabet book delights all readers, young and old!

Kalman, Bobbie, and William Belsey. *An Arctic Community.*

Crabtree Publishing Company, 1988. KP
Bright photographs accompany factual text, introducing children and adults to the lives and traditions of the people of the Rankin Inlet. Native people of this region prefer to be called *Inuits,* which means "the people."

Lepthien, Emilie U. *The Cherokee.* Children's Press, 1985. KP
These beautiful photographs of Cherokee life describe the Cherokee Nation from its earliest days to the present. Useful sections for young children are found in the first pages, which explore hunting, fishing, and Cherokee life.

_____. *The Choctaw.* Children's Press, 1987. KP
This book is part of an excellent series on American Indians. The history and traditions, as well as present-day lifestyle of the Choctaw, are carefully documented in simple text and colorful photographs. Others in this series include *The Apache, The Cherokee,* and *The Seminole.*

_____. *The Seminole.* Children's Press, 1985. KP
Photographs of Seminole families, past and present, embellish this informative text that covers tribal life in Florida on and off the reservation. A section about crafts and a helpful glossary are also included.

Longfellow, Henry Wadsworth. *Hiawatha's Childhood.* Puffin Books, 1984. KP
Richly detailed illustrations by Errol LeCain capture the vision of Longfellow's classic poem.

Luling, Virginia. *Indians of the North American Plains.* MacDonald Educational Ltd, 1978. KP
Detailed illustrations and easy-to-read text acquaint children with the lifestyle of the Plains Indians.

Maher, Ramona. *Alice Yazzie's Year.* Coward, McCann and Geoghegan, Inc., 1977. P
A poem for each month describing cultural concerns is set against a young girl's feelings. November's free verse poems make a strong statement against celebrating the time when land was being taken away from the American Indian.

Martin, Bill, Jr., and John Archambault. *Knots on a Counting Rope.* Henry Holt and Company, Inc., 1987. KP
When Grandfather and Boy-Strength-of-Blue-Horse review the events of Boy's birth and early years unfolds, a story of courage and abiding love between granddad and grandson unfolds. Ted Rand's watercolor illustrations are a handsome addition to this literary experience.

Martini, Tery. *Indians.* Children's Press, 1982. P
Numerous color photographs and a brief text describe five American-Indian groups living on the coast, desert, plains, swamps, and woodlands. A distinction is made between past and present.

Morgan, William Collector. *Navajo Coyote Tales.* Ancient City Press, 1988. NK
Young readers enjoy the adventures that entertained Navajo children on long winter nights

as they gathered around the fire in their hogans.

Munsch, Robert, and Michael Kusuqak. *A Promise Is a Promise.* Annick Press Ltd., 1988.   NKP
Fresh pastel illustrations capture the eye of young children as they listen to the story of the imaginary Inuit creature, Qallysillug, who lives under the Arctic ice floor and grabs children if they come too near the cracks in the ice. This traditional tale is set against modern changes that life has brought the Inuits.

Miller, Montzalee. *My Grandmother's Cookie Jar.* Price, Stern, Sloan Publishers, 1987.   KP
After Grandmother's death, Grandfather's stories of Indian people of long ago instill in a young girl a sense of the importance of passing on the rich legacy of one's culture.

Nashone. *Where Indians Live: American Indian Houses.* Sierra Oaks Publishing Company, 1989.   KP
This one-of-a-kind book by an American Indian is an excellent reference for finding out how American Indians lived in the past and how they live today. Clear information is given about temporary and permanent homes.

Nelson, Jenny. *The Weavers.* The University of Columbia Press, 1983.   P
Gathering, soaking, and splitting bark; roasting roots; weaving designs with a spider web, a snake's track, a bear—all this is learned from the elders. This informative book, which is free

of stereotypes, suggests weaving activities.

Newman, Gerald. *The Changing Eskimos.* Franklin Watts, 1979.   KP
Children learn about the Inuits and the distinct and diverse lifestyle they enjoy in the northern towns.

Opinski, Alice. *The Navajo.* Children's Press, 1987.   P
One important focus of this book is separation of the modern from the traditional. A young reader can enjoy the simple text, rich vocabulary, and striking photographs. Other favorites by Alice Opinski are *The Eskimo, The Inuit and Yupik People*, and *The Sioux.* Photographs in *The Sioux* offer interesting designs for tipis. The Seminole describes hide painting.

Ortiz, Simon J. *The People Shall Continue.* Children's Press, 1977.   P
This "epic story of Native American People" gives the history of the American Indians' survival despite the inhuman way they have been treated since their homeland was invaded. Children can begin to understand their plight.

Red Hawk, Richard. *Grandfather's Story of Navajo Monsters.* Sierra Oaks Publishing Company, 1988.   NKP
Most children like to talk about monsters sometime in their early childhood years.

Rogers, Jean. *Runaway Mittens.* Greenwillow Books, 1988.   NK
A marvelous story related by Alaskans. When they see radiators, curtains, ice fishing, and teapots, children begin to understand modern-day Indians of North America.

Roth, Susan L. *Kanahina: A Cherokee Story.* St. Martin's Press, 1988.
Collages of natural materials inspire children to illustrate their own version of the retelling of this traditional Cherokee story about a terrapin's tricks to outwit a pack of wolves.

Siberell, Anne. *Whale in the Sky.* E. P. Dutton, 1982.   K
A thunderbird, raven, salmon, and frog are upstaged by a terrible whale that gasps and shivers. Include this tale when creating a totem pole. The art is striking, and the text lends itself to dramatization.

Smith, Kathie Billingslea. *Sitting Bull.* Julian Mossner, 1987.   P
Young readers explore the life and times of Chief Sitting Bull. Indian customs and traditions are explained as the author clarifies the plight of the American Indian.

Smith, Mary Lou M. *Grandmother's Adobe Dollhouse.* New Mexico Magazine, 1984.   P

Architecture, art, food, and the cultures of New Mexico are depicted in this unique book for children and adults. In addition to the careful research, readers are given many Spanish nouns and a guide for pronunciation.

Sneve, Virginia Driving Hawk. *Dancing Tepees—Poems of American Indian Youth*. Holiday House, 1989. KP
Poems from the oral tradition of American Indians come alive through the simple but meaningful drawings of Stephen Gammell. Excellent for reading to children, its illustrations suggest possible designs.

Steptal, John. *The Story of Jumping Mouse*. Lothrop, Lee & Shepard Books, 1984. KP
An unselfish spirit realizes its dream for greatness. A simple mouse becomes a powerful eagle in this Great Plains legend. There is a richness about the black and white illustrations, but one is curious to see the splendid characters of a bison, a magic frog, and a wolf in full color.

Vallo, Lawrence Jonathan. *Tales of a Pueblo Boy*. Sunstone, 1987.
The author and storyteller recalls stories about Rabbit, which are part of his memories from childhood, when his desire for exploring cultures was beginning.

Villaseñor, David, and Jean Villaseñor. *Indian Designs*. Naturegraph Publisher, Inc., 1983. KP
Indian designs of the Greater Southwest are reproduced to encourage research into the original culture of this country.

The children will also enjoy the following books. Look for them in your library.

Bealer, Alex W. *The Picture Skin Story*.
Clark, Ann N. *In My Mother's House*.
Friskey, Margaret. *Indian Two Feet and the Wolf Cubs*.
Glubok, Shirley. *The Art of the North American Indian*, and *The Art of the Southwest Indian*.
Goble, Paul. *The Great Race*.
Jones, Hettie. *The Trees Stand Shining*.
Kusugak, Michael Arvaarluk. *Baseball Bats for Christmas*.
McDermott, Gerold. *Arrow to the Sun*.
Miles, Miska. *Annie and the Old One*.
Scott, Ann Herbert. *On Mother's Lap*.
Sleator, William. *The Angry Moon*.

Books and Periodicals for Adults

American Indian Education Handbook. American Indian Education Handbook Committee. California State Department of Education, 1982.
A splendid book that describes American-Indian terminology and makes suggestions for using it. The section entitled "Teaching about Americans" directs educators in creating learning environments for young children that help them assimilate an accurate picture of American Indians and their contributions to American life.

Boloz, Sigmund, and Debbie Hickman. *Just Beyond Your Fingertips: American Indian Children Participating in Language Development*. Eric/Cress, 1987.

Ideas for establishing or improving a language program, a review of the issues in early literacy, and a discussion of ways to involve parents. Activities with a holistic approach for kindergarten through third-grade students make this book a valuable tool in providing a quality program. Modeled by a Navajo primary school.

Calloway, Colin G. *The Abenaki*. Chelsea House Publishers, 1989. Fifty-three volumes.
One of an excellent series of fifty-three volumes of historical and present-day facts about American Indians, including information about the crafts of each tribe and their significance. This collection, which is also called *Indians of North America*, contains a bibliography, a glossary, and detailed photographs.

Fitcher, George S. *How the Plains Indians Lived*. David McCay Company, Inc., 1980.
Plains groups have always held a fascination for children. Numerous illustrations add to the descriptions.

Franklin, Paula Angle. *Indians of North America: The Eight Culture Areas and How Their Inhabitants Lived Before the Coming of the Whites*. David McKay Company, Inc., 1979.
This book is devoted to describing important rituals, ceremonies, and the Indian way of life before Europeans intruded.

Gomez, Gregory. "Wide Opened Arms..." *Pre-K Today*, Vol. 2, No. 3 (November/December, 1987), pp. 40-41.
Mr. Gomez, a Lipan-Mescalero Apache, suggests a read-aloud

story to use with children at Thanksgiving and reminds the reader of numerous American-Indian contributions.

Hausman, Gerald. *Turtle Dream/Collected Stories from the Hopi, Navajo, Pueblo, and Havasupai People*. Mariposa Publishing, 1989.
Adults enjoy these stories to share with children reflecting native customs, a foot race in Hopi Country, a ride on Turtle's back, and the adventures of a turquoise horse.

Hughes, Phyllis. *Pueblo Indian Cookbook*. Museum of New Mexico Press, 1986.
Authentic recipes using present-day cooking methods enable teachers to share the rich heritage of the Pueblo Indians with children.

Indian Peoples of the Southwest. Our Voices, Our Land. Northland Press, 1986.
Photographs by Stephen Trimble and Harvey Lloyd are an important part of this literary experience and lend it authenticity as well as striking beauty. It is a major addition to every classroom.

Jacobson, Daniel. *Indians of North America*. Franklin Watts, Inc., 1983.
From "The American Indian Movement" to "Zuni," this book serves as an excellent reference for adults and older children studying American Indians.

Kincade, Kathy, and Carl Landau. *Festivals of the Southwest*. Landau Communications, 1990.
Native American themes and other ethnic events are included in this guided tour to the festivals of Arizona and New Mexico.

Levine, Francine. *Beyond Bows and Arrows: Resources for Teaching Young Children About Native Americans*. The Olive Press, 1987.
This is a welcome addition to any library of resources that informs adults about the sensitive nature of exploring American-Indian cultures. "A Thanksgiving Myth" is an excellent handout for teachers making plans in November. The history of Thanksgiving and directions for activities are illustrated with pen and ink designs and descriptive drawings.

Luling, Virginia. *Indians of the North American Plains*. Silver Burdett Company, 1979.
A large book with big photographs and illustrations in bright colors, this work is especially helpful in preparing a cultural awareness unit. Adults appreciate the section on "present and future," which discusses some of the politics concerning American Indians.

Macfarlan, Allan, and Paulette Macfarlan. *Handbook of American Indian Games*. Dover Publications, Inc., 1985.
Children delight in learning a new game that is old. Remind them that these games, which require no equipment and can be played on the spur of the moment, are gifts of the American Indians who lived a long time ago.

McLuhan, Terry C. *Touch the Earth*. Simon & Schuster, 1976.
These passages, emphasizing the importance of harmony between humans and nature, were written by Indians.

Nelson, Margaret F., and M. Frances Walton. *Ohoyo Ikhana: A Bibliography of American Indian Native Curriculum Materials*. Okoyo, Inc., 1982.
This bibliography contains excellent resources, curriculum materials, and journal articles with accurate information on the American Indian.

Price, Christine. *Arts of Clay*. Charles Scribner's Sons, 1977.
This book for older children and adults examines the many uses for pots and bowls. The illustrations inspire young children in their pottery creations.

Silver Cloud. *Indian Heritage of the Southwest*. Distributed by Smith Southwestern, Inc. P.O. Box 24098, Tempe, AZ 85282, 1989.
The beliefs, customs, and description of the American Indian, past and present, are the main thrust of this all-too-brief book which contains useful photographs for classroom projects. Navajo, Hopi, Papago, Apache, Zuni, Acoma, and Taos Pueblo groups are included.

Ts a A Szi. Tsa Azzi Graphics Center, P.O. Box 12, Pine Hill, NM 87321.
A journal published quarterly to disseminate information about the Navajo cultures.

Walters, Anna Lee. *The Spirit of Native America/Beauty and Mysticism in American Indian Art*. Chronicle Books, 1989.

The author, Oklahoman Pawnee and Otoe-Missourian, is the director of the Navajo Community College Press and a specialist in books about American Indians. Photographs of museum items that describe the American Indians' past include a Sioux buckskin dress, a Kiowa bag, a birch-bark chest, buffalo-hide gloves, cradle boards, and leggings.

Yue, Charlotte, and David Yue. *The Pueblo*. Houghton Mifflin Company, 1986.
Everything you have ever wanted to know about the Pueblo Indians homes can be found here. Vividly illustrated, this book describes how these villages were built to accommodate both community and ceremonial needs.

Films, Filmstrips and Videos
American Indian Videos: Hopi and Navajo. Distributed by Smithsonian Institution. PI
Stories describing religious and seasonal rituals, family life, and traditional arts. Order from Department 0006, Washington, DC 10073.

dePaola, Tomie. *The Legend of the Bluebonnet*. Distributed by Educational Record Center, Inc., 1985. KP
This "1985 American Library Association Notable Children's Filmstrip" can be adapted for prekindergarten use. Available from Educational Record Center, Inc., 1575 Northside Drive, N.W., Atlanta, GA 30318.

_____. *The Legend of the Indian Paintbrush*. Filmstrip distributed by Educational Record

Center, Inc. (Address given above) NKP
Beautiful folk art illustrates the legend.

Girl of the Navajos. Distributed by Coronet Film and Video. 1977. PI
The observations of a young Navajo girl enable children to become aware of Navajo traditions in this video and 16 mm film. Seeing a hogan from the inside, making dolls with clay from a creek bed, and making friends in a special place are of interest to children. Suggested for grades one through six, this film also educates adults about Navajo customs and traditions. Order from 108 Wilmot Rd., Deerfield, IL 60015.

Legends of the Indians: The Legend of the Corn. Video distributed by Films for the Humanities, Inc., 1985. PI
Learning from his elders is of utmost importance to this young Chipewa boy. Lessons to be learned include "Everything that nature gives us is precious" and "Death is not to be feared." Dramatized by excellent Ottawa Indian actors, this legend handed down to Basil H. Johnston has a rare authenticity. Children are allowed a glimpse of this culture from a time many years ago, and the use of tribal language and traditional dress make the video an important cultural experience. Write to Films for the Humanities, Inc., P.O. Box 2053, Princeton, NJ 08543.

"The Life of a Kwakuitl Family: Living at Alert Bay," from the series *Six Native American Families*. Distributed by the Society

for Visual Education, Inc., 1976. 11:20 min. KPIA
A child narrates this story of a Northwest family of fishermen. Children love the bright photographs and beautiful music. A potlatch is described, striking totem pole art is presented, and the relationship of the Kwakuitls to the natural environment is shown. This is a must for every classroom that would like to understand the daily life of a contemporary Indian community. SVE, Department BM, 1345 Diversey Parkway, Chicago, IL 60614.

"The Life of a Mohawk Family: Living at Akewesasne," from the series *Six Native American Families*. Distributed by the Society for Visual Education, Inc., 1976. 11:05 min. P
This outstanding filmstrip does an excellent job of contrasting life in the big city with life on a rural Iroquois reservation on Mohawk land in upper New York state. A game of lacrosse being played, baskets being made, and Indian jewelry being created are shown; a walk in the woods to "rejoice in the simple beauty of a leaf or a butterfly or a box turtle" will enthrall children and adults.

"The Life of a Navajo Family: Living in Monument Valley," from the series *Six Native American Families*. Filmstrip distributed by the Society for Visual Education, Inc., 1976. 13:20 min. P
To live in Monument Valley means living in either a traditional or a modern hogan. Children learn about weaving rugs and herding sheep, but they also learn that Navajo people work

with heavy equipment in the mines, or in the electronics field as highly skilled laborers. Cradle boards are shown and described as a modern way to carry babies.

"The Life of a Pueblo Family: Living at Acomo," from the series *Six Native American Families*. Filmstrip distributed by the Society for Visual Education, Inc., 1976. 15:10 min. P
Acomo chants and words in the Acoma language accompany this beautiful filmstrip about a modern Pueblo family depicted in the wonderful faces of a grandmother, grandfather, and young children. A view of the cliffs and canyons covered with rock paintings and the Great American Desert, with its cacti, sage, and wild flowers, evokes the love of the Pueblo for the land.

"The Life of a Seminole Family: Living at Brighton," from the series *Six Native American Families*. Distributed by the Society for Visual Education, Inc., 1976. 8:45 min. P
This colorful filmstrip examines two different Seminole lifestyles. Children are interested in the cowboys and the pictures showing a traditional style of Seminole-type housing with a thatched roof of palms. Children and adults learn a great deal about the spectacular environment of the Everglades.

"The Life of a Sioux Family: Living at Rosebud," from the series *Six Native American Families*. Distributed by the Society for Visual Education, Inc., 1976. 12:10 min. KPIA

Life on the Rosebud Reservation in South Dakota is a life without modern conveniences and often one troubled by poverty and resistance to governmental domination. Mary Crow Dog, a Lakota Sioux Indian, narrates this authentic filmstrip. Older children and adults can learn from the problems described in this narration; young children learn from the first four frames about games, crafts, daily chores, and family structure. Music taped during dances and ceremonies provides authentic sound background.

Navajo Moon. Distributed by Films for the Humanities. Photographed on the Navajo reservation, this excellent video documentary dispels many myths about the American Indian as it follows three Navajo children through their day. The Navajo way is explained with sensitivity and understanding. This film describes powwows as being popular events with the Navajo people. A love of music and animals, learning to prepare wool for weaving, sand painting, and learning about the traditions buried in the long ago are presented in this one-of-a-kind film about the largest tribal group in North America.

Pow Wow! Distributed by Coronet Film and Video, 1980.
The powwow, "a reaffirmation of the faith," includes the art of constructing a tipi and features dancing, singing, and tribal crafts and skills. This 15-minute video documentary of a powwow held at Haskell Junior College in Lawrence, Kansas, reminds one that "the wacipi is the throbbing pulse of the living culture." The color photography of scenes with dancing and interviews enhances the importance of preservation of the old ways.

Richard's Totem Pole. Distributed by Coronet Film and Video. 1981
Richard, a 16-year-old Gutksan Indian, joins his father in the carving of a new family totem. Set in the Canadian Rockies and British Columbia, this video shows the rich heritage of the Native people and stirs an appreciation for Indian customs.

Summer Legend. Distributed by Churchill Films, 1987.
The legend of summer is told by Canadian Indians in this beautiful video. The story about how giant winter held the Micmac people in his icy grip is brilliantly illustrated in a subtle watercolor splash, accompanied by lovely voices and delicate musical renditions.

Materials and Experiences
Navajo Dolls. Claudia's Caravan, No. 28G.
Man and woman in traditional dress; made by Navajo people.

Navajo Weaver Doll. Claudia's Caravan, No. 27G.
No school should be without a Navajo doll, complete with a loom and a baby.

Ceremonial Drum. Craft Shop. Drum designed for ceremonial purposes, crafted from a hollowed log and animal skin. A handsome addition to every classroom.

Ceremonial Drum. Craft Shop. Select from drums made by American Indians. Other cultural artifacts are also available. Your purchase makes a donation to the Save the Children Fund and "gives a hardworking craftsperson the opportunity to make a better life for children." Order catalog from Craft Shop, 2515 E. 43rd St., P.O. Box 182226, Chattanooga, TN 37422-7226.

American Indians. Educational Teaching Aids.
Twenty-four posters present traditional and contemporary American-Indian contributions.

Contributions of Native Americans—Navajo Dyes and Weavings. Historic Indian Publishers, 1982.
Recipes for making dye surround the edges of this beautiful poster with photographs of vegetables suitable for dyes used in weaving. Order from Historic Indian Publishers, P.O. Box 16074, Salt Lake City, UT. 84116

Native American Personalities. Claudia's Caravan.
Fourteen 11-1/2 X 16-inch posters with an informative guide for older children and adults.

Native American Tribes. Cherokee Publications, 1989.
A colored map of the United States with five areas of American-Indian tribes defined. Information about each group adds to the attractiveness of this poster. Order from Cherokee Publications, Cherokee, NC.

North American Indian Personalities. Cole.
Twenty color photographs of contemporary and historical personalities from numerous professions.
North American Indians/Social Studies Posters. Distributed by Shack Industries.
Twenty brightly colored portraits with easy-to-read biographies. Order from 3300 W. Cermak Rd., Chicago, IL 60623.

Notable Native North Americans. Educational Teaching Aids.
Splendid posters of famous American Indians, including Chief Joseph.

Records and Audiocassettes
American Indian Songs and Chants with the Bala Sinem Choir. Distributed by Music for Little People.
This American-Indian group sings traditional songs from numerous Indian cultures.

Changes with R. Carlos Nakai. Distributed by Claudia's Caravan.
This flute music performed by a Navajo-Ute is in part improvisational, with some traditional melodies.

Corn Dance from the Chippewa Indians: Authentic Indian Dances and Folklore. Kimbo Educational Records.
This includes history, cultural tradition, and dances of the Chippewa tribes.

Earth Spirit with R. Carlos Nakai. Claudia's Caravan.
This is another splendid flute concert with this talented Navajo-Ute composer.

Coyote and Native American Folk Tales, with Joe Hayes. Trails West Publishing Company.
This cassette relates the adventures of Coyote as told by a favorite storyteller in many classrooms in the Southwest.

Journeys with R. Carlos Nakai. Claudia's Caravan.
This tape provides American Indian music for classroom use. It has a pleasing sound, with flute as the main instrument.

Lakota Wickijo Olowan, with Kevin Locke. Distributed by Music for Little People.
Locke's flute embraces the listener with tranquil, dream-like songs of the Sioux.

Music of the North American Indian. Canyon Records and Indian Arts.

Myth, Music, and Dance of the American Indian. Claudia's Caravan.
This tape includes a bilingual book of Indian songs and dances.

Reflections: Indian Stories, told by Tsonakwa. Distributed by Music for Little People.
An Abenaki tribesman relates myths and legends.

"Shee-nasha," from *Little Johnny Brown* album with Ella Jenkins. Distributed by Smithsonian Folkways.
This Navajo song was taught to Ella Jenkins by children on the Navajo reservation in Arizona. Children learn this song quickly.

Sounds of Indian America. Indian House.
Recorded live at the Inter-Tribal Indian ceremony, this tape is a favorite. A descriptive catalog listing numerous cassettes and records of songs is available from this distributor, including titles from various groups in the U.S. and Canada. Cassette packages include background information about the recording of these authentic sounds and are a useful way to explain how American Indians take pride in their rich musical heritage.

Catalogs and Supply Houses
Authentic Indian Designs, A Dover New Book Catalog by Maria Naylor. Dover Publications, Inc., 31 E. 2nd St., Mineola, NY 11501.
Designs taken from beadwork, blankets, woodwork, totem poles, and baskets are illustrated. You can also order copyright-free geometric, symbolic figures and plant and animal motifs taken from Navajo blankets, Hopi pottery, and Sioux buffalo hides.

American Indian Education: A Directory of Organizations and Activities in American Indian Education. Compiled by Elaine Roanhorse Benally, Pam Coe, and Joan Hill, 1988. Order from ERIC Clearinghouse on Rural Education and Small Schools (ERIC/CRESS), 1031 Quarrier St., P.O. Box 1348, Charleston, WV 25325.
Names of organizations in American Indian Education are provided; annotated lists were to be updated in 1990.

Bilingual Materials Development Center (BMDC) booklet, Box 219, Crow Agency, MT 59022.
Teachers can browse through this booklet to select curriculum materials, including books, flannel board materials, wall charts, curriculum guides, posters, and more. The goal of the center is to enhance the self esteem of Indian students.

Burke Museum Publications, University of Washington DB-10, Seattle, WA 98195.
Current editions of books for children and adults that are not usually found at local bookstores include authentic stories, research reports, and exhibit catalogs.

Canyon Records and Indian Arts, 4143 N. 16th St., Phoenix, AZ 85016.
A remarkable library of records and cassettes of American Indian music for the classroom and library, including tapes of music played on handmade wooden flutes.

Claudia's Caravan, P.O. Box 1582, Alameda, CA 94501.
Multicultural books and resources for children and adults.

Global Village. 2210 Wilshire Blvd., Box 262, Santa Monica, CA 90403.
Anti-bias products for children, educators and parents.

LeBaron's Native American Artifacts by Larry Baron. Order the Larry Baron Catalogue, 11145 Pink Coral, El Paso, TX 79936, (915) 592-0511.
An assortment of dolls, drums, baskets, pots, metals, masks, and numerous artifacts may be ordered from this anthropologist and teacher. He personally selects quality native goods from the areas where they are made.

Music for Little People, Box 1460, Redway, CA 95560.
A variety of multicultural musical selections, ethnic musical instruments, and videos.

Society for Visual Education, Inc, Department BM, 1345 Diversey Parkway, Chicago, IL 60614-1299.
Multi-ethnic filmstrips featuring children's literature and social studies themes.

Supernow's Oklahoma Indian Supply, 301 East W.C. Rogers Blvd., Skiatooh, OK 74070.

Trails West Publishing, P.O. Box 8619, Santa Fe, NM 87502.
Joe Hayes favorites are included in this marvelous selection of Indian legends recorded on videos, audiocassettes, and in books.

Troll Learn and Play, 100 Corporate Drive, Mahwah, NJ 07430.
Native American legends introduce children to great stories "with factual background information." Included are Navajo, Eskimo, Cherokee, Cheyenne, Algonquin, and Hahah legends. Also available are Indian Hero Series for ages 9-12.

World Wide Games: Exceptional Handcrafted Games. Colchester, CT 06415.
A selection of beautiful games from all over the world.

CHINESE AND CHINESE-AMERICAN CULTURES

A study of China—both the mainland (People's Republic of China) and Taiwan (the Republic of China)—promotes a sense of common heritage as children explore family life, arts and culture, customs and festivals.

China's culture is 5000 years old. Chinese customs and traditions have had an effect on the neighboring Asian nations, as well as far-reaching effects in countries throughout the world, including the United States, where the Chinese have made valuable contributions in the arts and in science. Today, many Chinese people live in the United States, enriching the American culture.

In the classroom, children learn about the Chinese people's love for nature and beauty, talk about festival customs, and explore and experience Chinese family life. They arrange brightly colored tropical flowers and dry vines in the Chinese style of floral art; they make holiday red lai see envelopes to celebrate the New Year; and they prepare rice and eat with chopsticks as is customary in Chinese families.

Hsiu-Huei, from Taiwan, is a doctoral student in Early Childhood Education at Teachers College, Columbia University. She was a valuable consultant in validating the contents of this unit and in interpreting the Chinese culture.

FAMILY LIVING

HOMES

Traditional Chinese rural and village homes were "one-dragon homes" for the extended family. They were covered with red brick, and the red-colored roofs of the aristocrats' homes were curved upward along the edges. Some villages were U-shaped, with a courtyard in the center and a red gate at the entrance. The yard was used for many family activities. Each home was marked by a banner with the family's name on it.

In the cities today, many people live in modern apartment buildings furnished in Western style. Those Chinese who have yards grow flowers and herbs for cooking.

Children can help make a traditional house using a large refrigerator box turned on its side. Cut out windows and a door. To simulate the red tile roof, cut two pieces of 36-inch-wide butcher paper the length of the box. Staple these pieces together to make a roof and attach them to the top of the box. Turn the corners up to make the curved eaves. Paint the roof red to give a clay-tile effect.

Let children build a wall around the house with blocks to make a courtyard and decorate the yard with plum blossom

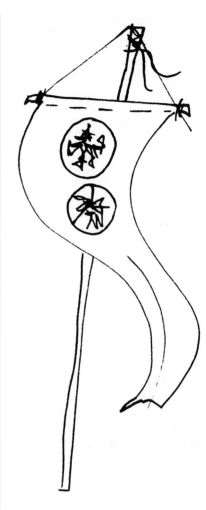

branches. (See the Creative Art Expression section.)

Make a banner as illustrated and place it in front of the house. Children hang paper lanterns around the room. (See Creative Art Expression.)

Banners

Children can make banners by painting Chinese characters on a 12-by-36-inch piece of paper. Glue a stick to the top of the banner, and then tie a string to each end of the stick to hang it in front of the home in the family living center. Banners may also be attached to paper sticks, made by tightly rolling up newspaper and securing it with tape.

Gate (*Men*)

Decorative gates have been used in China for centuries. Gates mark entrances to courtyards, public buildings and parks. In the past they designated the entrance to a village surrounded by a wall. Today gates are painted in bright colors, often red or blue, with hand-painted decorations in red, blue, white, or green. The color red used on buildings is a symbol of nobility.

Make a Chinese gate, as illustrated, for the entrance to the family living center. It should be high enough for children to walk through. Cut the gate from heavy cardboard or build a wooden frame, paint it red, and add gold trim. A gate cut from red poster board makes a frame for your classroom door while studying the Chinese culture.

Flower Arranging (*Ch'a-hua*)

Chinese women learn the art of flower arranging in the Japanese and Western styles, as well as in the traditional Chinese style. In the Chinese style they use few flowers; to one or two flowers they may add a branch of bamboo, a branch of blossoms, or a sprig from a fir tree. After children have seen pictures of Chinese flower

arrangements, supply fresh flowers, branches, and vases so that they can practice this art. Artificial flowers may be substituted.

Many florists give away flowers that they cannot use. Check with a local florist a day or two before you plan to do the activity and ask them to save some flowers for you. Ask parents to save large juice cans to use as vases. Let children arrange flowers in the cans, using crushed paper to hold the flowers in place.

DRAMATIC PLAY

Make the following items available for dramatic play. Most of the items are described in this unit.

—bamboo scrolls
—capes
—children's pajamas with embroidered symbols, available at import stores.
—Chinese and American dolls
—Chinese kites
—chopsticks
—cushions for tea party
—farmers' hats
—lacquerware
—low table
—mai tai (baby carrier)
—men's clothing—pants, shirt; quilted silk jackets
—paper fans
—parasols
—puppets and masks from import shops
—rice steamer
—small stuffed animals—lion, tiger, dragon, panda
—teapot and teacups
—women's clothing—pants, skirt, blouse with stand-up (Mandarin) collar

CLOTHING

One of the first things young children want to do when exploring a culture is to try on traditional clothing. Have clothing available for children to examine, or let them make their own by adding a creative touch to an existing garment or using a pattern and starting from scratch. Involve the children in determining what tools are needed, selecting materials, and deciding where to cut.

Baby Carrier (*Mai Tai*)

Some mothers in China use a wide wrap-like garment called a *mai tai* to carry their babies close to their bodies while working or shopping. A mai tai is made by cutting a piece of fabric as illustrated. The baby is placed in the front or back of the mother's body. The long ends are tied and knotted diagonally across the mother's body, in the front or back, from shoulder to waist. Make several mai

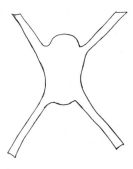

tai and have them available to use with dolls in the home center. Children enjoy carrying their baby dolls tied close to their bodies. Remind children that African mothers use a similar baby carrier and compare them to carriers used in the United States that are derived from a similar design.

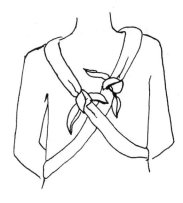

Children's Clothing

The style of boys' and girls' clothing is the same as worn by children in the U.S., except for special celebrations when traditional clothing is worn. Girls wear pants or skirts with blouses in red, pink, or purple; boys wear blue or gray pants and white shirts. Kindergarten children wear aprons to protect their clothing. Children wear uniforms at school, each school having its own style and color.

Put the appropriate clothing in the dramatic play center so that children can dress to go to school in China.

FOOD

The hot, rainy climate in China is needed for growing tea and rice. Chinese people eat rice, which is cooked in a rice steamer, at every meal. In northern China, noodles or dumplings are served instead of rice.

(Safety note: Be sure to obtain parental permission before allowing children to eat anything in case of allergies or diet restrictions.)

Rice

Cook rice, following the directions on the package. Let children help with the whole process. Print the recipe on a chart so that children can follow it. Include illustrations so that nonreaders can follow.

While the rice is cooking, children can talk about the pro-

cess. Some children may want to copy the recipe to take home. Serve the rice in small bowls and let children eat it with chopsticks.

Chinese Rice Balls
1 C short-grain white rice
1 1/2 C water
1/2 t salt
sugar

Put the rice in a pan, add water, and let it soak for 30 minutes. Cover and bring to a boil. Reduce heat to simmer. Cook until all the water has been absorbed. Let set for 5 minutes. Cool. Butter or spray oil on hands. Form rice into walnut-sized balls. Roll balls in sugar and enjoy.

Chopsticks (*K'uai Tzu*)

Chinese believe that food tastes better when eaten with chopsticks. Meat and vegetables are cut into bite-sized pieces and stir-fried together. When food is eaten with chopsticks, every bit of each piece can be tasted. Buy chopsticks in Asian stores. Let children use them to

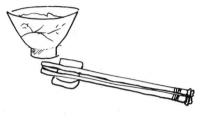

eat rice, noodles, chips, or small crackers.

Fruits and Vegetables

Bring Chinese fruits and vegetables to school and explain how they are grown and how they taste, so that children can see the food before it is processed. Frozen or canned foods may be used if fresh ones are not available. Fruits include apples, oranges, bananas, pineapple, papaya, and melon. Vegetables include corn on the cob, napa lettuce, bean sprouts, snow peas, long string beans, taro (similar to potatoes), Chi-

nese cabbage, water chestnuts, and bamboo shoots.

Fruit soup

One Chinese dessert is made from several kinds of fruit in season. Cut the fruit into small pieces and serve it in fruit juice.

School lunch

Chinese children take their lunch to school in a metal or plastic box with a handle. It is heated at school. Lunch may include rice, broccoli, chicken or pork, eggs (boiled, scrambled, or fried), and fruit.

Plan to have a Chinese lunch. Send parents a list of foods for children to bring. Schedule a day when children bring their Chinese lunch to eat at school.

Spring Rolls

As the name indicates, spring rolls are served most often in spring, when vegetables are freshest and peanut oil is plentiful.

1 T cooking oil or shortening
1/4 lb shredded pork or chicken
1/4 lb bean sprouts
2 green onions, chopped
1/2 C celery, chopped
1 T soy sauce
10 spring roll wrappers
1 egg , beaten, or water
2 C peanut oil

Heat oil in frying pan. Add meat and stir fry for 2 minutes. Add the next four ingredients and stir fry for 2 minutes. Put about 1 T of the mixture in the center of each wrapper. Fold the two opposite corners to the center. Then begin at one of the other corners and roll to the other side. Moisten edge with beaten eggs or a few drops of water and press. Deep fry rolls

in hot peanut oil for about 3 minutes. Drain on paper towels.

Children enjoy dipping the spring rolls in honey or soy sauce. They also enjoy filling and wrapping the rolls. Make the filling and let it cool. Provide small bowls of filling, beaten eggs, and wrappers for children. Let them wrap their own egg rolls, but ask a parent to do the deep frying.

Chinese Pretzels

5 C flour
1 C sugar
5 eggs, beaten

Mix the ingredients to make a ball of dough. Flatten the ball until it is the thickness of a chopstick. Cut into strips, about 5 inches long and 2 inches wide. Fold each strip of dough in half lengthwise and cut into thirds. Unfold the dough. Take one end and fold it under the same end. The cut strips will be curled. Fry pretzels in enough oil to cover them. When they are light yellow, place them on a paper towel to drain.

Since the authentic recipe for Chinese Pretzels is much too difficult for young children to make, have parents make them to bring to class.

Ramen Noodles

Noodles are a favorite Chinese dish. Soup mix with Chinese noodles is sold in most grocery stores and is very easy to prepare. Children love to eat the noodles out of small cups with chopsticks.

Fortune Cookies

It has been reported that fortune cookies were created by a Chinese-American man in San Francisco in the 1800s. They are served in Chinese restaurants in America. Chinese who come to America have never heard of fortune cookies. Buy these cookies for a snack. Read and talk about appropriate fortunes inside the cookies.

Teahouse

A teahouse is a place where friends visit and drink tea. The house is furnished in traditional style. People sit on cushions on a platform around a low table. There are also Western-style tables with chairs or stools. Art objects by Chinese artists are displayed. The kind of tea served—brown or jasmine in Taiwan—varies in the different provinces. Plum preserves, peanuts, cookies, or dessert pretzels are served with the tea.

Arrange a teahouse in an area of the classroom. Add a table, cushions, teacups, a teapot, place mats, napkins, and a place to display art objects the children have created. Children make the place mats using Chinese designs. Show children

how to set the table and serve the tea. Invite another class or parents to tea and have the children serve them.

Good Luck Oranges and Chinese Tea Snack Tea Ceremony (*Chanoyu*)

In China, oranges are presented to friends to wish them good luck. Pass out oranges for a nutritious snack. Oranges and apples may be arranged in a pyramid for display. Purchase Chinese tea and let children make it and serve themselves from a real china teapot.

Morning Market (*Tsay shs*) and Evening Market (*Yeh shs*)

The Chinese buy vegetables and other foods in the morning market. The evening market is a large area of numerous small shops where food, clothing, toys, and many other items are sold. At the shop where sweet play dough is sold, children create articles in the shop. The teahouse is an important place to relax and visit.

Let children make a small shop from which to sell Chinese items, or let each class prepare a different food—spring rolls, rice balls, noodles—and then bring it to market to be sold. This is a good outdoor activity. Fans, kites, scrolls, and other items made by children can be sold.

TRANS- PORTATION

When Chinese leave their homes to shop or travel, they use many types of transportation. The bicycle is the most popular way to travel. Thousands of bicyclists are on the streets when people go to work or to school. A small family can ride on one bicycle. Boards or baskets are hung on the bicycle to carry goods from place to place.

The number of motorbikes and motorcycles is increasing, and cars are being used in the cities. Electric trains are dependable and run on time. Many people travel by bus. In rural areas, horse-drawn carts and wagons are used to take farm products to market. For some people, the only way to travel is to walk.

Talk with children about the ways Chinese travel. Discuss who can ride a bicycle, who has ridden on a train, and who has traveled on a bus. Make a graph of the numerous ways Chinese travel and have children mark those they have experienced.

Have available a toy train, small toy bikes, and motorcycles for children to use in the dramatic play and in the block center.

CREATIVE ART EXPRESSION

Creativity means starting with ideas generated by children. The role of the adult is to foster creativity by asking questions, supervising the projects, and providing reinforcement. Provide many choices of materials.

CHINESE ARTISTS

The ability of the Chinese artists and craftsmen has been evident for thousands of years. Their works of art are unique in design and color and reflect a deep respect for nature. Because Chinese children learn the basic elements of the arts, many people engage in the arts in their daily lives and appreciate the work of their artists.

A Painter

Chang Ta-ch'ien, an outstanding Chinese painter who died at the age of 85 in 1983, was famous for his fearless trip during wartime to copy cave paintings and to make rubbings of them. He created his own style of painting, but he also used the painting styles of the past. Art was his life. He surrounded himself with beauty in his home and the gardens near his home. His collection of unusual stones is one of the finest in the world.

Look for a book of Chang Ta-ch'ien's paintings in the library. As you show them to the children, talk about the things he painted and his use of light and dark colors. Compare his paintings to illustrations in children's books.

Chinese Artists of Today

Contemporary Chinese artists whose work has been exhibited by the Pacific Cultural Foundation in Taipei, Taiwan, include the following: Chung-i Chiang, known for watercolor paintings; Jief-fu Chou, recognized for the "Year of the Rooster" paintings; and Wang Nung, a painter whose art has been exhibited in the United States. Maya Lin, a young Chinese-American architect, designed the Viet Nam Veterans Memorial in Washington, D.C. and the Civil Rights Memorial in Atlanta.

A Poet

Wang Junchih, whose pen name is Yungtze, has published eleven collections of poetry since 1953. She also translates children's stories and has won national and international awards.

Distinguished Chinese-American Artists

Jong Kingman, artist.

Amy Tan, author of *The Joy Luck Club,* a novel comparing Chinese mothers born in China with their American-born daughters in California.

Ann-Ping Chin, author of *Children of China,* a look at home and school life in China based on interviews with children.

Maxine Hong Kingston, author.

Lin Yutang, author.

Help children find information about Chinese artists and illustrations of their work. Locate Chinese American artists in your community and invite them to show and talk about their work.

DECORATIVE ART
●●●●●●

Scrolls

Popular motifs for many Chinese artists are flowers, dragons, bamboo, butterflies, and lanterns. Imitating the Chinese finger painters, children can use watercolors to draw with their fingers on a 12-by-36-inch scroll. They complete the scroll by gluing bamboo sticks to the top and bottom of the paper. A scroll may be hung but is rolled up and tied for storing.

Children at The Learning Tree make scrolls after the seeing the film or hearing the book *Big Bird in China* by Jon Stone. Read the book *Step into China* by Neil Johnson.

Brush Painting

Chinese paintings depict delicate impressions of life. Traditional ancient art shows landscapes with mountains, rivers, trees, birds, and flowers in very pale colors. Vases and pottery, lacquerware, and other items are decorated by artists with beautiful, intricate designs of

flowers, scenes and people. Today some Chinese artists paint in bright, bold colors.

Display famous prints or pictures of traditional brush paintings, and explain that artists painted them many years ago. As children paint with watercolors, suggest that they try to reproduce the traditional pale colors. To produce a different effect when brush painting with watercolors, have the children wet the paper before they begin to paint. Also, suggest that children experiment with several different sizes of brushes. Chinese school children paint outdoors during good weather.

Two excellent books to read to children before beginning this activity are *Tye May and the Magic Brush,* by Molly Bang, and *Liang and the Magic Paintbrush,* by Demi.

Let children arrange their paintings for a school art exhibit and invite parents to attend.

Calligraphy

Painting large black characters or letters with black ink on special white paper is called calligraphy. Each artist develops an individual style. The paper is long and narrow. When finished, the paper is rolled into a scroll. A special black ink is used. Black tempera may be substituted, but sticks of Chinese black are preferred.

Elementary age children learn calligraphy, painting characters with a brush and ink. Provide Chinese characters as illustrated so that children can copy them. Brushes and ink are available in many art and stationery stores. (See Symbols in the Language Development section for Chinese characters.)

Flags

The flag for the Republic of China (Taiwan) is red with a white sun on a blue rectangle in the upper left corner. The flag for the People's Republic of China (mainland China) is dark

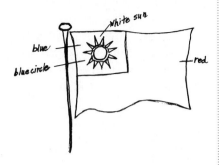

red with one large gold star and four smaller stars.

Provide fabric or construction paper and paint, crayons, or marking pens for children to use to make flags. Attach flags to paper sticks made from rolled newspapers. Ask children to use their creativity to figure out how to fasten the flag to the stick. Have a parade of flags or display them in the classroom.

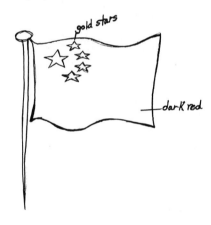

Chinese Knot

A Chinese knot is made of many different knots, with a special decoration tied onto it. These knots are used for decorations in the home, and men wear them for special occasions. The making of a Chinese knot is an art in China. Young children learn to tie simple knots and gradually learn to make the more difficult ones. Mothers use this art in their homes.

Some children may wish to try making a simple knot. Have a Chinese knot available for children to examine. Provide different lengths, 12 inches or longer, of brightly colored heavy cord or yarn and have children select several pieces. Knot the pieces together at one end. Attach the knotted end to a shape of heavy cardboard by pushing it through a hole cut in the cardboard. Use tape to secure it.

Let children choose from gold and red paint, marking pens, glitter, sequins, and pieces of jewelry to decorate the pieces of cardboard. Then ask them to tie the cords in knots. Hang the knots in the classroom or pin them to the children's clothing. The complexity of the knots will vary, of course, according to each child's developmental level.

Jade

Jade is a very precious and beautiful stone in China. The most valued color is a clear, dark green. Other colors of jade are white, gray, brown, blue, yellow, bright red, and black. Jewelry and carvings and vases are made of jade. Show a piece of jade to the children and read to them about this precious stone.

A famous Chinese jade carver is Hing Wa Lee. Display pictures of his work. Jade carving is a very revered art that is passed from father to son. Mr. Lee is the former president of the Hong Kong Gem Carvers Association.

Children can make beautiful "jade" jewelry using soda and cornstarch clay shaped into beads. (See Creative Art Expression in the Mexican/Mexican-American Cultures unit.) Let children paint their beads using a mixture of equal amounts of tempera paint and white glue. (When the mixture dries, it is shiny.) Then they can string their beads to make necklaces, bracelets, or earrings. (See Creative Art Expression in the African and African-American Cultures unit.)

Paper Making

The Chinese were one of the first cultures to invent the art of paper making. Paper was made in China as early as 105 A.D. The earliest paper was made from tree bark, hemp, rags, and fish nets. Later, bamboo pulp was used. The traditional methods of making paper are still used in China today. Display books and pictures of paper making in China.

Children enjoy making paper. You will need a large tub or dish pan; paper scraps—newspaper or any kind of paper; several large, long-handled wooden spoons; a screen such as a small window screen or a fry pan spatter screen; stacks of newspaper; and an iron.

To make the paper, children can tear and shred paper into small pieces and put them into the tub. Young children enjoy this activity. While tearing the paper, discuss what happens to paper when it gets wet. Fill the tub half full of water to cover the paper scraps. The children can then use the large spoons to stir the mixture. Soak it overnight. The next morning, pour off the water and refill the tub with clean water. Let children stir the mixture several times during the day. Ask them to bring lint from home clothes dryers to add to the mixture. Stir it again.

After about four days, when this mixture has become very soupy, dip the screen into the tub. Lift out a thin layer of pulp. Place the screen so that the water can drain off. After draining for a few minutes, quickly flip the screen upside down on a table covered with several layers of newspaper. Ask children to rub and pat the back of the screen vigorously. Then gently lift the screen off of the pulp and cover the pulp with another layer of newspapers. Repeat this process until each child has made a sheet of paper. Let the paper pulp dry overnight.

The next day, remove the newspaper on top of the pulp. Iron the paper until it is dry. Peel paper from the bottom newspaper.

Explain to children that they have made paper using the same method the Chinese used many years ago. After the paper is dry, it may be decorated with block printing. A book that explains this process is *Writing It Down* by Vikki Cobb.

Block Printing

Children enjoy this version of block printing, which can be done on their handmade paper.

To make printing pads for block printing, place a wet paper towel that has been folded to make a small square into a flat dish. Make one printing pad for each color you plan to use. Sprinkle powdered tempera paint on the towel in each dish. Let stand 5 minutes until the paint is moistened. Be sure to use red and metallic gold paints, Chinese festival colors. Make available several different gadgets for printing, such as spools, canape cutters, carved vegetables such as potatoes, and similar items.

To print, give each child a sheet of the handmade paper. Children select gadgets, press them on the printing pad, and then print on the paper. They continue choosing gadgets and colors until their paper is decorated to their satisfaction.

Fans

Beautiful hand-painted fans are popular in China. Provide an assortment of fans from China for children to use.

To make fans, have available various sizes, shapes, and colors of construction paper, tag board, or poster board. Children can usually fold construction paper easily to make a pleated fan. Some children may wish to paint a picture on the paper, as is the custom in China. They then fold the paper in accordion-style pleats and staple the pleats together at one end. A ribbon may be added to the stapled end for decoration and for carrying.

Another way to make a Chinese fan is to cut a 9-by-12-inch piece of poster or tag board into an oval shape. Use a hole punch to put holes around the outside of the oval, two inches apart. To imitate the soft water color designs of Chinese arts, provide brightly colored tissue paper for the children to cut into shapes such as butterflies and flowers.

Show them how to place several patterns on the oval, overlapping them, and then paint tissue pieces with vinegar. The colors will bleed and transfer to the oval fan. Glue a wooden tongue depressor to each side of the fan for a handle and let children sew colored yarn through the holes.

Lanterns (*Teng lung*)

Lanterns can be made of plastic or paper and come in many shapes, sizes, and colors. They are decorated with delicate designs and are carried for many festivals. Each member of the family carries a lantern at the Lantern Festival (see Celebrations). Lanterns may also decorate the store fronts. Purchase lanterns at import stores and hang them in the classroom.

To make a lantern, each child will need one 12-by-18-inch sheet of colored construction paper; one 12-by-18-inch sheet of bright yellow tissue paper; colored pipe cleaners; 12-inch-

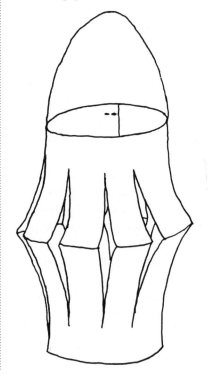

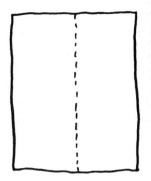

long crepe paper streamers in assorted colors; and stickers of butterflies, birds, and flowers.

Let children draw pictures on the construction paper. Then fold it in half lengthwise. Lay the paper so that the fold is at the bottom. Draw a line across the paper one inch from the top. Then children cut slits about one inch apart from the fold to the line. Unfold and staple the short sides together. Show children how to attach a pipe cleaner handle and add crepe paper streamers to the bottom of the lantern. They crush a sheet of yellow tissue paper to place inside the lantern to make a light.

Kites (*Feng cheng*)

Many kinds of kites are flown in China by children and adults. Chinese were the first to create kites. They were not used as toys, but rather to send messages, or sometimes to lift men over rivers. The Wright Brothers in America used kites to create the first airplane.

Designs of kites are different in each region of China. Kites of the South are often made in the shape of light and fragile butterflies to catch the soft wind. In the Northern region, where the winds are stronger, kites are larger and stronger and often made in the shapes of birds,

fish, animals, or geometric shapes. There are many wonderful stories and Chinese folktales about kites, including *The Emperor's Kite* by Jane Yolen and *The Dragon Kite* by Thomas P. Lewis. An excellent book about kites is *Catch the Wind: All about Kites* by Gail Gibbons.

To make butterfly kites, cut two or three butterfly shapes from different colored sheets of 12-by-18-inch construction paper. Let children paint designs on the butterflies for decoration. Connect the butterflies to each other, stapling them wing to wing. Staple colored crepe paper streamers to the

wings. Tie a string to the top of the kite and fly it outdoors.

Children may also create their own shapes and designs for making kites.

Paper Cutting

Chinese children begin the art of paper cutting at about age eight, cutting designs in paper without cutting the edges of the paper. The snowflakes American children cut each winter are a simple version of Chinese paper cutting. The paper cutting of Chinese artists is quite intricate.

Packages of Chinese paper cuts, with several cuts in each, are available at import or stationery stores. Allow children to examine these delicate pieces in order to gain an appreciation for the art form.

Paper Folding

Children in China begin to learn simple paper folding in kindergarten. Later they learn to fold animals, houses, birds, people, bicycles, and many other things.

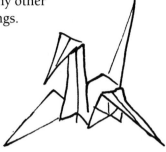

Some children are interested in learning to fold paper. Many books are available with instructions for paper folding. Any type of paper may be used, but origami paper or typing paper works best.

To make a drinking cup, start with an 8-inch square of paper. Fold the square in half to form a triangle. Crease each line sharply. Fold the left corner to the middle of the right edge; fold the right corner to top of the left fold. Fold down the triangle flaps at the top of the cup. To open the cup, press the fold lines in slightly. Pour some water into the cup and take a drink!

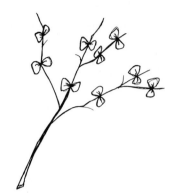

Plum Blossoms

The plum blossom is the national flower of China and is the symbol of good health and long life. It is used in Chinese paintings, jade carvings, stories, and poems.

Children can make plum blossom branches by cutting pink tissue paper into three-inch bow shapes as illustrated. Hunt outdoors with the children to select small branches from shrubs or trees. Wrap and twist the pieces of tissue paper around the twigs of the branches to resemble blossoms. Put branches into oatmeal box vases weighted with sand. Let children decorate their vases with construction paper and paint.

Dragons

The dragon and lion are considered lucky symbols in China. The dragon is a national symbol, responsible for giving gifts and for helping bring rain and for keeping peace. The lion is given the same respect as the dragon.

When the dragon is used for a dance during the New Year celebration, its length can be from one inch to one mile. To create a simple dragon, provide materials for making a mask, and let children create the mask. Attach a long piece of cloth, wide enough to cover several children. Children may decorate the cloth to resemble a dragon's body, and then dance under the cloth, following the leader in a dragon dance.

Another kind of dragon head may be made out of a cardboard box; a 16-by-24-inch box is an appropriate size, large enough for a child's head to fit through a hole cut in the bottom near the back end of the box.

Score the box as illustrated for the dragon's eyes—do not cut all the way through the cardboard. Then cut eye holes as shown. Push the two side sections of the box in to make the eye sockets. Dampen the box first to make it easier to push.

Cut the mouth section on the front end. Cut cardboard ears and spine as illustrated and attach.

Have children paint the outside of the box with green tempera paint and the mouth with red. Let it dry. Then children can cut out white jagged teeth, glue them inside the mouth,

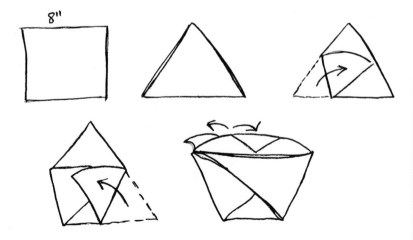

and attach a long red paper tongue. To make the mouth open and close, attach a long rubber band with a brad fastener to the upper and lower jaws. Use small plastic butter tubs to make eyeballs;

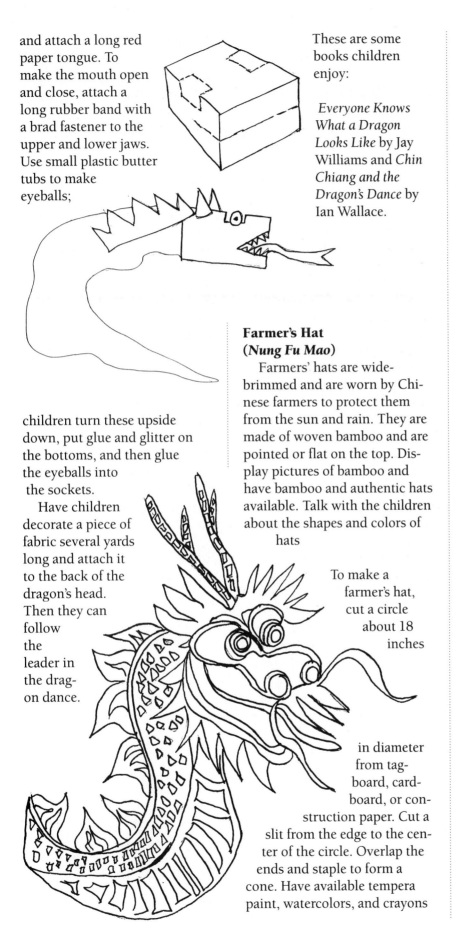

children turn these upside down, put glue and glitter on the bottoms, and then glue the eyeballs into the sockets.

Have children decorate a piece of fabric several yards long and attach it to the back of the dragon's head. Then they can follow the leader in the dragon dance.

These are some books children enjoy:

Everyone Knows What a Dragon Looks Like by Jay Williams and *Chin Chiang and the Dragon's Dance* by Ian Wallace.

Farmer's Hat (*Nung Fu Mao*)

Farmers' hats are wide-brimmed and are worn by Chinese farmers to protect them from the sun and rain. They are made of woven bamboo and are pointed or flat on the top. Display pictures of bamboo and have bamboo and authentic hats available. Talk with the children about the shapes and colors of hats

To make a farmer's hat, cut a circle about 18 inches in diameter from tagboard, cardboard, or construction paper. Cut a slit from the edge to the center of the circle. Overlap the ends and staple to form a cone. Have available tempera paint, watercolors, and crayons

so that children can select the colors needed to make their hats resemble the shades of bamboo. Some children are able to manage the cutting and painting, but others may need help.

Junks

Chinese use boats called junks on the Yangtze and Yellow Rivers, which flow across mainland China. Some people live on junks. Others sell fish, other foods and crafts to people along the riverbanks. In southern China, junks are used on the sea. Some Chinese travel from China to Hong Kong by boat.

Suggest that children make a junk that will float, selecting from a variety of materials, including wood scraps, styrofoam, and cardboard. Encourage children to experiment to find out if their junks will float.

Pottery and Porcelain

Chinese porcelain and pottery are beautiful works of art. Each dynasty (emperor) created a special design. Most porcelain is painted a delicate green, gray-green, white, orchid, dark red, or blue and white. Hand paintings of flowers, birds, and people decorate the pieces of art.

Vases are some of the most beautiful works of art. Show Chinese pottery and porcelain to the children.

Young children can make dishes of potter's clay. If natural clay is used, it may be possible to have the dishes fired in a kiln. Let children paint their clay dishes with red, green, blue, or gold paint.

Red Envelopes (*Lai see*)

During the Chinese New Year celebration (see Celebrations section), small red envelopes called *lai see* are given as gifts. Red is the popular color in

China. The envelopes contain money and special wishes. The envelopes are decorated with gold calligraphy. Red envelopes are given to express wishes for good luck and happiness, similar to American greeting cards.

To make a red envelope, cut red tissue paper or red wrapping paper into 6-inch squares. Let children make play money out of scraps of paper. Place a piece of this money in the center of the red square. Fold all corners to the center, slightly overlapping them. Use gold stickers to hold the corners together; notary seals are ideal. Let children use gold paint pens to decorate the envelopes. Then the envelopes are ready to be given to a special friend.

Chinese Play Dough

Chinese children use a special kind of play dough for decorations or for eating. Because it is special, they have an opportunity to use play dough about once a year.

For a decoration, children make animals, toys, fruit, or flowers. They then put their design on a bamboo stick, similar to a hot dog stick. The play dough is dried thoroughly.

In the Chinese recipe, wheat or rice flour are mixed with water to a consistency of bread dough. The dough is divided into several parts and artificial color is added to each part. For eating, some Chinese add sugar, others add salt, and some eat it plain.

Let children use this play dough recipe to create objects to place on sticks but not to eat.

Basic Play Dough

2 C baking soda
1 C cornstarch
1 1/4 C water
Food coloring

Mix soda and cornstarch in a saucepan. Gradually add water. Bring to a boil over medium heat, stirring constantly until the mixture begins to thicken. Remove it from the heat. Put the dough on a plate and cover it with a damp cloth. Let it cool. Knead the dough until smooth. Divide it and add color. Mold the dough into the desired figure and let it dry.

NATURE AND SCIENCE

By appreciating, exploring, and observing nature, children become more aware of the world around them. The children learn how to cherish life and value the gifts of nature. Guide children to understand the great respect Chinese have for nature.

Famous Chinese Americans

The following Chinese Americans are making important contributions to various fields of study in the United States and the world:

Dr. Tsung Dao Lee and Dr. Chen Ning Yang, Nobel Prize winners in the field of science

Dr. Chien-shung Wu, the world's foremost experimental physicist

Dr. Choh Hao Li, biochemist

Gim Gong Lue, horticulturist

Information about these people may be found in current newspapers and magazines.

The Great Wall (*Ch'ang Ch'eng*)

The Great Wall is the longest wall in the world, and it was built many, many years ago. Talented Chinese builders completed it and the thousand-mile Grand Canal without the use of any machines. Show pictures of these two great engineering masterpieces. Discuss with older children the magnitude of these achievements, considering the time they were built and the technology available. An excellent film for children is *Big Bird in China*, which describes the Great Wall and provides an introduction to Chinese customs.

To create a Great Wall in your classroom, get four cardboard pattern boards from a fabric shop. Unfold the boards and attach two of them together, end to end, using large brad fasteners and cloth duct tape. Cut six-inch slits along the top of the two boards. Fold down every other flap as illustrated. Attach one side of the Great Wall to each side of the door frame. Arrange the wall to lead to the home center or any other center in the classroom. Children can pretend they are walking on the wall as they come into the room. Let children draw squares on the wall to represent the individual stones.

Children can build a Great Wall and dig a Grand Canal in

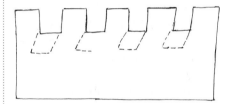

the sand outdoors. These activities help children gain an appreciation of these unique Chinese accomplishments.

ANIMALS
. . . .

Silkworms

Plan to introduce the Asian cultures and raising of silkworms when mulberry leaves are available. Parents and children alike delight in this adventure.

Place the silkworm eggs in a large glass container, aquarium, or fishbowl. After the eggs hatch into worms, place a piece of nylon net over the opening of the container. Silkworms must be fed mulberry leaves every day. They feed on the mulberry leaves until it is time to spin the cocoon, about three weeks. The silkworm secretes a fluid that hardens into silk thread. The worm winds this thread around itself to form a cocoon. When the moths come out of the cocoons, in about three weeks, children may examine the cocoons more closely.

Children may then observe the process of reproduction and the laying of new eggs. To store the eggs for next year, place them in an air-tight container in the refrigerator. More information about silkworms may be found in a children's encyclopedia.

Silk thread is made by unraveling the fiber of the cocoon and twisting strands together to achieve the desired thickness. Beautiful clothes are made of silk. Men's shirts, women's pants and blouses, and children's clothing are made of fabric woven from silk thread. Elaborate designs are embroidered on the silk. This clothing is worn only for special occasions. Show silk fabric and clothing to the children. Have them feel the fabric and talk about it. An excellent resource on silk is the January, 1984, issue of *National Geographic.*

Fish

Fish is a main food for the Chinese. Taiwan is an island, and many people who live near the coast can catch their own fish or buy them at the markets. Mainland China is a very large country where many people do not live near the ocean. Fish is transported along the Yangtze and Yellow Rivers by boat and sold along the rivers.

Let children draw fish of different sizes and colors on paper. Then show them how to attach a paper clip to the head of each fish and place it in a container. Tie a string to a magnet with a small hole in the middle and use it as a fishing line to catch the fish in the container.

Panda

The world first heard about the loving panda in China about 100 years ago. It looks like a bear. Today it is one of the most endangered animals in the world.

Pandas live in the mountains in the lush bamboo forests of China. An adult panda can weigh about 300 pounds or more and eats about 40 pounds of bamboo a day. But bamboo is becoming scarce in the forests, and the panda has less food to eat each year.

Baby pandas weigh a few ounces at birth. They have black ears, eyes, shoulders, and legs, with a white face and body.

The mother handles and cuddles her baby, keeping it close to her body, warm and safe. She holds her baby against her body with her paws. Pandas have acute hearing and a strong sense of smell. They climb trees easily at the first sign of danger.

Pandas are very playful and affectionate with people. Pandas given to the U.S. as a gift from the Chinese have captured the nation's imagination; Ling-Ling and Hsing-Hsing live at the national zoo in Washington, D.C.

Children can make panda masks or puppets to create a puppet show or role-play a story.

Display pictures, books, and stuffed or plastic toy pandas. Talk with children about the black and white features on the panda's face.

To make a panda mask: provide black and white construction paper, lightweight paper plates, glue, craft sticks, and masking tape (see illustration). Assist in cutting as needed. Children enjoy using plastic moving eyes when making panda puppets.

Pets

Because many people live in China, each family has very little space. Children are able to keep only small pets. Some of their pets are silkworms, small goldfish, rabbits, and birds. Children enjoy watching them. People can be seen in the park during the early morning observing and listening to birds. Older men take their birds in covered cages to the park for an airing. They open the cages and throw out seeds for their birds.

If you do not have these pets in your classroom, ask parents or friends to lend one pet at a time for a day or a week so that children can learn

more about them. Learning activities include observing and sharing observations.

PLANTS

Bean Sprouts

Bean sprouts are an ingredient in many Chinese recipes. To grow bean sprouts, plant dried beans in small containers. Transplant some of the seedlings to the outdoor garden. Cut and taste the other bean sprouts.

Put dried lentils into a large pan or jar. Cover them with a wet paper towel. Keep the paper towel moist. The lentils sprout very soon. Children can eat the sprouts during the week as they sprout.

Canned and fresh sprouts are available in grocery stores. Provide several different kinds for children to taste.

Bamboo (*Chu—chu*)

Bamboo grows as high as tall trees in America. It is strong and is used to make chopsticks, furniture, house walls, baskets, umbrellas, musical instruments, and many other useful items. It is also used for food.

Show bamboo to the children. Explain how it grows and how it is used. Bring a can of bamboo shoots for a tasting party. Ask the children how they taste. Look for other things made of bamboo to share with children.

If it is available, cut bamboo and bring it into the classroom. Let children touch, smell, and find words to describe bamboo.

Flowers

Many kinds of flowers grow in China, including carnations, daisies, and lilies. The Chinese have a deep appreciation for flowers and some are very special to them. The yellow lily (*chin hsuan*) is the symbol of mothers. When given to a mother, an original poem is also given. When chrysanthemums bloom, parties are held to view them, and people write poems about them.

In brush painting, the three basic flowers are plum blossoms, orchids, and chrysanthemums. Flowers are exported all over the world, especially orchids and chrysanthemums. Find some of these flowers in your community. Talk about the color, shape, size, and fragrance of each. Bring pots of chrysanthemums into the classroom.

LANGUAGE DEVELOPMENT

Learning about cultures through activities of interest to children encourages new language. Chinese show respect to others with a bow or a handshake—that is, through body language.

Vocabulary

The following words may used in labeling pictures and objects in the room.

ch'ang—Great Wall
ch'a—tea, principal drink in China
chu—bamboo, a tall plant with many uses
do yah—bean sprouts, roots of bean used for food
feng-cheng—kite
hsiung mao—panda
k'uai tzu—chopsticks, thin bamboo sticks used in pairs for eating
lung—dragon, symbol of China used in many folktales
mi—rice, grown in China and eaten at all meals
nan hai—boy
nu hai—girl

nung fu mao—farmer's hat
pan tsu—dishes (plates, bowls, cups)
teng-lung—lantern
wa-wa—doll

Additional words and terms may be found in the various sections of the unit.

Symbols

Use books, pictures, and posters to introduce children to Chinese characters. These characters, which are like pictures, comprise their alphabet. Each character is a whole word or idea. Several books in the bibliography include Chinese characters. Some children copy them or use them as labels.

Chinese is written in columns from top to bottom and right to left. See the Creative Art Expression section for suggestions on using symbols.

ba—father

da—big

ma—mother

nan hai—boy

nu hai—girl

seeow—small

su—tree

Chinese Words and Phrases
Ni hao (nee how)—How are you?
Zai jian (dsi jien)—Good-bye

Hsieh hsieh ni (shee shee nee)—Thank you
Ching (Cheeng)—Please
Wo ai ni (wo ai nee)—I love you

Chinese Numbers

Because there are various dialects used in different regions of China, there are several pronunciations for each number.

i (yee)—one
uhr (er)—two
sahn (sahn)—three
suh (suh)—four
wu (woo)—five
liu (leo)—six
chi (chee)—seven
ba (bah)—eight
ju (jeo)—nine
shur (shur)—ten

Chinese varies greatly, depending upon the region where it is spoken and the dialect.

Chops (Seals)

Young children write their names with a scribble, a drawing, the first letter of their name,

or their first name. For many years a Chinese custom has been to use a seal, which is called a name chop, to sign names to letters. A chop is similar to a rubber stamp with the person's name on it. This art is still practiced in China. The chop is made by extremely skilled artists and used to sign important papers. Artists sign their works

with their special chop. The chops are printed in red.

Have children ask their parents if they have stamps with their names on them; if they do, ask them to send a sample to school. Rubber stamps with letters and pictures are widely available. Provide a variety of stamps and red ink pads for children to use. Children also enjoy looking for the chop prints on authentic Chinese artwork and materials.

Here is The Learning Tree chop:

Good Luck Seals

On New Year's morning Chinese-American children break the good luck seals on doors and windows. Provide strips of paper, approximately 12 by 25 inches, and marking pens. Let children copy Chinese symbols and characters on a banner and then attach it across a door opening. The messages on the banner-like seals convey messages of Good Luck, Long Life, and Good Health.

Learning to Speak English

Teachers who have one or two young Chinese children who do not speak English have a responsibility to help them learn English. In a classroom where there is a great deal of interaction among children, the Chinese child learns English from the other children.

A non-English-speaking child will also progress in learning English if you spend extra time with him or her each day. Young children learn languages easily. When groups of non-English-speaking children attend one school, special programs for learning English are often provided. Chinese children enrich the culture of the class as the American and Chinese customs and lifestyles are shared.

Dramatization

Plan a dramatization of a story children enjoy. These are two stories suitable for dramatization: *Tye May and the Magic Paintbrush,* by Molly G. Bang, and *Yeh-shen: A Cinderella Story from China,* by Ai Ling Louie. Ask the children questions to help decide what characters and props they need. Let the children act out the roles of the characters, using the dialogue as they remember it. Encourage them to add their own words and their own interpretation.

The Three Bears in China

This old favorite was rewritten by young children at The Learning Tree. The bears became a panda family that lived in a bamboo forest in China. The porridge and spoons were changed to rice and chopsticks. With authentic props available in the classroom, the children used their imagination and creativity to dramatize part of another culture and to discover similarities and differences between cultures.

Shadow Play

Stories can be dramatized in many ways. The shadow play is used in China. In this group activity, one person reads the story, while children dramatize it with puppets behind a screen that is lighted on the back side. Children see shadows of the

characters in the story. Each child has one or two characters. A clothed character can be fastened to a stick, or hand puppets can be used. Dramatize a favorite Chinese story. Invite children to make the characters in the story.

Stories

The literature of a country or region of the world expresses the culture of that country. Stories, especially those written by authors who are natives of the country, provide authentic

information about the culture. Stories are powerful sources of vocabulary and language development. They also provide many ideas for creative expression.

One modern-day Chinese author, Hsiao-Yeh, makes up stories after dinner with his family. His love of reading and stories stem from the time his own father read to him. The stories made up by Hsiao-Yeh and his sons have been published as *Hsiao-Yeh's Children's Fables*.

Many older books about the Chinese stereotyped them. The stories and illustrations did not show them realistically. Children should be exposed to books that show people as they live. Several popular children's stories are old favorites. They need to be examined by the teacher before using them with children.

The best of picture books about China have been illustrated by Ed Young, an artist born in Shanghai. In his illustrations, he uses watercolors, the old Chinese art of painting, and pencil drawings to convey the text.

Symbols in Stories

Chinese literature includes many symbols. Certain animals symbolize directions: dragon—east; tiger—west; tortoise—north; phoenix—south. Certain colors specify seasons: black—winter; green—spring; red—summer; white—autumn. The symbol of the dragon is the most important because it is considered wise and good. Many stories in Chinese folklore include the dragon.

Folktales

To expose children to folktales is to give them an insight into the thinking of a culture. The folktale is the clearest form of beliefs of a culture. Young children become familiar with folktales through listening and dramatizing these tales. Many folktales are now being adapted for young children.

Developmental stages of young children that make the enjoyment of folktales possible are a belief in magic, a developing imagination, and an understanding of language. When reading Chinese folktales, explain to children that these are make-believe stories, like "The Three Bears" or "The Three Little Pigs."

Three-Character Classic Poetry

Classic Chinese poetry emphasizes morality and character building, including obedience, respect for one's elders, contentment with life, and peace and tranquility. Poetry memorized in childhood may be remembered for life.

Three-character classic poetry is comprised of six characters, three in each line. The meaning of the Chinese characters may be translated into English phrases to convey the thought. Books of these poems have been printed for years. Today these poems are available in China in books or cassettes.

Beginning at about age three, young children memorize many classic poems under the guidance of parents and teachers. At ages four and five, children begin to write their own poetry. These are examples of classic poetry: "The sun rises early, and I rise early, too;" "The big dog barks, and the little dog jumps." Children at The Learning Tree wrote this classic poem:

The rain comes down,
The rain is softly falling;
I want to play, my friend
wants to play.

Invite children to create their own three-line poems.

Proverbs

Proverbs are learned in China to express truths in unique language. Recall some of our American proverbs. Primary-age children may be able to explain the meaning of these Chinese proverbs:

A wise bird selects its tree.
A single kind word keeps one warm for three winters.

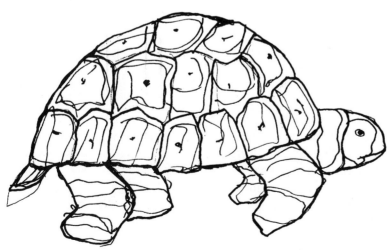

MUSIC

Chinese music has a different, unique sound quality unfamiliar to Western ears though familiar instruments—flutes, cymbals, lutes, gongs, wooden blocks, drums—produce it. A big red drum is a typical musical instrument.

String Instruments

Chinese play string instruments. The samisen is a three-stringed instrument similar to a banjo. The pipa is a string instrument similar to a guitar. Chinese also play a type of mandolin.

Introduce children to as many Chinese instruments as possible. Import or Asian shops may have some of them. Small bamboo flutes are inexpensive and children enjoy playing them. Encourage children to create their own music after listening to Chinese music, imitating the melodies and rhythms. Invite a musician to bring Chinese instruments to class to demonstrate. Show pictures of the instruments. Check the PBS television and radio schedules for broadcasts of Chinese music.

Gong

The Chinese gong is a unique musical instrument. Traditionally, it was used to announce special events, such as the arrival of an important visitor.

Make a gong from a large silver or metal tray. Silver (or silverplate) makes a more pleasing sound. You will need a tray that has filigree around the edge or open handles. Attach a leather loop through a hole near the edge. Pad a wooden mallet with pieces of soft cloth, covered with a larger piece of cloth or sheepskin. Children can hold and strike the gong. It can also be hung on a stand. The gong makes a wonderful sound and can be used to summon children or get their attention in the classroom.

Listening

Play selections from the Chinese recordings suggested in the Resource section. Ask children to listen for the sounds of the flutes, bells, and especially the gong. The music may inspire children to create stories and poems.

Many Asian stores have records and tapes of popular music from China. Teresa Ten is a popular vocalist in China today. Children at The Learning Tree enjoy her voice and music. They refer to her music as the "New Chinese Music." Teresa Ten's music is available from Polydor Publishing in Hong Kong.

Chinese Children and Music

Today modern and traditional instruments are played in China. In Taiwan, classes in violin, piano, and bamboo flute and other traditional instruments are taught. A few young children learn to play the violin using the Japanese method.

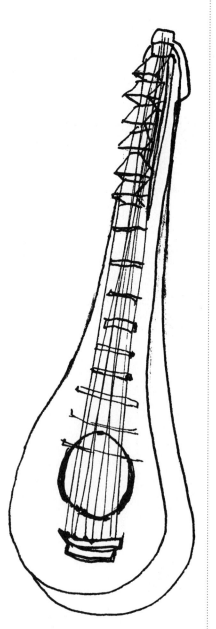

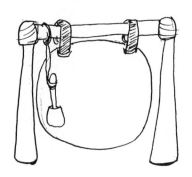

DANCE

Folk Dance

Many Chinese children learn traditional folk dances. The girls are especially interested in performing the dances. Children enjoy moving to the beat of Chinese music. Provide long, narrow, brightly-colored scarves similar to those used in China—about 8 to 12 inches wide and 3 to 5 feet long. As the children dance, the scarves float in the air. Crepe paper streamers also provide the desired effect.

DRAMA

Puppet Theaters

Marionette puppet theaters present dramas in the parks in special puppet theaters. The puppets are dressed in elaborate, beautiful costumes. Locate marionette players in your community. Invite them to demonstrate how marionettes are manipulated.

Beijing Opera

This drama is an ancient art in which important Chinese values are dramatized. The story is sung by players wearing masks. The opera includes music, dance, mime, and acrobatics.

Skilled Chinese acrobats perform in America, and at times their performances are televised. Talk about the meaning of mime and acrobatics and the training needed for these arts.

Beautiful painted masks similar to those used in Chinese opera are available at import stores. Have them available for children to use when they perform their own dramas. Provide paper plates and bright colors of tempera paint for children to create masks.

GAMES AND MANIPULATIVES

Today the Chinese are interested in team sports. Traditionally their games were not competitive, reflecting a cultural value of this society.

Shuttlecock, spin the top, and jump rope are Chinese folk games. Folk dances with long scarves are a favorite activity for girls.

Shuttlecock (*Jentz*)

Shuttlecock is played using a weighted game piece that has feathers attached to the top of it. Each child has a shuttlecock. The object of the game is to see how long the shuttlecock can be kept in the air using only the feet. In the United States this game has been adapted and is known as Hacky Sack.

Children make a shuttlecock using feathers, a small metal washer, and two pipe cleaners. Have them loop the pipe cleaners through the sides of the washers and attach feathers to the washers by wrapping and twisting the pipe cleaners around the ends of the feathers.

Spin the Top (*To Lo*)

Chinese tops range in size from tiny to very large. The larger the top, the stronger the string or rope needed to start the spinning. Display pictures of books about these very large toys.

Jump Rope (*T'ao Sheng*)

Chinese and American children play jump rope the same way. One child or a group jumps, depending upon the length and weight of the rope. Counting Game (*Jen-dow, Shih-toe, Boo*)

This counting game may used to select the person who will be "it." Children play Scissors, Paper, Stone, chanting "Jen-dow, Shih-toe, Boo" as they play. Players shake fists up and down twice and then stretch their fingers out on the third beat ("Boo"). Five fingers stretched out are paper; two are scissors; a clenched fist is stone. If one player is paper and the other scissors, scissors wins because it cuts paper. If the two players are scissors and stone, stone wins because it can break scissors. If two players are paper and stone, paper wins because it can wrap itself around stone. If both players bring their hands down in the same position, they repeat the game. The loser becomes "it."

Elementary School Athletics (Grade One and Up)

All schools offer athletic classes. In Taiwan, parks, sports grounds, gardens, and play areas are available to schools. Each class begins with a ten-minute physical exercise period. All ages in China exercise regularly. Classes are also taught in traditional activities like table tennis, gymnastics, and kung-fu.

Relay Games

Relay games are played in two teams. The children in each team pass a small ball from one child to the next as fast as they can. The first team to finish wins.

Tug-of-War

Tug-of-War is a popular school activity. Two teams pull on opposite ends of a rope to see which can pull the other team across a line.

Kung-Fu

Many boys and girls begin to practice martial arts at about the age of seven. The movements must be done very fast. Kung-fu helps children protect themselves and feel stronger. It must be learned from a person trained in kung-fu. Invite a kung-fu expert to demonstrate this art to the children.

T'ai Chi

T'ai Chi is an art, a form of exercise, and a martial art. It is practiced all over China, sometimes accompanied by music. It consists of a set of slow, graceful exercises involving all parts of the body; the mind and body must work together. The Chinese create their own movements or imitate those of kung-fu. Many Chinese practice t'ai chi at sunrise in the parks and on the hills.

Have children do exercises outdoors very slowly, bending only at the waist. Be certain all parts of the body have been exercised.

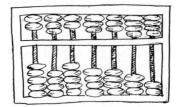

Abacus

The abacus has been used for thousands of years to calculate mathematical problems. Special classes for learning how to use the abacus are taught, usually beginning at about age eight, though some begin as young as four. Children learn modern mathematics in school. Children can calculate answers on the abacus very quickly. Contests are held each year.

The abacus is an appropriate piece of equipment for all ages from two, on up, depending on the child's developmental skills. Two-year-olds enjoy manipulating the beads. Three-year-olds are able to identify the object. Four and five-year-olds begin to count the beads. Older children can use it for mathematics.

Have several different kinds and sizes of abacuses available for children to use.

Chinese Tangram

The tangram is a puzzle that originated in China. Children are fascinated with this puzzle, which consists of seven pieces—five triangles, one square, and one rhomboid. When fitted together, these shapes make a design or picture. Hundreds of pictures can be created from these seven pieces.

Tangrams may be purchased from many educational supply companies. They provide excellent problem-solving activities, as well as developing form dis-

crimination and visual perception. Discovery Toys offers an inexpensive tangram, including design sheets. A beautiful hand-crafted walnut set is available from World Wide Games in Colchester, CT 06415.

Chinese Character Lotto

Lotto or matching games can be made using Chinese characters. Select the characters representing numbers or simple characters shown in books.

Mah Jongg

This Chinese game has four sets of beautiful square ivory-like pieces with engraved symbols on top of each piece. It is played in a manner similar to dominoes.

Young children enjoy playing with the pieces and examining the symbols. Older children may play the Chinese version of the game. Mah jongg is available at Chinese gift shops and other game suppliers.

SPECIAL EVENTS

Community Resources

Search in your community for Chinese resources. Attend a Chinese New Year's festival if possible. Chinese restaurants and shops are valuable learning resources. A favorite trip for The Learning Tree is a visit to a Chinese market. Check the local museums and newspapers for art exhibits. Call local schools and colleges for additional resources.

Invite a Chinese family to come to school to share their culture. Clothing, food, games, stories and poetry, and artifacts are of interest to children.

CELEBRATIONS

Holidays are frequent and popular in China, especially in Taiwan. The whole country closes down. Chinese traditions are preserved through holidays. New clothes, special foods, decorations, and fireworks characterize the celebrations. Banners are made for some holidays. The most important holidays are described here.

Chinese New Year (*Yuan Tan*)—Celebrated on the first day of the lunar calendar, varying from January 21 to February 19

New Year's Day is the most important and happiest holiday of the year and is celebrated by Chinese all over the world. A family dinner is part of the festivities, and it includes fish, a symbol of prosperity. Homes are decorated in red, a symbol of happiness to all Chinese. Door signs express good wishes such as, "See joy when you raise your head." There are also parades and dragon or lion dances, followed by fireworks. New Year is a time of gift-giving. (See "Lai see" in Creative Art Expression.) On New Year's Day, debts are paid, accounts settled, and grudges forgotten.

Lantern Festival—Last day of the New Year festivities

On the last day of the New Year celebration, the family joins the parade, each member carrying a lighted lantern. They go to the carnival, which has puppet shows, operas, and dragon dancing in the streets. Dragons symbolize royalty. Special food is a dumpling of rice with a sweet filling. (See "Lanterns" in Creative Art Expression.)

Children's Day—April 4

This day honors children who have been outstanding in school in academic achievement, extra-curricular activities, or citizenship. One or two children from each class in each school, beginning with the first grade, are honored. They attend

a special ceremony at the city hall, where the mayor speaks to them. The children receive a certificate and a gift and attend a special movie. Plan a Children's Day for your classroom. Have a ceremony to tell something special about each child, and then award each with a special ribbon.

Dragon Boat Festival—May 28 to June 28

This festival is the biggest event of the summer, the official beginning of the season. Teams race against one another in long boats (sculls) decorated with a dragon's head in front of the boat.

Moon Festival—September 15-16, 15th day of the 8th lunar month

The moon is believed to be at its brightest during the Moon Festival, when the Chinese give thanks for the harvest, as Americans do at Thanksgiving. Love and beauty are celebrated. A decorated moon cake, as round and yellow as the moon, is eaten. The roundness of the cake symbolizes the moon and family unity. Chinese Americans also celebrate this festival. Serve moon cake, available at Asian bakeries and grocery stores, for a snack.

Chinese National Day—October 10

This is independence day for Taiwan. Children attend a special ceremony at city hall, where there are acrobatic shows, dancing, the flying of banners, and showing of animals and crops. Many families attend the fireworks display in the evening.

Winter Festival—Around December 21

Winter festival is celebrated within the family at the beginning of the season.

RESOURCES

N Nursery
K Kindergarten
P Primary
I Intermediate
A Adult

Books for Children

Few contempoary Chinese books are available in the United States. We hope more Chinese books will be translated into English and that there will be more children's books written by Chinese Americans.

Bales, Carol Ann. *Chinatown Sunday, The Story of Lillia*. Reilly and Lee Books, 1975. KP
A large picture book reveals the life of a ten-year-old living in Chicago. Older children see the ways they are like Lillia and ways they are different. Chinese-American children can identify with a story that describes the life of a girl who is asked daily, "Are you from China or Japan?"

Bang, Molly. *Tye May and the Magic Brush*. Greenwillow Books, 1981. NK
A wicked emperor learns a lesson from a young girl. The story is a favorite for dramatization.

Behrens, June. *Gung Hay Fat Choy*. Children's Press, 1982. KP
Ideas for celebrating the Chinese New Year are suggested through colorful photographs and an informative text.

Brown, Tricia. *Chinese New Year*. Henry Holt and Company, 1987. P
Photographs introduce the lively traditions of the Chinese New Year.

Cayseuter, Frances. *Tales of a Chinese Grandmother*. Charles E. Tuttle Co., 1985. IA
For older readers and adults, this treasury of Chinese folklore explores Chinese customs and beliefs as shared by the grandmother of the Ling family.

Chang, Kathleen. *The Iron Moonhunter*. Children's Book Press, 1987. P
This story based on the building of the Central Pacific Railroad tells about the Chinese Americans' bitter past.

Daley, William. *The Chinese Americans*. Chelsea House Publishers, 1987. I
From the series "The Peoples of North America," this text detailing the past and present of the Chinese people in America is an excellent resource.

Demi. *Chen Ping and His Magic Axe*. Dodd, Mead, and Company, 1987. KP
This retelling of a Chinese folktale about honesty can easily be dramatized by children. A greedy man, a poor little boy, and an old man with a white beard are the principle charac-

ters in this story that describes an encounter with a stranger that results in magical powers being acquired by a common axe.

_____. *A Chinese Zoo. Fables and Proverbs.* Harcourt Brace Jovanovich, Inc., 1987. KPI
In a most unusual way numerous animals are described.

_____. *Liang and the Magic Paintbrush.* Holt, Rinehart, and Winston, Inc., 1980. NK
An adventure filled with magic delights young children as they learn how good wins over evil.

Eco, Umberto, and Eugencio Carmi. *The Three Astronauts.* Harcourt Brace Jovanovich, Inc., 1989. KP
A Chinese, a Russian, and an American land on Mars and learn a lesson. Watercolor collages present this story with a message children should hear.

Fyson, Nance Lui, and Richard Greenhill. *A Family in China.* Lerner Publications Company, 1985. P
A glimpse of twelve-year-old Wang Chinn Ling's home in the Liaoning province of China shows children how people can share and work together for the good of everyone.

Gerstein, Mordicai. *The Mountains of Tibet.* Harper Trophy Books, 1987. P
This is a beautifully illustrated book about choices.

Haskins, Jim. *Count Your Way Through China.* Carolrhoda Books, Inc., 1987. KP
Young children learn numbers one through ten in Chinese and

are introduced to concepts about Chinese culture. This is one of a series about eight diverse cultures with bright illustrations.

Heyer, Marilae. *The Weaving of a Dream.* Puffin Books, 1986. P
This talented author and illustrator presents a tale of fantasy and reality with illustrations that sing. This Chinese folktale is enjoyed by all, but the text is for the older children.

Hou-tien, Cheng. *The Chinese New Year.* Holt, Rinehart, and Winston, 1976. KP
The Chinese art of paper cutting is presented in this story about the elaborate and festive New Year's celebration.

Jacobsen, Peter Otto, and Preben Sejir Kristensen. *A Family in Hong Kong.* The Bookwright Press, 1985. P
The Cheng family introduces the reader to their life in Hong Kong, including cooking in the traditional way, eating rice with chopsticks, fishing in the South China Sea, visiting skyscrapers, and enjoying a city with neon advertisement signs.

Jensen, Helen Zane. *When Panda Came to Our House.* Dial Books, 1985. NK
Pencil drawings illustrate this story of an imaginary friend who comes for tea. The glossary of Chinese terms and definitions adds to this literature experience, which is rich in art and ideas for activities.

Johnson, Neil. *Step into China.* Julian Messner, 1988. P
Color photographs, Chinese calligraphy, and descriptive text

give insight into modern mainland China and her people.

Levine, Ellen. *I Hate English!* Scholastic, Inc., 1989. P
Children learn about the importance of a person's language through Mei Mei as she moves from speaking Chinese to English words. A lesson in sensitivity about cultural differences is very well presented.

Levinson, Riki. *Our Home Is the Sea.* E. P. Dutton, 1988. KP
Accurately detailed paintings add dimension to this factual story of a modern-day child of Hong Kong and his desire to follow the traditions of his father and his father before him.

Lobel, Arnold. *Ming Lo Moves the Mountain.* Greenwillow Books. 1982. NK
Subtle watercolors and a clever text enliven this folktale which is suitable for dramatization.

Louie, Ai Ling. *Yeh-shen, A Cinderella Story from China.* Philomel Books, 1982. KP
This story about a poor girl of long ago and her mean stepmother is illustrated in pastels and watercolors. It is excellent for dramatizing.

Luppi, Andrea. *Republic of China: As Exemplified by Its People and Life in Taiwan.* Magnus Edizioni, 1982. P
This picture book reveals present-day Taiwan, with all its tradition and contemporary ways. The brief introduction is helpful.

Mahy, Margaret. *The Seven Chinese Brothers.* Scholastic Inc., 1989. P

This beautifully illustrated text pays a great deal of attention to detail describing the amazing powers of the brothers.

Niang, Bang Gu. *Seven Clam Sisters*. Zhaohua Publishing House, No. 21 Chegongzhuang Xilu, Beijing, 1982. KP
This story relates the adventures of Bai Hai as he searches the sea for pearls.

Reuter, Bjarne. *The Princess and the Sun, Moon, and Stars*. Pelham Books, 1986. KP
Attention to cultural details makes this a beautifully illustrated folktale.

Roy, Ronald. *A Thousand Pails of Water*. Alfred A. Knopf, Inc., 1978. K
This is a delightful story of a small boy's efforts to save a great white whale.

Sadler, Catherine Edwards. *Two Chinese Families*, Atheneum, 1981. P
The photographs in this book are interesting to children, but the text is for older children.

San Souci, Robert D. *The Enchanted Tapestry*. Dial Books, 1987. KP
This Chinese fable, illustrated in watercolor and pencil, weaves a story with a happy ending.

Sen, John. *Hsiao San's Magic Brush*. Asian-American Bilingual Center, 1980. KP
A magic brush takes a homesick Chinese American, Hsiao San, toward Peking over the Great Wall of China, and across the mountains, ending in Hong Kong. Chinese children will especially enjoy seeing a text written in Chinese.

Soend, Otto S. *Children of the Yangtze River*. Pelham Books, 1985. NK
This book describes the modern-day communal life in China, and explains how a family celebrates with the red good-luck sign, firecrackers, and lanterns. Detailed illustrations are included.

Stock, Catherine. *Emma's Dragon Hunt*. Lothrop, Lee & Shepard Books, 1984. NK
This beautiful story about ancient Chinese dragon myths enables children to see beyond the dragon stereotypes.

Stone, Jan. *Big Bird in China*. Random House/Children's Television Workshop, 1983. KP
An excellent introduction to the rich culture of China is presented; also available in video.

Tang, Yungmei. *China, Here We Come! Visiting the People's Republic of China*. G. P. Putnam's Sons, 1981. P
Black-and-white photographs and interesting text tell the story of a visit by a group of thirteen-year-old American students to mainland China.

Tompert, Ann. *Grandfather Tang's Story*. Crown Publishers, Inc., 1990. NKP
Using her interest in tangrams, the author spins a tale about two friends. Changing the arrangement of the puzzle pieces on each page changes the course of the adventure.

Torre, Betty L. *The Luminous Pearl: A Chinese Folktale*. Orchard Books, 1990. KP
Wa Jing becomes the perfect suitor for Princess Mai Li as she looks for an honest and brave husband.

Wallace, Ian. *Chin Chiang and the Dragon's Dance*. Atheneum, 1984. NK
A young Chinese-American boy loses his courage when the first day of the Year of the Dragon arrives. A description of a Chinese family's celebration—exchanging gifts of fine tea, new clothes, and Lucky Money—can suggest activities for classroom experiences focusing on the New Year. Fine watercolor drawings support the text.

Waters, Kate, and Madeline Slovenz-Low. *Lion Dancer Ernie Wan's Chinese New Year*. Scholastic, Inc., 1990. NK
An attractive, informative book describes an actual celebration with the Wan family in New York City.

Whitaker, Janet. *Visiting Junjun and Meimei in China*. Press Syndicate of the University of Cambridge, 1988. PI
Actual photographs depict daily life of ten-year-old Junjun and eight-year-old Meimei in a small village inland from Shanghai. Detailed text enables young readers to gain insight into the life of Chinese children.

Williams, Jay. *Everyone Knows What a Dragon Looks Like*. Four Winds Press, 1976. KP
Mercer Mayer illustrated this clever tale about a young boy—a gate-sweeper—who becomes a hero.

Wyndham, Robert, ed. *Chinese Mother Goose Rhymes*. Philomel Books, 1989. NKP
Traditional Chinese rhymes and poems are translated into English, with Chinese characters included on each page. Enchanting paintings illustrate these rhymes about nature, children, and families.

Ying, Mei. *Magic Deer.* Foreign Language Press, (24 Baiwanzhaiang Road, Beijing, China), 1982. K
Colorful crayon drawings embellish this tale of Magic Deer and his dangerous adventures.

Yolen, Jane. *The Emperor and the Kite.* World, 1967. KP
An emperor of ancient China learns about giving love and attention. Illustrated by Ed Young, a Shanghai born artist who paints in the style of the old Chinese artist.

_____. *The Seeing Stick.* Thomas Y. Crowell, 1977. KP
Delicate drawings set the stage for this Chinese folktale about the lesson learned by the emperor's daughter with the help of an old man and his seeing stick.

_____. *The Seventh Mandarin.* Seabury Press, 1970. P
The wind carries the huge dragon kite outside the palace grounds where the seventh mandarin discovers the poor Chinese. He helps these people. Ed Young was the Caldecott winner for his illustrations.

Young, Ed. *Lon Po Po.* Philomel Books, 1989. KP
This is a beautifully illustrated

Chinese version of "Red Riding Hood." *Lon Po Po* means "Granny Wolf."

Children will also enjoy these books. Look for them in the library.
Grosvenor, Donna K. *Pandas from the National Geographic Books for Young Explorers.*
Lewis, Thomas P. *The Dragon Kite.*
Martin, Patricia Milles. *The Rice Bowl Pet.*
Otsuka, Yuzo. *Suko and the White Horse.*

Books and Periodicals for Adults

Carpenter, Frances. *Tales of a Chinese Grandmother.* Charles E. Tuttle Company, 1985.
This book of stories, copyrighted in 1937, still enchants "anyone not too old in spirit to enjoy folktales."

Cheng, Hou-tien. *The Chinese New Year.* Holt, Rinehart and Winston, 1976.
This is an excellent description of holiday activities with text for older children.

Dowdee, Dorothy. *Chinese Helped Build America.* Julian Messner, 1972.
This history book contains accurate information about the plight of Chinese people working on the railroad and their mistreatment as immigrants. An interesting chapter on festivals and holidays describes "lai see" (the red envelopes used at New Year's); the Dragon Boat Festival; and the Moon Festival at harvest time, when large, round cakes decorated to look like the moon are eaten. Photographs are interesting to children.

Jones, Claire. *The Chinese in America.* Lerner Publications Company, 1972.
This book of historical facts about Chinese immigrants is written for older children and is also interesting to adults researching immigration and early history of "life behind the Great Wall of China."

Sinorama. Kwang Hwa Publishing, Inc. Greenway Plaza, Suite 216, Houston, TX 77046.
This monthly bilingual magazine is colorfully illustrated and covers a variety of current topics, including the following: arts, medicine, the environment, education and children, people and society, communications and language. Each issue has a cover story on a current topic.

Sung, Betty Lee. *An Album of Chinese Americans.* Franklin Watts, Inc., 1977.
The life, customs, and traditions of Chinese Americans, from their earliest migration to this country to the present day, are discussed and highlighted by many descriptive photographs.

Takahama, Toshie. *Origami Toys.* Shufunotomo Co., Ltd., 6, 1-Chome, Surugadi, Kanda, Chiyvdu-ku, Toyota, Japan, 1981.
Fifteen simple models, including the captain's shirt, can be made with children or demonstrated by an adult.

Tan, Amy. *The Joy Luck Club.* G. P. Putnam's Sons, 1989.
Amy Tan's own life has found its way into her first novel. A foot in both cultures, Chinese and

American, this author gives us a sensitive view of a group of Chinese women.

Films, Filmstrips, and Videotapes

Big Bird in China. Random House/Children's Television Workshop, 1983.   KP
This video gives an excellent introduction to the rich culture of China. It is also available as a book.

China: Sichuan Province. National Geographic Society, 1988.
Suggested for intermediate and adult viewing, this film or video gives excellent background information for older children and adults on the centrally located province. People's Republic of China Live includes scenes of mealtime, markets, the road to China, games, martial arts, and river port activity. The quality of this film is exceptional.

Folktales from Two Lands. Distributed by Churchill Films. 16-1/2 minutes. Ages 4-13.
Two favorite stories for young children illustrate the similarity of folk themes and human nature. Children delight in tales about magic wishes. The animated tales capture the interest of all children. A teacher's guide suggests activities and follow-up discussion.

New Year's Day in Chinatown. Produced and distributed by Society for Visual Education, 1982.
The "long, long body of the dragon" captures the young child's imagination as Terry, a young Chinese-American boy, explains this holiday that is important to Chinese contemporary life and is gaining interest worldwide. A handout suggests ideas for follow-up activities. Although labeled for primary grades, we believe some teachers will find it useful for children five and six years old.

Otsuka, Yuzo. *Suko and the White Horse*. Weston Woods.
Suko's love for the White Horse dominates this tale of Mongolia that explains how the horsehead fiddle became an instrument preferred by Asians. The watercolor illustrations are very pleasing. Available as video, 16mm film, and filmstrip.

Sui Mei Wong: Who Shall I Be? Distributed by Coronet Films and Video.   P
An eleven-year-old Chinese American girl's dream of being a ballet dancer conflicts with her parents' desire for her to maintain pride in her heritage. Children learn about Chinese food and family manners.

World Cultures and Youth: Shao Ping the Artist. Coronet Films and Video, 1987.
This story of Shao Ping and her best friend allows a glimpse at a day in the life of a masterful acrobat in Shanghai and acquaints viewers with the lifestyle of a Chinese family.

Materials and Experiences

Dolls—Asian Boy, Asian Girl. Claudia's Caravan, Nos. 19G, 18G.
Thirteen-inch vinyl dolls in Asian category. Continue to search for distinct groups, especially Cambodian, Japanese, and Chinese.

Ethnic Dolls. Child Craft, Nos. 182758, 182774.
Asian Boy and Asian Girl dolls promote ethnic pride.

Mien Dolls. Claudia's Caravan, No. 31G.
Handcrafted cloth doll in traditional dress.

Games and Manipulatives

Asian Girl Body Puzzle. Educational Teaching Aids, No. 8779D-E9.
Scaled to life-size proportions, this puzzle is 3 3/4 inches long when assembled.

Chinese-English Flash Cards. Claudia's Caravan.
Chinese characters with English words and pictures introduce basic vocabulary.

Posters and Pictures

Asian Personalities. Kaplan, No. 1791.
Four full-color prints are 11 1/2 by 16 inches.

Asian American Posters. Educational Teaching Aids, No. 2725-99.
Fourteen color posters, with information on each.

Contemporary Asian Americans. Distributed by Cole.
Fourteen colorful 11-by-16-inch study prints depict famous Asian Americans, including Chinese Americans.

Records and Audiocassettes

Children's Songs in Chinese. Claudia's Caravan, No. 102H.
This cassette with songbook is about special occasions. Selections are sung by Cantonese children. Text provides an expe-

rience with Chinese characters (English translation).

Jenkins, Ella. "A Train Ride to the Great Wall" on *I Know the Colors of the Rainbow: In the People's Republic of China with Ella Jenkins*. Educational Activities, Inc., LP record AR595. Music emphasizes appreciation for other cultures and languages.

"Empress of the Pagodas".on *Making Music Your Own. Integrated Listening Selections*, Columbia Records. Music for listening.

McKenna, Siolihan. *Chinese Fairy Tales*. Distributed by Music for Little People, Box 1460, Redway, CA 95560. Cassette of ancient Chinese fairy tales containing wise Confucian values. Suggested for ages five to ten.

Catalog
China Books and Periodicals, Inc., 2929 24th St., San Francisco, CA 94110.
Write for catalog describing twelve Chinese magazines in English; music, games, and materials for learning Chinese; children's hats and pouches; and books. Some items are available as software or on cassettes.

JAPANESE AND JAPANESE-AMERICAN CULTURES

Japan has a long history. The Japanese developed their culture and the arts early in their history. In recent times, vast changes have occurred in Japan. Today it is an industrial country. The Japanese have developed many unique and useful products that are purchased by other countries, including the United States. The Japanese are known and respected worldwide, and though they enjoy many Western customs, their basic traditional culture remains.

Not all of the activities included are appropriate for all ages. Allow children to choose activities and use a creative approach so that they accomplish their goals according to their developmental levels. Share the background information provided as appropriate. Enlist the help of Japanese families and Japanese-Americans in your community to clarify children's questions about Japanese culture.

Keiko Miyashita of Tokyo, a doctoral student at the University of North Texas majoring in early childhood education, was a valuable consultant in validating the contents of this unit and in interpreting Japanese culture.

FAMILY LIVING

Family life in Japan has a foundation of strong family ties. Many changes have occurred in Japan since the 1950s, but the basic Japanese character remains. The blending of traditional Japanese and Western lifestyles seems to affect all facets of society.

HOMES

Today homes may have both Japanese and Western-style rooms. Some have a traditional Japanese-style tatami room for guests. More and more, families live in small apartments or condominiums because houses are expensive and space to build them is limited. Furnishings and appliances are comparable to those in the United States.

Japanese-style homes are built of wood and have tile for the roof. Most of them are one story, though some have two stories. Floors are covered with carpet and linoleum. Some homes still use straw floor mats (*tatamis*). Sliding doors (*fusuma*) are built into the outside wall to increase air circulation. The inner walls (*shoji*) are flexible. They are wooden frames with paper or cloth stretched over them. All homes have an entrance hall (*genkan*) where street shoes are removed.

A room with paper walls can be constructed by attaching one end of a 36-inch wide roll of butcher paper to one wall. Stretch the paper across the room, around a card table or chair, and then attach it to another wall to make an enclosure. Let children cut doors in the paper wall.

In the family living center, include low tables and put cushions and tatamis on the floor. Suggest that children and adults take off their shoes before entering this area.

Futon

A *futon* is a beautiful, bulky quilt—or two quilts—spread on the floor or on a folding mattress for sleeping. It may also be used on a western-style bed. It is rolled up for storage during the day. Futons used with frames are increasingly popular in the United States; they are sold in furniture stores.

Tatami

A *tatami*, a rice straw mat, is used as a floor covering in Japanese-style homes. The size of a room is determined according to the number of tatamis that will fit into it. A low table is used when Japanese sit on the tatami. Some floors in other rooms are carpeted. Shoes are always removed at the door to prevent soiling the tatami.

The tatami is popular for use at the beach in the United States. Rolled ones are available in many department stores and

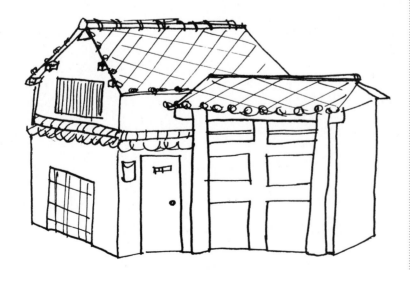

import shops. They are inexpensive and add a special atmosphere when learning about the Japanese culture.

Children can make tatamis by weaving 1-by-18-inch strips of paper through slits cut in a 12-by-18-inch piece of construction paper. Staple the ends of the strips to the large piece of paper to hold them in place. Lay the mats together in one part of the room.

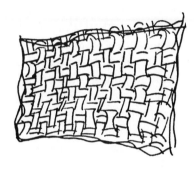

Carrying Infants

Japanese mothers carry their infants on their backs. A wide piece of fabric, long enough to reach from one shoulder to the other, holds the infant to the mother's back. It is fastened in front with two belts that are attached to each side of the fabric, crisscrossed, and fastened in the front.

Tokonoma

The *tokonoma* is a special place of beauty in a Japanese home. The love of nature and art is symbolized with a flower arrangement on a low table and a display of a scroll painting or calligraphy on a scroll.

Let children take turns providing objects from nature and art for this place of beauty.

Ikebana

The traditional Japanese art of arranging cut flowers began about 500 years ago. Three basic sprays are used to signify the sky, the earth, and people. The arrangement expresses the harmony of the balance of nature.

The flowers, with unwanted leaves removed, are arranged in a vase and used to decorate the home. Today, Japanese also make modern floral arrangements.

Have pictures and resource books available to acquaint children with Japanese flower arranging. Children can pick fresh flowers, leaves, and greenery. Ask the local florist for unused flowers. Also provide artificial flowers, vases, and clay. Using these materials, children can arrange flowers to appear as if they are growing. If the arrangement is for the New Year, use pine branches and white chrysanthemums. See Family Life section on Flower Arranging in the Chinese and Chinese-American unit.

Gardens

Many Japanese create formal gardens using plants, rocks, statues, and pools. These gardens are works of art that have been made for 1000 years. The aim is to show the natural beauty of the outdoors. Plants, shrubs, and rocks are symbols of this beauty. For new homes in the cities, space is not readily available for gardens, so public gardens are important.

The miniature hill garden has a pool filled with large goldfish, symbol of the sea. Mounds of earth and the arrangement of rocks symbolize the mountains.

The dry garden has a place for white sand shaped in ripples, with blue rocks placed as a reminder of a waterfall. Let children select a place out of doors to create a garden. They can choose rocks and small trees or bushes and place a container of water in a shallow hole they have prepared. Add wind chimes (*furin*) to the garden scene (see Creative Art Expression).

SCHOOL LIFE

School Bag

Japanese children carry a notebook, pencil box, and lunch in a school bag. Kindergarten children carry a backpack or a bag with a strap over the shoulder. Elementary-age children carry *randoseru*, leather backpacks.

Homework

Japanese parents place a high priority on their children's education. The responsibility for helping them is taken very seriously. Primary-age children spend one to two hours a night on homework. Some children begin *juku*—private tutoring—several nights a week to prepare for the difficult examination at the end of the elementary grades.

DRAMATIC PLAY

Provide the following Japanese articles for role-playing:

—child-sized kimono and sash for obi
—chopsticks
—electric train
—furoshiki
—futon for dolls
—kabuki hand puppets
—kokeshi dolls
—lacquerware
—miniature cars
—paper fan
—rice bowl
—robot
—sandals
—small teacups without handles
—sneakers
—tatami
—teapot
—top for spinning
—U.S.-style doll
—U.S.-style puppets
—umbrellas in bright colors
—Western-style boys' and girls' clothing

CLOTHING

One of the first things young children want to do when exploring a culture is to try on traditional clothing. Have clothing available for children to examine, or have them make their own by adding a creative touch to an existing garment or using a pattern and starting from scratch. Involve the children in determining what tools are needed, selecting materials, and deciding where to cut.

Furoshiki

Japanese carry the same kind of shopping bags as Americans. They also wrap items in a *furoshiki*, a square piece of cloth that is tied at the corners. It may be very small, or it may be large enough to carry a quilt. Some are cotton and some are silk; some furoshiki are plain, and others have designs of birds or flowers. The furoshiki is handy because it can be folded and carried in a purse and used for any shape or size of item. Special gifts are carried in a silk furoshiki.

To tie the furoshiki, place the item in the middle of the cloth. Tie the two diagonally-opposite corners together, then tie the other two corners together.

Children can make their own furoshiki by using colored marking pens to draw pictures and designs on inexpensive silk scarves. They enjoy using them in dramatic play to carry things. Authentic furoshikis may be purchased at Asian or import stores.

Kimono

The *kimono* is a unique Japanese style of clothing.

A formal kimono is worn by women for special holidays—especially the New Year, ceremonies, and family celebrations. Many styles and colors are worn. It is loose and fitted to each woman. Formal kimonos are made of plain silk, and some are decorated with embroidery.

Men and women wear simple cotton kimonos at home, especially during the summer. Men wear them at home when relaxing. Both women and men, however, wear Western-style clothing in their daily lives.

Kimonos are sold at import shops. Display informal kimonos, especially those for children. Kimonos may be made by cutting the collar and cuffs from a man's dress shirt and using a three-yard length of fabric to wrap around the waist for an obi.

Obi

The *obi* is a wide sash worn around the waist over a kimono. If children want to try on the traditional obi, show them how to tie a wide strip of brightly colored fabric about three yards long around their waist over a kimono or plain robe.

Footwear (Kutzu)

Geta, zori, and sandals are traditional Japanese footwear. They have a Y-shaped thong that is gripped between the big and second toes and passes over the top of the foot.

Geta are wooden clogs worn with a sock *(tabi)* that has the big toe in it. Geta are worn with a summer kimono. *Zori* are rubber or straw sandals worn by women, mainly with traditional kimonos. Some zori soles are covered with leather or fabric.

Today the Japanese wear many kinds of footwear. Tennis shoes and slippers are popular in the same styles as in America. Children wear sneakers to school; they have special slippers to wear indoors.

Shoes are removed in the entrance hall when Japanese enter their homes. Some families provide special slippers for everyone—including guests—to wear indoors.

To make geta, children put their feet on a piece of cardboard and draw around them to make a sole. Cut out the sole. Staple a strip of fabric to each side of the sole and to the point between the big toe and the second toe. The strips hold the geta on the child's feet.

FOOD

Rice and fish are basic foods in Japan. The Japanese arrange food artistically because they believe food should be pleasing to the eye as well as to the palate. Acquaint children with foods eaten in Japan, which are sold—fresh or canned—in most grocery stores.

(Safety Note: Be sure to obtain parental permission before allowing children to eat anything, in case of allergies or diet restrictions.)

Meals

The evening meal is the main one of the day. Food is placed in an artistic manner on beautiful dishes of various colors and shapes. It is eaten with wooden or plastic chopsticks *(hashi).* Each person has a personal set of chopsticks to use.

The menu is mainly rice (served at each meal): fish, meat, and vegetable dishes; soup; pickled vegetables; and *miso.* Sometimes Western dishes are also served.

Discuss with children the foods they eat at their main meal. Compare Japanese and American meals.

Rice (Kome)

A Japanese person eats an average of one-half to three-fourths of a pound of rice every day. Rice is grown in valleys in

the mountain areas and on the plains. The heavy spring and summer rains are an especially good climate for growing high-quality rice. Today, many families cook rice in their electric rice cookers.

Involve children in cooking rice. Try brown rice. Copy the recipe from the package onto a chart, using words and pictures. Children can participate in the whole process—measuring, stirring, and serving. While the rice is cooking, talk about the nutritional value of brown rice, review the cooking process, and show children how much rice is in a half pound. Some children may want to copy the recipe to take home. Serve the rice in small bowls and let children try eating it with chopsticks.

Rice Cakes (Mochi)

Rice cakes are prepared for the New Year. They are made with a paste of pounded steamed rice that is shaped into dumplings and added to soup or baked.

Red Rice (Sekihan)

Japanese celebrate happy occasions with red rice and sea bream *(tai),* a fish prepared with the head and tail. Glutinous rice (sticky rice) is steamed with red

beans, which turn the rice red. Red is considered lucky because it is associated with fire and sun.

Fish

Japanese eat eight times more fish than Americans do. For this reason, their diet is low in fat. Fresh fish shops are everywhere, selling cod, mackerel, sardines, tuna, sole, octopus and others. Fish is eaten stewed, salted, smoked, broiled, baked, and raw.

Prepare different varieties of fish for children to taste. Talk about the nutritional value of fish.

Octopus

An excellent hands-on activity is to let children examine a real octopus or squid, which can be purchased at a grocery store that carries fresh seafood. Purchase a whole octopus, wash it, and place in a gallon jar. Cover it with alcohol. This preserves it for a while and controls the smell. Take it out of the jar and place it on a large, flat tray for children to examine. They will be interested in finding its beak, counting its legs, and especially feeling its tentacles.

Sushi

Sushi is popular with visitors in Japan. It is a combination of slightly vinegared rice, slices of raw fish, and minced vegetables that are arranged in layers or mixed together and wrapped in seaweed. Sushi is widely available in the United States.

For a snack, show children how to cook and season rice and top it with kipper snacks, sardines, or tuna and a vegetable. Fish may be eaten separately and dipped in light soy sauce.

Fruits and Vegetables

Fruits in Japan include tangerines, pomegranates, persimmons, mandarin oranges, round yellow watermelons, grapes, and peaches. Vegetables grown in Japan include daikon radishes, spinach, cabbage, and others that are also available in America.

Desserts

Dessert is usually fresh or dried fruit or a Japanese rice cracker (*senbei*) or cake served with tea.

School Lunch

A typical school lunch usually includes a rice ball or bread, meat or fish, and fruit; or a ham and cheese sandwich and fruit; and cold tea or milk. Plan a school lunch day when children bring a typical Japanese lunch.

Introduce the children to the foods common in Japan. Bring one food at a time to discuss the shape, color, and size. Compare it to similar foods children eat, and taste them. All the foods described above are sold in grocery stores.

Soybeans *(Daizu)*

A great treasure for the Japanese is the soybean. Because soybeans are high in protein and grow in many countries, this nutritious staple could solve world hunger. Japan does not have sufficient land to grow enough soybeans for its own needs. It buys more soybeans from other countries than any other nation in the world.

If soybeans grow in your community, take an excursion to a soybean field. Ask the farmer to explain the process of growing and harvesting them. If a trip is not possible, invite a farmer to bring soybeans to the classroom and talk to the children about how they grow. Then use some of the recipes that follow for tasting and cooking experiences.

Japanese add soybean products to many foods. In addition to the kinds that follow, they use soy oil and soy sauce and add soy flour to cakes, candy, and ice cream. Candy made with soybeans is available in Asian markets.

Miso

Miso is fermented soybean paste. It is a popular strong and salty seasoning used for miso soup and many other dishes.

Yuba

Heat soy milk until a sheet forms on the top. Skim off the tissue-thin sheet, and then dry, roll, and slice it. Use it in soup or as an appetizer.

Soybean Milk

Boil soybeans and strain.

Tofu

Tofu, or soybean curd, is made from the liquid of boiled soybeans. This gelatin-like curd is cream colored and is used in many Japanese dishes. A softer "silken" creamy tofu is used for dressings, dips, and sauces. It is available in the produce section of grocery stores.

Tuna-Tofu Meatballs

Use a favorite meatloaf recipe and substitute tuna for beef.

Add tofu, grated cheese, and light soy sauce. Shape mixture into small balls, roll them in sesame seeds, and steam or bake. Cooked, mashed soybeans can be substituted for tuna.

Bean Sprouts (*Moyashi*)

Bean sprouts are an ingredient in many Japanese recipes. To grow bean sprouts, plant dried beans in small containers. Transplant some of the seedlings to the outdoor garden. Cut and taste the other bean sprouts.

Canned and fresh sprouts are available in grocery stores. Provide several different kinds for children to taste.

Bamboo Shoots (*Takenoko*)

Read about bamboo in the Nature and Science sections of all the Asian units. Show bamboo to the children and talk about how it grows and is used. Open a can of bamboo shoots for tasting. Ask children to describe the taste. If the children cannot think of a descriptive word, suggest one or two to get them started.

Daikon Radish

Daikon is a giant, white, sweet radish used widely in Japan. It is a healthy food, with lots of Vitamin C to aid digestion. Daikon is eaten raw, cooked, or pickled. Sometimes it is added to soups or vegetables, or it may be grated and eaten with meat and fish. A healthy meal is *sashimi*—raw fish dipped in soy sauce with tofu and daikon. For colds, a drink is made of one-quarter cup of daikon mixed with a small amount of ginger and added to hot water.

Daikon radishes can be found in the produce section of grocery stores. Look for pieces of white radish six to ten inches long. Involve the children in making a daikon salad—in washing the leaves, measuring the ingredients, and other tasks.

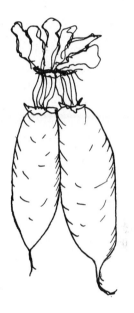

Daikon Radish Salad

Daikon radish about 4 inches long
1 can minced clams (optional)
Shiso or lettuce leaves
1 1/2 T mayonnaise or favorite dressing
White sesame seeds
Salt

Peel skin off daikon. Slice into thin strips about 1 1/2 inches long. Salt lightly and toss until a little soft. Wash and drain, squeezing out water. Cut shiso into thin strips and add to daikon; add clams if desired. Toss dressing with all ingredients. Sprinkle sesame seeds on top. Serves 4.

Tea

Japanese enjoy eating snacks and drinking tea in their tea-rooms. Bean cakes and rice crackers are served with the tea. Green tea (*gyokura*) is favored. The making of pottery was influenced by the tea ceremony, in which special dishes were used.

Children can have a tea party sitting on cushions around a low table. Buy green, herbal, or caffeine-free tea and prepare a weak brew in a small teapot. Let children serve each other using small cups without handles. Serve with rice crackers or rice cakes.

Milk

Calpis (fermented milk), soy milk, or plain milk may be served.

Seasoning

Japanese season food lightly, just to enhance its natural flavor. The main seasonings are soy sauce, sake vinegar, and sugar and salt used sparingly. Sugar was introduced in Japan during the last century, and it is used sparingly.

Foreign Foods

Japanese enjoy foods from other countries in their many restaurants. They also prepare them at home. Favorite foreign foods are fried eggs, hamburgers, bread, curry and rice, and spaghetti. They also eat at American fast food outlets throughout Japan.

Gelatin Blocks (*Kanten*)

Kanten is a special treat often served to Japanese children. American children know this treat as "pick-up Jel-lo" or "Knox blox." Serve it at a Japanese tea party. Mix in a large bowl and stir to dissolve:

3 3-oz. packages of orange dessert

4 small envelopes of unflavored gelatin

4 C boiling water.

Pour the mixture into a shallow pan. Refrigerate until jelled, about 1 hour. Cut into 1-inch squares. Serves 10 children.

In Japan, this treat is sometimes served in orange baskets: Cut oranges in half. Scoop out the fruit and add it to the gelatin mixture. Spoon gelatin into the orange "baskets" or allow it to set in orange halves; slice into quarters and serve when set.

Noodles with Seaweed (*Ki Soba Arame*)

The ingredients needed for this dish are available in whole foods, natural foods, and grocery stores specializing in Asian foods.

1/2 lb. Japanese buckwheat noodles (*ki soba*) or thin spaghetti
1 T sesame or vegetable oil
1/2 C sesame seeds
3 chopped green scallions
1/2 C crushed *arame*—thin, hair-like seaweed
1/4 C light soy sauce
A few shakes of powdered ginger

Cook noodles, drain, and set aside. Heat sesame oil and saute scallions, crushed arame, and sesame seeds. Add soy sauce. Pour mixture over noodles. Mix well. Serve hot or cold.

Markets (*Ichiba*)

An *ichiba* is a group of small markets or shops that are open all day. Some are fish or farmers' markets. Japanese buy fresh fish, fruits, vegetables, and other foods in the morning. Some shops sell clothing, dishes, and other household items. The Japanese carry their purchases in a furoshiki (see Clothing), though many use the same kinds of bags used in America. Customers can eat in the restaurants in the ichiba.

Let children set up a general store where Japanese items can be bought with play money. Children can take turns being the store owner and the shoppers. Inexpensive items made in Japan—fold-out paper fans, toys, chopsticks, and small paper umbrellas—can be purchased at import shops and variety stores and sold in the general store. Flowers made by the children may be added to the store's inventory. Cherry blossoms, irises, chrysanthemums, and azaleas, originally from Japan, could also be sold. Add any items that have been created by children, such as kites, pottery, lanterns, and flags. Suggestions for creating items are in the Creative Art Expression section.

TRANS-PORTATION

The most useful transportation in Japan is the train (*denshu*) which comes in many varieties. Crowds of people travel to work on the trains daily. When the last passenger cannot get into the train far enough to let the door close, and the passengers are too polite to ask him to wait until the next train, a "pusher-in," wearing a uniform and white gloves, pushes him into the train.

The Japanese bullet train is known all over the world. It is always on time, very clean, and very fast, traveling 120 miles per hour. It is a very safe way to travel due to its design—it stops automatically during earthquakes—and regular maintenance.

The number of cars in Japan has increased rapidly, causing traffic congestion. To avoid this, many take the train or bus to work. Huge underground parking garages have been built.

Bicycles (*jitensha*) are a popular way to travel to the train, to work, and to other places. Japan is second only to the Scandinavian countries in the number of bicycles per capita.

Taxis are uniquely designed so that passengers enter through an automatic door at the back of the vehicle.

Kindergarten children walk to school or ride the school bus.

Display children's trains. Invite parents to show their special trains. Provide an electric train for children's dramatic play and ask them to describe train rides they have enjoyed.

CREATIVE ART EXPRESSION

By LeeAnn

Creativity means beginning with ideas generated by children. The role of the adult is to foster creativity by asking questions, supervising the projects and providing reinforcement. Provide many choices of materials.

Only some of the many Japanese arts are included in this book. Traditional arts continue to flourish, while twentieth-century Japanese designs have been influenced by Western arts. Japanese have art all around them, especially in their homes.

Japan honors its actors and artists, naming them "National Living Treasures." Artists are encouraged to pursue their talents through government support that allows them to work totally without financial pressure.

Myoshin Nakamura, 82, is the leading artist in Aikawa, Japan. She writes poetry, composes songs, and teaches calligraphy to local children.

DECORATIVE ART

Fans (*Sensu*)

Beautiful fans are a heritage of Japan. The first fans were made to cool people's faces during the hot weather. Later it was polite to carry a beautiful fan while dancing. Fans are made of special paper and painted by hand. Designs include outdoor scenes, landscapes, birds, flowers, or handwritten poems. Today fans are used for dances and decorations.

Start with one 8 1/2-by-11-inch piece of construction paper. Lay the paper so the 11-inch length is at the bottom. Let children paint a picture or design on the paper. Show children how to fold the paper in accordion-style pleats, with the 8 1/2-inch width at the bottom and staple the pleats together at one end. Add a ribbon so that the fan may be carried when not in use.

Flag (*Nisshoki*)

The flag of Japan is the "flag of the rising sun." It is white with a red circle in the center that represents the sun.

To make the flag, cut a piece of white fabric or strong white paper, such as butcher paper, any size the child desires. Let the child use paint, crayons, or marking pens to make the flag as illustrated. Attach the flag to a paper stick made from rolled newspaper. Let children use their creativity in figuring out how to fasten the flag to the stick. Children can have a parade of flags or display them in the classroom.

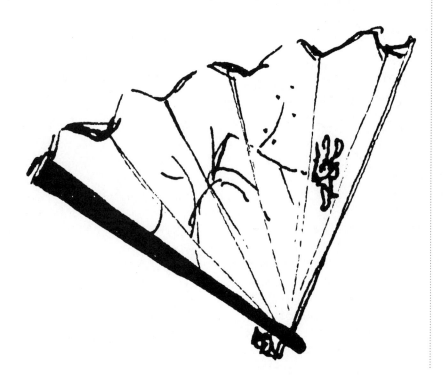

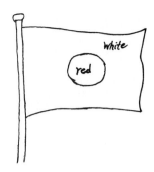

Wind Chimes (*Furin*)

Wind chimes, or *furin* are often hung in gardens to catch a gentle breeze. They are usually made from small pieces of hand-painted glass or small shells. Furin are sold in import and garden shops. Have one available for children to examine. Hang it in the classroom and listen for the pleasant song made by the wind.

Children can use metal lids from frozen juice cans to make furin, decorating the lids with acrylic paint designs, glitter, sequins, marking pens, or different shapes and sizes of stickers. Attach different lengths of string, six to twelve inches long, to each lid with a small piece of colored duct tape and tie the strings through holes punched in the bottom and rim of a small foil pie pan. Attach a colored pipe cleaner to the center of the pan for a hanger. Children listen as the wind plays a tune.

Pottery and Ceramics

Japanese artists have created ceramics and pottery for thousands of years. The art of making pottery was brought from China. Gradually the Japanese developed their own style. Some regions have unique styles, such as *arita-yaki*, *kutani-yaki*, and *mashiko-yaki*.

Today, traditional and modern ceramics are created in Japan. Two companies manufacture china dinnerware that is popular in the United States: Noritake, which makes fine china; and Mikasa, which makes stoneware, fine china, and casual dinnerware. Invite someone from a china department to show Japanese fine china.

Japanese vases, ranging from the inexpensive to the very expensive, are sold in stores. Share some of them with children, discussing the shapes, lines, and decorations. Let children make vases or dishes out of clay and paint them with red, green, blue, and metallic gold tempera paint.

The potter Shogi Hamata is a "Living Treasure" of Japan. He studied pottery in England and brought about a revival of handmade pottery in the 20th century. Toyozo Arakawa is another leading potter.

Calligraphy (*Sho*)

Calligraphy is the art of writing Japanese characters artistically on a scroll (*kakemono*). A brush with black ink is used to make the large characters on a long narrow piece of white paper. Japanese children learn this art in school, beginning in the third grade.

Scrolls are displayed in the tokonoma or other room. On January 2, words and poems are

written in calligraphy for the "first writing of the year." (see Calligraphy in the Korean unit for additional information).

Provide long, narrow white paper, several sizes of brushes, and black ink sticks or tempera paint. Let children lay their paper on the floor and then write their names, Japanese characters or English letters, messages, or their own creative ideas. Contact a calligrapher to demonstrate this art to the children.

Dolls (*Ningyo*)

Japan manufactures many kinds of dolls today, in both Japanese and European styles. They make traditional and new types of dolls that represent almost every nationality in the world.

Warrior dolls are displayed during the Boys' Festival, and colorful hina dolls are shown during the Girls' Festival. The most popular are the *hakata* and *kokeshi* dolls.

Hakata dolls are molded from clay, fired, and painted. The detailed painting and colors that are used, especially on the faces, make them appear real.

Kokeshi dolls are traditional wooden dolls. These dolls have a round body and head. A face is painted on the head in two or three colors, such as red, blue, and yellow. Lines or a chrysanthemum may be painted on the body. These dolls, used for decorations, have a rustic charm.

Children can celebrate their own doll festival. Make a display stage with a beautifully decorated screen for the background. Let children paint a cardboard pattern board (from fabric shops) with black or metallic gold paint. Small, pink tissue paper flowers may be attached to the screen to resemble peach blossoms, which are in bloom during the Doll Festival in Japan.

Children bring their favorite dolls to display in front of the screen. Tea and kanten are served. Parents are usually happy to help with this project.

Daruma Doll

A favorite toy in Japan is the *daruma* doll. It is a roly-poly doll with no arms or legs. It is weighted on the bottom so that whenever it is pushed over, it always pops back to an upright position. It is a special doll for the New Year.

Daruma dolls may be made from plastic Easter eggs or the egg-shaped container in which some panty hose are packaged. Mix two tablespoons of plaster of Paris with two tablespoons of water. Pour this mixture into the bottom half of the egg and let it dry. Fasten the egg halves together with tape and let children use marking pens to draw features on the dolls.

Painting

Japanese paint in light, delicate colors with oil or watercolor paints. Various sizes of brushes are used with the watercolors. Many different beautiful effects may be achieved using assorted sizes of brushes. Lines and shades of color add to the beauty of the picture. Mountains and rivers, cherry blossoms, and other flowers, birds, bamboo, and scenes from nature are favorite motifs.

Pictures and banners are painted by a member of the family to decorate the tokonoma, or Japanese or Chinese paintings are purchased. In Japanese-style homes, paintings done in a Japanese style on special paper or silk are displayed. Today, Japanese and Western styles of paintings are popular.

Fish Banners (*Koinobari*)

Fish banners are flown on Boys' Day (see Celebrations). Use a long, white paper bag or cloth to make a fish banner. Bakery bags are an excellent size. Look at pictures of fish with children to acquaint them with fish scales, then let children draw fish scales on the sides of the bag and head features on the end of the bag. Tie a string to each side of the fish. Children hold the strings and run so the fish catches the wind.

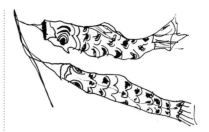

Another way to make a fish banner is to cut two large fish shapes from 12-by-18-inch pieces of white butcher paper. Show children how to staple the two fish together, leaving only the mouth open. Then they can paint features and designs on the fish, using watercolors, marking pens, and crayons. Attach a string to each side of the mouth for flying the fish.

Kites (*Tako*)

Kite-making is an art in Japan. A Japanese painter and sculptor, Fumio Yoshimara, creates kites that have been exhibited around the world. He constructs various sizes, from tiny kites to huge kites that are eighteen feet across. Kites are made of nylon or paper. The many stories and songs about

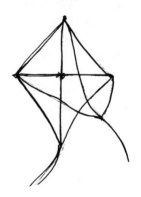

Japanese kites show their popularity.

On New Year's Day, many shapes of kites can be seen—animals, brightly colored fish, octopi, turtles, and miniature birds and insects. A simple kite has a diamond shape. During the Cherry Blossom Festival, boys engage in kite fights, flying huge kites that have sharp objects or bits of glass attached to the string. Each team tries to cut the string of the other team's kite. (See Creative Art Expression in the Chinese unit for making kites.)

Origami

Origami is the art of Japanese paper folding, which has been practiced for centuries. The art of origami was taught to daughters by their mothers. Origami items were first used on gifts to signify good luck, a practice that continues today. Animals, flowers, and familiar objects are made using basic folds.

Any kind of colored paper thin enough to fold easily may

be used. Packets of origami paper can be purchased at import or Asian stores. Newspaper or wrapping, packing or shelf paper may also be used.

All schools in Japan teach origami from nursery and kindergarten levels through the elementary grades. Origami helps develop small muscle coordination and sequencing skills.

Follow the instructions in these books, listed in Resources, or similar ones: *The Joy of Origami* and *Origami Toys*, both by Toshie Takahama.

Samurai Hat

Children are fascinated by stories of the brave and strong *Samurai*, early Japanese warriors. In Japan, origami Samurai helmets are often made by parents and put on gifts to young sons in the hope that they may grow to be healthy and strong.

Children can make Samurai helmets by using the steps in the illustration to fold a 22-by-22-inch square of butcher paper. When completed, let them paint the helmet with metallic gold paint.

Two excellent Japanese folktales about Samurai warriors are *The Warrior and the Wiseman,* by David Wisiewski, and *Issunboshi: The Inchling,* by Momohio Ishi.

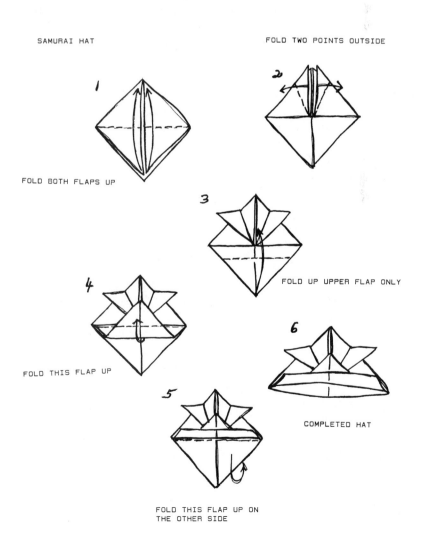

SAMURAI HAT

1

FOLD BOTH FLAPS UP

FOLD TWO POINTS OUTSIDE

2

3

FOLD UP UPPER FLAP ONLY

4

FOLD THIS FLAP UP

5

FOLD THIS FLAP UP ON
THE OTHER SIDE

6

COMPLETED HAT

NATURE AND SCIENCE

Japanese enjoy and appreciate the beauty of the natural environment. They have preserved this harmony between nature and man for centuries. They travel to the mountains to view the changes in nature each season.

ANIMALS

Pets

Cats, dogs, and birds, especially parakeets, are favorite pets. A Western breed of dog, the akita, is a popular pet today. Kindergartens have chickens and rabbits.

Discuss children's pets and compare them with those of Japanese children. Some children may wish to dictate or write a story about their pets. Older students look for information in the library about the akita, which is also popular in America. Share the stories and information with the class.

Crickets

Children in Japan keep musical insects as pets. Many kinds of insects sing, but crickets and beetles are the most common. Children catch or buy them and keep them in bamboo cages. These pets are said to bring good luck.

A cricket gets used to its home and owner in a few days. It recognizes the child's voice and enjoys the cucumber slices fed to it. In the summer, insect concerts are held in the park. The main event is freeing the

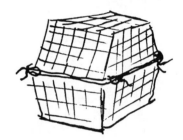

insects so that they can lay eggs before they die.

Display a small insect cage and hunt for crickets. Put them into the cage. Children can make their own cages for insects using berry baskets and pipe cleaners by placing two baskets together and fastening their rims together with pipe cleaners.

Pheasant (*Kiji*)—The National Bird

The pheasant, which is found in Japanese folklore, has been the official national bird since 1947. The male pheasant, a colorful bird, has a red face and dark green neck, breast, and stomach. Its back is purplish and its tail has many black stripes. The female is light brown with black spots and a short tail. The pheasant lives mainly in the woods near grassy or cultivated fields. It makes its nest on the ground and lives on berries and insects.

In the United States, pheasants are quite a delicacy and are also common game birds.

Display pictures and books about pheasants. If they live in your area, ask children to bring in pheasant feathers, bones, and photographs of them.

Cranes (*Tsuru*)

The Japanese crane is called a "special natural monument." This bird, sacred in Japan, symbolizes happiness and a long life.

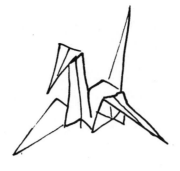

A crane may live to be 50 years old. This graceful bird grows to about five feet tall. Its body is white, its legs and tail are black, and its head is black and white with a red crown. Its shrill voice can be heard for up to two miles. In the winter, the crane stands on one leg while it warms the other one under its body. Cranes build their nests on the ground. When one crane begins to dance, soon all of them are dancing.

Thousands of cranes lived in Japan, but by 1952 only 33 remained. A refuge was built to protect them. Today Japan has more than 300 cranes. Each year, when the cranes return, many Japanese travel to welcome them back. Children in rural northern Japan feed corn to cranes during recess when the birds fly in. Cranes can toss a corn husk into the air and catch it before it reaches the ground.

Origami books have instructions on how to make a crane which older children may wish to try. Show pictures of cranes. Compare the size of a crane to something or someone that is five feet tall.

Whales (*Kujira*)

In Japan whales are named "Lords of the Ocean" because they are the largest creatures on earth. Some measure 45 feet long and may weigh 40 tons. In the summer they feed in cold, food-rich waters, and in the winter they travel as far as 10,000 miles to warm water.

Whales form family bonds and are care-giving parents, protecting and nurturing the calves. They play in the moonlight, talk to one another, do acrobatics, and blow bubbles in the water.

Since the Japanese do not have enough land to raise cattle, the whale industry provides meat. Whales are an endangered species that must be protected and laws for this purpose have been in effect since 1931. Dr. Akito Kawamira is a Japanese scientist who is a recognized authority on whales.

Children are fascinated with whales and often draw them. Show pictures of them, including those from the National Geographic or other authentic sources. Children also enjoy singing "Baby Beluga," a song on Raffi's *Baby Beluga* album. This song has a special message about saving the whales.

See the Islands section in this unit for information on how to use a "whale" in water.

Fish (*Sakana*)

Japan leads the world in consumption and processing of fish. Fish caught in the Sea of Japan provide high-protein food. Bright lamps used on

Japanese squid-fishing boats to attract squid can be seen by astronauts in space capsules.

Fish Print *(Gyo taku)*

The Japanese word for fish is *gyo* and for print is *taku*. Making fish prints is a very interesting activity for children and it produces an "object of art."

Use a fish you have caught or buy one at the market. A fish with large, rough scales makes the best print.

Let children wash the fish and place it on paper towels. Cut a lemon in fourths. Let children squeeze lemon juice on the fish and then gently wipe it dry with paper towels to remove dirt and slime.

Squeeze a small amount of water-soluble block printing ink into a styrofoam meat tray. Roll an ink roller through the paint. Apply a coat of ink to the fish with the ink roller. Be sure the fish's mouth, tail, and fins are coated with ink.

Hold a sheet of rice paper (available at art supply stores) or thin typing paper a few inches above the fish. Let the paper fall onto the fish. Gently press the paper so that all of the fish, including the fins and tail, are printed. Place the print on a 12-by-18-inch sheet of colored construction paper and let it dry. When dry, attach the print to the paper mat with a dot of glue on each corner. Display the prints or use them to decorate fish banners.

After all the fish prints have been made, recycle the real fish. Children can wash off all the ink, then bury it in the garden or yard for valuable fertilizer.

Dissecting Fish

Children may wish to dissect a fish or cut it apart for a detailed examination. Place fish on a board. Make a slit with a knife from the anus to the head in order to expose the stomach cavity. Cut away the rib section. Use a picture or drawing to tell children the names of the organs. Children may draw an outline of a fish on paper. Remove organs from the fish and place them in the appropriate place on the fish diagram. Label the fish organs with words. Remember to inspect the craw to see what the fish had for supper.

Pearls *(Shinjyu)*

Jewelry made of pearls is admired worldwide. Pearls develop on pearl farms. It takes an oyster three years to make a pearl.

Baby oysters grown in tanks for 60 days. Then they are put into baskets in Ago Bay in cold water until they are older. Next they are put on a rack where they relax and open their shells so an implanter can insert a tiny "shell bead" into each oyster. They are then put in baskets in cold water. The oyster coats the bead with layers of nacre to make a pearl.

The Japanese use pearls for jewelry and to decorate statues and other art objects. Pearls of poor quality are ground fine and used in cosmetics, calcium tablets, some medicines, and toothpaste.

Show children pearl necklaces and other items made of pearls. Let children examine them. Talk about the beauty of the pearl and the length of time it takes for one pearl to develop. Bring examples of items that contain ground pearls.

Silkworms *(Kaiko)*

Japanese have woven beautiful silk for many years. They use it to make clothing, to paint on, and for other items. (See Silkworms in the Nature and Science section in the Chinese unit for a description of how silkworms produce silk thread and how to grow silkworms in the classroom.)

Bring silk items for children to examine and display Japanese pictures painted on silk.

Snow Monkeys

Japanese macaques (muh kacks) live in the mountains of northern Japan. They are called snow monkeys because of their ability to survive in the cold, snowy winters. Snow monkeys are a tourist attraction. They swim and soak in the hot springs in the mountains.

Provide books and pictures of snow monkeys so that children may discover more about this unique animal.

PLANTS

Cherry Blossoms (*Sakura*)— National Flower

The beautiful pink or white cherry blossom symbolizes Japan. Long ago, writers of myths referred to the cherry blossom as a national symbol. Japan has cherry viewing (*hanami*) spots all over the country to enjoy the blossoms in the spring. Huge crowds gather to see the fragrant blossoms in bloom. It is a time to appreciate nature, sing, have picnics, and hang traditional lanterns in the trees. Some Japanese tie poetry to the branches. Others view them in the moonlight and are inspired to write poems.

Place tree branches in clay pots filled with wet sand. Let children decorate the branches with small pieces of pink tissue paper to resemble cherry blossoms.

When the trees in your community are in bloom, take a nature walk. Describe the different kinds of blossoms and their sweet fragrances.

Flowers (*Hana*)

The chrysanthemum (*kiku*) is also a Japanese symbol and is part of the Imperial Crest.

Iris, azaleas, and camellias are among the many flowers in Japan. Look for them in yards, parks, or at a nursery. Bring as many as possible to the classroom for at least one day. Elicit new language when talking about the size, color, smell, and shape of these flowers.

Trees (*Ki*)

Many fruit trees grow in Japan, including tangerine, pomegranate, persimmon, peach, and mandarin orange. If these grow in your community, take a nature walk to identify them.

Children can make a nature bracelet as they walk. Put a masking tape band around each child's arm, sticky side up. As the children walk, they attach leaves to the bracelet. Then talk about the leaves and compare them.

Bonsai

The art of creating dwarf trees, *bonsai*, developed in Japan. A tree is planted in a ceramic pot or in a shallow, oblong pan. The tree will last for years if it is cared for properly. It is kept small by controlling its growth. Fast-growing shoots are removed, and small branches and leaves are trained to grow up and sideways. Pine and other evergreen, flowering, and fruit-bearing trees are used.

Provide shallow trays or pots, plants, potting soil, and pictures of bonsai. Some children may wish to plant a small tree. Keep a daily chart of the plant's growth. A bonsai can be purchased for the room. Invite someone who practices the art of bonsai to bring examples to show children. Your local florist may be able to recommend an expert.

Bamboo (*Take*)

Bamboo is one of the world's most useful plants. (See Bamboo in all Asian units.) The many varieties of bamboo grow faster and taller than any other plant, growing as many as four feet in as little as 24 hours. In Japanese-style homes made of wood and paper, the ceilings, rain spouts, and gutters are constructed of bamboo. In Kyoto, many bamboo items can be purchased—baskets, flutes, plant pots, flower stands, dolls, scarecrows for gardens, garden fences, and umbrella frames. Look for items made of bamboo to share with children.

GEOGRAPHY AND THE ENVIRONMENT

Islands

Japan is a country of islands. It has four main islands, with three-fifths of the land on the island of Honshu, and about 4,000 smaller islands. No one lives more than 60 miles from a coast.

To give children a concept of an island, make one in a water/sand table. Place a large, flat rock in the center of the table. Fill the table with water until only the top of the rock is out of the water. Small plastic houses, people, and animals may be used to inhabit the island. Small boats, plastic fish, octopi, and whales may be put in the water.

Mt. *Fuji-san*

Over half of the small country of Japan is mountainous. Forests cover the mountains, and many clear lakes can be found. Mt. *Fuji-san* is the highest mountain in Japan. It is a dormant volcano that last erupted 250 years ago. The upper half of the mountain is covered with snow most of the year. Mt. Fuji-san has often been portrayed in art and poems. All Japanese hope to climb it once in their lifetime to see the magic rays of the morning sun above the clouds. In the moonlight, above the snow-covered mountain, the stars shine like gems.

Show pictures of Mt. Fuji-san to the children. Talk about its height and shape, and discuss snow on the mountains in general.

Volcanoes

The fact that Mt. Fuji-san was once an active volcano is interesting to children and creating an active volcano is a popular activity.

Use a plastic 35-mm film container for the base. Children can place the container in the center of a small plastic tray, make a volcano-shaped mountain out of potter's clay, and put it around the film container, covering it except for a small opening at the top.

When the clay has dried, let children pour one teaspoon of baking soda into the container. Mix red food coloring with vinegar. Give each child a three-ounce paper cup full of the vinegar mixture and let them slowly pour the vinegar into the volcano. Watch as the hot lava flows over the sides of the volcano!

Protection of the Environment

Many countries in the world are becoming aware that the earth's environment must be protected. The fast development of Japanese industries has caused air, water, and noise pollution. The country has made much progress in controlling its pollution through strict laws passed in 1970.

Ask a representative from an agency for environmental protection to talk to the children about what they can do to protect the environment in their community. Read *If I Built a Village,* by Kazue Mizumuru, author and illustrator.

Garbage

Japan has very little landfill space for garbage and so has developed a recycling system. One way to recycle that is new for Japan is to sell items at garage sales and flea markets. A second method is to burn trash in an incinerator. Nonburnable trash is separated out and then melted or disintegrated and made into new items. For example, glass is melted and made into new glass, and paper is dissolved into pulp and made into new paper. (See Paper Making in the Chinese unit.) A third method is to change the way a product is made. An example is the Japanese development of a water-resistant paper garbage bag that can burn.

TECHNOLOGY AND SCIENTISTS
....

Automobiles (*Jidosha*)

Japan leads the world in manufacturing cars. It buys the raw materials from other countries and builds the cars in Japan and other countries.

Many Japanese cars are built and sold in America. Look for pictures of Toyotas, Nissans, and Hondas. Identify these cars on the streets in your community. Compare the size of Japanese cars with American cars.

Place toy cars in the dramatic play area. Show children "matchbox" Japanese cars. Make an automobile book of Japanese and American cars. Children cut out pictures of cars and paste them in the book. Label each car. Magazines, mail advertisements, and car shows are sources for pictures.

Robots (*Robot*)

Japan has developed many kinds of electronic equipment, such as transistor radios, televisions, cameras, and pocket calculators. It leads the world in producing and using robots in industry. They are operated by micro-computers. In restaurants and department stores, customers may be greeted by a talking robot dressed in a kimono. In auto manufacturing plants, robots with shoulder, elbow, and wrist joints weld steel parts together and spray paint new cars. Robots can put an electric motor together and screw in light bulbs. They can load and unload metal blocks. Robots can work faster than people and be programmed never to make a mistake.

Children enjoy creating a robot using all sizes of boxes, cardboard tubes, egg cartons, and paper cups. Provide a variety of materials for them to use, along with masking tape, glue, and paint.

Science and Schools

By the 1990s, every school in Japan must have at least one computer for students' use.

Children in the elementary grades plant flower and vegetable gardens. They have responsibility for their care.

Excursions are included in the school program. Popular trips are to factories—auto factories, food factories, and robot factories.

To keep the environment clean, children and teachers clean the schools daily, with a special cleaning at the end of vacations.

Japanese Nobel Prize Winners

Hideki Yukawa, 1949, Physics
Shinichiro Tomonage, 1965, Physics
Liona Esaki, 1973, Physics
Eisaku Sato, 1974, Peace
Kenichi Fukei, 1981, Chemistry

LANGUAGE DEVELOPMENT

Children learn about the Japanese culture through pictures, books, and from Japanese or Japanese Americans who share their culture. Information new to children encourages language. Japanese also communicate through body language—for example, in bowing at the waist, they show respect to others.

Vocabulary

The following words may be used in labeling pictures and objects in the room:

densha—train
furoshiki—square piece of fabric to carry items
futon—bedding
hana—flowers
ie—house
jitensha—bicycle
kimono—woman's traditional dress
koinobori—carp banner for Boys' Day
kujira—whale
kutzu—any kind of footwear
Mt. *Fuji-san*—highest mountain in Japan

ingyo—doll
obi—wide sash worn at waist over a kimono
origami—art of paper folding
robot—robot
sakana—fish
sho—calligraphy
tako—kite
tatami—woven straw mat, used on floor

Symbols

Use books, pictures, and posters to introduce children to Japanese characters. Explain that each character is a whole word or idea. Compare Japanese characters to American writing in which several letters make a word.

The Japanese written language is derived from three different groups of characters. Kindergarten children learn 50 characters. By third grade, children have learned 880 characters, and by the sixth grade, 1800. By high school graduation, students know 8,000 characters. The literacy rate in Japan is 99%.

Traditionally Japanese books are printed in columns, right to left. Today many books are printed as those in Western countries.

Japanese typewriters have been difficult to manufacture because of the number of characters in the Japanese language.

Foreign Language

All Japanese students are required to take three years of English, usually during junior high school. Many complete six years of English.

What Does the Rooster Say, Yoshio?, by Edith Battles, illustrates a unique method of communication between an English-

speaking and Japanese-speaking child.

Vowels

When Japanese words are translated into English, the vowels are always pronounced the same: *a* is pronounced "ah," as in *father*; *e* is pronounced "eh," as in *pet*; *i* is pronounced "ee," as in *see*; *o* is pronounced "o," as in *bone*; *u* is pronounced "oo," as in *stool*.

Japanese Words and Phrases

Sayonara—Good-bye.
Konnichiwa—Hello.
Ohyo—Good morning.
Arigato—Thank you.
Dozo—Please.
Do itashimashite—You're welcome.
Sukidesa—I love you.
San—Mr., Mrs., Miss. Added to adult names, as, "Alan-san."
Chan—Added to child's name, as "Jan-chan."

Japanese Words

chichi—father 父

chisai—small 小

danshi—boy 男子

haha—mother 母

jyoshi—girl 女子

ki—tree 木

mori—forest 森

okii—big 大

onna—female 女

otoko—male 男

Japanese Numbers

ichi—one 一

ni—two 二

san—three 三

shi—four 四

go—five 五

roku—six 六

shichi—seven 七

hachi—eight 八

ku—nine 九

ju—ten 十

Read *Count Your Way Through Japan* by Jim Haskins.

Bilingual Books

Books written in English letters and in Japanese characters show that the written language of each country is different. Since the Japanese language does not include the sounds of *L, Q, V,* or *X;* it may be difficult for Japanese-speaking children to pronounce these sounds.

A bilingual book to use is *Chocho Is for Butterfly: A Japanese-English Primer* by Jeannie Sasaki and Frances Uyeda. Some books by Taro Yashima include Japanese characters.

Animals and Folk Literature

Japanese authors have used many animals symbolically in their tales. Some of the animals and the symbols they represent follow.

The dragon is the most important beast in folk literature. Legend has it that the dragon, or king, lives in a palace on the bottom of the sea.

The fox is a symbol of abundance in some stories and a mischief-maker in others.

The cat is a symbol of friendliness, welcome, and prosperity.

Many buildings and homes are decorated with the monkey because it is believed to protect children.

The toad is thought to have superior magical powers that hypnotize people and animals and change evil into good.

The turtle and crane are symbols of long life.

The tiger is admired for its strength.

A related book is *Magic Animals of Japan* by David Pratt.

Japanese Illustrators and Artists

Prominent Japanese illustrators of children's books include Allen Tay (Japanese American), Yasue Segawa, Kazue Mizumura, Fuku Akino, Eiichi Mitsui, Chihiro Iwasake and Yoshi. The children's books by Taro Yashima, a Japanese author and illustrator whose books were published in the 1950's and 1960's, continue to be popular today.

As stories and poetry are shared with children, include the names of authors and illustrators, pointing out their individual styles. A valuable source is *Literature for Children about Asians and Asian Americans* by E.C. Jenkins and M.C. Austin.

Yasunari Kawabataf was awarded the Nobel Prize for Literature in 1968.

Stories

The literature of a country or region expresses its culture. Stories, especially those written by authors who are natives of the country, provide authentic information about the culture. Stories are powerful sources of vocabulary and language development. They also provide many ideas for creative expression.

Folktales

Exposing children to folktales gives them an insight into the thinking of a culture. Folktales reflect the fundamental beliefs of a culture. Young children become familiar with folktales through listening and dramatizing.

Dramatization

Plan a dramatization of one of the stories children enjoy. Through asking them questions, let the children decide what characters and props or equipment they will need. Children can act out the roles of the characters using the dialogue as they remember it. Encourage them to add their own words and their own interpretation.

The Beautiful Princess
ISSUN BOSHI

BY LORI

Haiku

Haiku, a poem of three lines, has a definite pattern. The first line has five syllables; the second line, seven; and the third line, five. The art of creating haiku is a gift from the Japanese culture. Favorite subjects for haiku are flowers, birds, snow, falling leaves in autumn, love, and similar topics. Japanese poetry usually shows a relationship between man and the world of nature. Haiku is read to children beginning at age eight,

and they begin to write their own at age ten.

Some children are interested in creating their own haiku. Encourage three words for the first line.

These haiku were written by six-year-old children at The Learning Tree:

Little curly dog
I saw him yesterday
He likes people too.

Dog smelling flowers
Brown and curly is he so
A boy saw him go.

A horse smells flowers
Big and gray and big white ones
Feels soft and warm too.

Read haiku to children often before they try to write their own. Select haiku to read aloud from books such as *Don't Tell the Scarecrow and Other Japanese Poems* by Issa and Others (Four Winds, 1970, K-4) and *Flower Moon Snow: A Book of Haiku* by Kazue Mizumura (Crowell, 1977).

Proverbs

The proverbs of a country are indications of its culture. Discuss with older children the meanings of these proverbs:
A hedge between keeps friendship green.
It's a long lane that has no turns.
To every bird its own nest is charming.

MUSIC, DANCE AND DRAMA

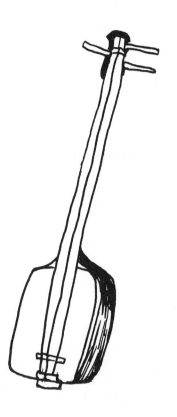

Japanese music (*ongaku*) has unique sound and rhythm that are very different from Western music. The influence of Western arts is evident in the music, dance, and drama created in the 20th century, and Western arts are popular among the younger people in Japan today.

Contemporary Japanese artists include Seji Ozawa, conductor of the Boston Symphony, and Midori (professional name), a young violinist who records classical music.

Instruments

Traditional instruments popular today are the *shamisen, koto,* and flute, which are often played together. The shamisen is a three-stringed instrument similar to a banjo. It is used to accompany singers or played as a solo instrument. The koto is a type of harp. The flute (*shakuhachi*) is made of bamboo and is similar to the recorders American children play in school. Fumiko Yonekawa plays the koto.

Listen to tapes, found in Asian stores, that feature these instruments. Identify the sound of each.

Many instruments of bamboo are available. Children can use them to accompany Japanese music.

Other familiar Japanese instruments are hand drums, cymbals, gongs, lutes, and wooden blocks. Today Japanese are familiar with Western instruments through their symphony orchestras.

Buy as many traditional Japanese instruments as possible. Check import and Asian stores. Let children create their own music and imitate Japanese tunes.

Listening

Music for listening follows. Children at The Learning Tree often accompany the music with their instruments.

Oriental Sunrise, by a Japanese flutist, distributed by Music for Little People.

"Chotto Matti Kudasai," from the album *I Know the Color of the Rainbow,* by Ella Jenkins.

"Hara Ga Kita," from the album *Everything Grows* by Raffi. It is the Japanese version of "Springtime Is Coming."

Japanese songs popular with children are "Japanese Rain Song," "Chi Chi Papa," and "Springtime Is Coming" from the album *Making Music Your Own* .

Suzuki Method

Shin'ichi Suzuki, a Japanese musician, believes that all children have innate musical talent that should be developed before the age of five. He introduced a method of teaching young chil-

dren, beginning at ages three and four, to play the violin. Playing a small violin, they learn the technique of playing the instrument and play simple melodies by ear before they begin to read the musical notes.

In Japan today, this method—taught in private lessons—is used to teach many kinds of instruments, including the piano. Many children in the United States have learned to play the violin using the Suzuki method. Invite a child trained in the Suzuki method to demonstrate how to play the violin.

The book *Preschool in the Suzuki Method* by Susan Grille provides additional information.

Music in School

In Japan, music is a very important part of the school program. Japanese children learn many songs. They learn to read music and to play three instruments in the elementary school—the harmonica, recorder, and keyboard. They are introduced to music from all countries and listen to Japanese and European classical music.

Young children add movements to their songs. Kindergartners also learn Japanese folk dances.

Traditional songs for young children with simple, short lyrics have been handed down for generations. Some of these are "How Old Are You, the Moon?," "First Star," and "Bird in the Cage." Look for these songs in music books.

Some songs for young children composed during the 20th century that show Western influence are "Dragon Fly," "Desert in the Moonlight," "Red Shoes," and "New Year."

Odori Dance

The traditional *odori* dance, *kabuki* dancing, is dynamic and grew out of Japanese folk dances. Songs are interpreted through hand and body movements. Other types of dance are taught today, some influenced by Western cultures. Ballet and modern dance are especially enjoyed. Various dances are performed at Japanese festivals.

Bunraku

Bunraku is a classical form of puppet theater. The puppets have a head, trunk, hands and feet. They are dressed in costumes and range in height from about 40 to 60 inches. A puppet is manipulated by three puppeteers, each operating one part of the puppet's body. The story is told in a special chant to the accompaniment of shamisen music. Tamao Yoshida is a master puppeteer and a master of bunraku in Japan.

Children can make small bunraku puppets by drawing and gluing features on cardboard tubes. Tagboard arms may be attached to the tubes and manipulated with a wooden kebob skewer or sturdy wire attached to each arm. Invite a Japanese puppeteer to demonstrate bunraku if one is available. Ask children to suggest how puppets may be used to tell a story.

Let children use the puppets available or create their own to role-play Japanese stories. Stick puppets are simple to make by attaching the face of a story character to the top of a stick.

Theater—*Noh* and *Kabuki*

Kabuki and *Noh* dramas are well-known throughout the world.

Noh is a dance and drama play accompanied by music. The actors wear special masks to represent different emotions. Reproductions of these masks are sold at many import stores. Display several so that children can examine and wear them.

Children can make noh masks out of paper plates. Discuss how to express anger, joy, and fright with children. Let them use paint, marking pens, and colored paper to decorate the masks. See the Creative Art Expression section in the Korean unit for ideas on how to create more elaborate masks.

Kabuki is a drama of dialogue, songs, and dances. A rhythm pattern is followed in the speaking and movements of the actors, who wear elaborate costumes and masks.

Puppets made to resemble kabuki actors are available at Asian stores. Children enjoy creating their own kabuki drama using these puppets.

Comedy Storyteller *(Rakugo)*

A *rakugo-ka* tells humorous stories to large audiences, mainly in dialogue form using gestures and facial expressions. Some stories are accompanied by a musical instrument. Types of stories include historical, human interest and those with moral themes. Children understand these adult stories, learning about history and their duty to society. Professional storytellers are ranked according to skill and experience. Rakugo continues to be very popular in Japan today.

The art of storytelling is being revived in the United States. Guilds have been organized in many communities. Invite a storyteller to perform for the children. Also provide times for children to tell favorite stories or to create and tell original ones. Talk about how children's families use storytelling.

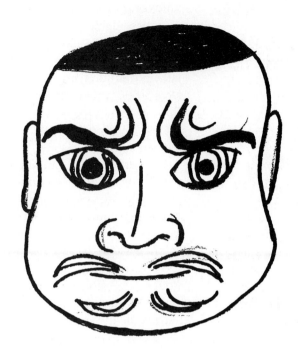

GAMES AND MANIPULATIVES

The Japanese engage in many kinds of sports and physical activities, including winter, mountain, team, and water sports. Favorite games for Japanese children are flying kites (see Creative Art Expression) and spinning tops.

Jenken

See Games in the Chinese unit for instructions on how to play the scissor-paper-stone counting game. Substitute the words *jan ken pon* for the chant before making the sign of scissors (*choki*), paper (*po*), or stone (*gu*). Adults often use jenken to decide turns, much like people in Western countries toss a coin to determine who will begin.

Kagome

Children stand in a circle. One child who is "it" stands blindfolded in the middle of the circle. The children sing to music. When the music stops, one child in the circle asks, "Who Am I?" The child who is "it" guesses. If the guess is correct, the child who asked the question is "it." If the guess is wrong, the child who is "it" stays in the middle of the circle and the game is repeated.

Shuttlecock

See Games in the Chinese unit.

Relay Games

Relays are popular in Japan. Divide the class into two teams. Line up each team in a row. The children in each team pass a ball or stick from the first child to the next as fast as they can. The first team to finish wins. Children may suggest many variations. Older children in Japan run relays on a track.

Marbles

Marbles for girls are called *ohajiki*, and for boys, *biidama*. A popular game, played especially by girls, is played by the same rules as used in America.

Tops

Spin the top (*koma*), a game well known in America, is usually played by boys with various sizes of tops.

Mah Jongg

A Japanese game of *mah jongg* is available in stores. See the Games section in the Chinese unit for a description of this game.

Songs of a Hundred Poets (Karuta)

This game is played in the home by adults and children eight or nine years and older and in regional and factory

tournaments. It is a popular game during the New Year holiday.

Waka are two-part poems of 31 syllables. The first part of the poem has three lines of five, seven, and five syllables respectively. The second part has two lines of seven syllables each. To play the game, cards with the second part of the poem are laid face up. Players sit around these cards, listening to one person read the card from the first part of the poem. The winner is the one who picks up the matching card first and who has the most cards at the end of the game.

The poems relate the wisdom of the ancestors, teaching Japanese culture through the game. It has been adapted for younger children. Proverbs, sayings of old, the first character of a poem, or pictures are on their cards.

Fuku Warai

This game is often played during the New Year celebration. *Fuku* means "good fortune." Draw a face without eyes, mouth, and nose. Draw and cut out these features from a separate sheet of paper. A blindfolded player tries to place the features on the face. The game is similar to Pin the Tail on the Donkey.

Another way fuku warai may be made is to draw and cut out a blank face from white contact paper. Stick the face on a metal tray or cookie sheet. Draw and color features of the face on a white poster board. Cut them out and attach small pieces of magnetic tape to the back of each one. Blindfold a player, who then tries to place the features on the face correctly

Hanetsuki

This game, which is similar to badminton, is played during the New Year Holiday with a birdie and paddle.

Baseball (*Yakyu*)

The Japanese are almost as interested in baseball as Americans. High schools, universities, and corporations have teams and tournaments. Boys begin playing baseball at any age. Girls play softball beginning in the elementary grades.

Young children enjoy T-ball. They may also enjoy pantomiming a baseball game.

Martial Arts

The most popular martial arts in Japan are *judo, kendo,* and *karate.* All arts must be done under the supervision of a master.

The aim of *judo* is to train the mind and body. *Ju* means "soft and gentle." The principle of judo is "softness overcomes hardness." Boys begin learning judo at the age of six. The two boys wear jackets, trousers, and the color of the belt they have earned. They stand on tatami mats while they grab and throw each other.

Kendo is a form of fencing. Traditionally, a sword was used for protection. Today bamboo swords are used. The players

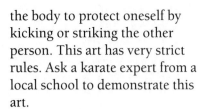

wear protective clothing.

Karate means "empty hands." It is the art of self-defense, using the body to protect oneself by kicking or striking the other person. This art has very strict rules. Ask a karate expert from a local school to demonstrate this art.

In the Japanese art of archery, called *kyudo,* a bamboo and wood bow and bamboo arrows are used. The purpose of this art is to discipline the mind and body.

Physical Education in School

In the mornings, whether at school or at home, children exercise to music on the radio.

Playground equipment for most kindergartens includes jungle gyms, slide, swings, and sand.

Some children begin gymnastics at age three or four. They learn to swim in the pool at school. From kindergarten through the university, all schools schedule "Olympic Game" competitions once a year.

Abacus

The Japanese have used the abacus for hundreds of years. Even with the electronic calculator, it continues to be popular because it is easy to operate. The abacus is a rectangular frame with thin, vertical bamboo rods. Each rod has beads on it, the beads on each rod representing a specific number. The beads are moved up and down the rods to carry out addition, subtraction, multiplication, and division.

Competitions are held to rank abacus operators by skill and speed. In some speed contests, abacus operators compete against calculator operators.

SPECIAL EVENTS

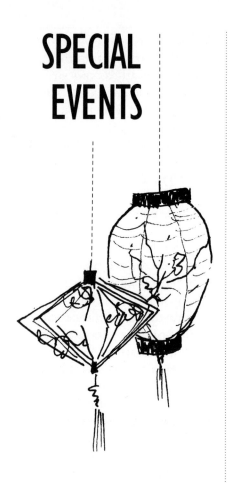

Children gain valuable understanding from real-life experiences.

Excursions

• Visit a Japanese garden (*ohana mi*). Viewing and observing flowers are important events in Japan.
• View Japanese art at the local museum. Check the newspaper for special Japanese exhibits.
• Visit a Japanese restaurant to view the decor.
• Find the numerous items made in Japan sold in stores, especially in electronics stores. Children identify electronic items at home with their parents' help.
• Visit an Asian shop to find items made in Japan.

Resource Persons

Invite Japanese guests to come to the center to show and explain the Japanese culture. Guests may include a gardener, manager or clerk of a store or restaurant, museum curator, college student, musician, and others.

For a family school event, invite a Japanese family to share its culture with the children. A suggested menu is steamed rice (*go-han*), teriyaki chicken (*yaki tori*), tofu soup, daikon salad (see Food) or American-style salad, and hot or iced green tea.

CELEBRATIONS

Festivals in Japan are occasions to celebrate with families and to wear traditional styles of clothing. The festivals and holidays described below are observed by the entire country. Japanese Americans observe some of these festivals. Find out how these festivals are celebrated in your community.

New Year's Day (*Ganjitsu*)— January 1

New Year, celebrated for three days, is an important holiday. Families celebrate by going to shrines or temples and visiting relatives and friends. The top of the gateway is decorated with rice straw ropes and pine branches. Banners are displayed. Children play the card game "Song of a Hundred Poets," battledore, shuttlecock (see Games) and fly kites. Acrobats may perform for the community. Rice cakes (*mochi*) are served as a special food.

Setsubun—February 3 or 4 (lunar calendar), the day before the beginning of spring

In the evening, people open the doors of their homes to drive away evil and bad luck. They throw handfuls of soybeans and shout, "Evil out! Good Luck in!"

Girls' Day—March 3

Wishes are expressed to girls for their future happiness. They dress in kimonos. A set of hina dolls, dressed in costumes worn in the ancient royal courts, is displayed on a tiered stand draped in red. Girls who have miniature furniture, dishes, musical instruments, and other similar treasures display them.

In San Francisco, Hina dolls are also displayed. They are decorated with peach blossoms and spring flowers. Red beans, rice cakes, and fruit-shaped candy are eaten, and a sweet drink, *shirozake*, made from rice gruel and mixed with fermented rice, is served.

Japanese American Festival—April 9 (date varies)

The Japanese Americans in San Francisco combine several Japanese festivals on this day. On the first Sunday the cherry blossoms are in bloom, they gather at the Japanese Tea Garden in Golden Gate Park for a celebration.

Boys' Day (*Tangono-sekku*)—May 5

This festival is celebrated to express the hope that each boy in the family will grow up to be healthy and strong and to be a success in life. Iris leaves are placed under the eaves to keep away evil. Special rice cakes wrapped in oak leaves are eaten. A giant paper carp banner is flown from a long bamboo pole in front of Japanese home, one fish for each son in the family. The carp is the symbol of power and strength. Boys display dolls dressed as warriors in armor

and as famous Japanese heroes, who represent strength and bravery. (See Creative Art Expression for instructions on making a carp banner.)

Star Festival (*Tanabata*)—July 7

This festival is based on a Japanese legend about the meeting of two stars on either side of the Milky Way. The traditional offerings are original stories and poems. Pieces of bamboo are placed in front of the houses or garden gates. Poems and proverbs are written on strips of brightly colored paper used to decorate the bamboo branches. On July 8, children take their decorated bamboo branches to the nearest stream to be carried away. Japanese eat peaches and melons on this day.

Festival of Souls (*Obon*)—Mid August

Families honor ancestors, returning to their home towns. Later, dressed in cotton kimonos, they gather for outdoor dances.

Night of the Full Moon (*Tsuki-mi*)—August 15 - September 13 (lunar calendar)

This is the time for moongazing during the autumn evenings. Decorations of Japanese pampas grass are used. *Dango,* a kind of dumpling, is made.

Seven-Five-Three Festival (*Shichi-go-san*)—November 15

Parents with boys age five, girls age seven, and either boys or girls age three, dress their children in colorful, traditional clothing and take them to the shrine. These three ages were chosen because odd numbers are considered lucky.

Christmas Eve—December 31

Some Japanese celebrate on Christmas Eve. Children enjoy receiving gifts from Santa Claus. Stores display Christmas decorations. "Sister Santa," a female Santa Claus, talks to the children.

NATIONAL HOLIDAYS
••••••••••••••••

Schools, corporations, and government offices are closed on each of the twelve national holidays.

New Year's Day—January 1

Coming-of-Age Day—January 15

The young people who reach the legal age are congratulated. They are now ready to make their own way in the world. Ceremonies are held in each

town for those who come of age during the year.

National Foundation Day—February 11

This day is set aside for the commemoration of the founding of Japan in 660 B.C. and the fostering of patriotic feelings.

Vernal Equinox Day (Spring)

Nature is praised and love of all living things is shown on this day.

Greenery Day—April 29 (since 1989)

Former Emperor Hirohito's interest in plant life is honored.

Constitution Memorial Day—May 3

Commemoration of the signing of the constitution in 1947 is observed, and hope for the future growth of Japan is shown on this day.

Children's Day (also Boys' Day) (Kodomo-no-hih)—May 5

On this day, wishes are expressed that the children will grow up and find happiness. Appreciation is also expressed to mothers.

Respect-for-the-Aged Day—September 15

This is a time to show respect and affection for the elderly who have devoted themselves to the society for so many years and to celebrate their long life. In cities and towns, the elderly are invited to entertainments and are given gifts.

Autumnal Equinox Day (Fall)

Ancestors are honored.

Health-Sports Day—October 10

This is a day to foster a sound mind and healthy body. Commemoration of the 1964 Tokyo Olympics and many sporting events are held.

Culture Day—November 3

Celebration of love and freedom, equality, and promotion of Japanese culture are the themes of this day.

Emperor's Birthday—December 23

The Emperor and Empress receive the good wishes of the people.

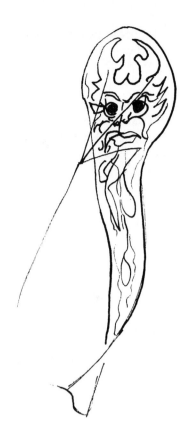

RESOURCES

N Nursery
K Kindergarten
P Primary

Books for Children

Ashley, Gwynneth. *Take a Trip to Japan.* Franklin Watts, Inc., 1980. P
The Boys' Festival and Girls' Festival of Dolls are described in this book designed for young readers. Photographs of deer, the sport of catching fish, and noodles and dumplings capture the interest of younger children.

Bang, Molly. *The Paper Crane.* Greenwillow Books, 1985. NK
This story is about a stranger who repays his benefactor in a mysterious way. The paper cut-out photographs, with their three-dimensional effect, are especially interesting.

Bryan, Ashley. *SH-KO and His Eight Wicked Brothers.* Atheneum, 1988. KP
Lovingly illustrated by Fumoi Yoshimura, this folktale from his childhood reminds us of the importance and power of acts of kindness.

Friedman, Ina R. *How My Parents Learned to Eat.* Houghton Mifflin Co., 1984. NK
This delightful tale, told through the eyes of a Japanese-American child, describes how an American sailor and a Japanese school girl learn each other's ways and form a loving relationship.

Elkin, Judith. *A Family in Japan.* Lerner Publications Company, 1987. P
This series of books presents information about families from around the world, from Aborig-

ines to Zulu. A day in the life of a Japanese sixth-grader, Dar-suke, introduces children to calligraphy, the Boys' Festival, and temples.

Garrison, Christian. *The Dream Eater.* Bradbury Press, 1978. NK
Watercolor on parchment gives a splendid effect in illustrating a tale about a baku who restored pleasant slumber to a village.

Ishii, Momako. *Issun Boshi, The Inchling; a Retelling of an Old Japanese Tale.* Walker, 1967. KP
A famous folktale about an old couple who wish for a child; a good story for dramatization. The themes include love of children and the need for identity.

Izawa, Yohgi, and Canna Funakoshi. *One Evening.* Picture Book Studio, 1988. NP
Brief text and soft, interesting illustrations describe a quiet evening with a man and his cat. One Morning, Izawa's first book, was voted one of the ten best children's books of 1987.

Kitamura, Satoshi. *UFO Diary.* Farrar, Straus and Giroux, 1989. P
A lost UFO explores this planet with the assistance of a small boy.

Lifton, Betty J. *Kap and the Wicked Monkey.* Norton, 1968. K-3
This story is one example of the way cranes are used as characters in many Japanese folktales. Magical animals illustrate the theme of kindness rewarded.

Marimoto, Junko. *Inch Boy.* Viking Penguin, Inc., 1986. NK
An inch-tall Issunboshi has the desire to become a Samurai, which takes him on an adventure into the Red Demon's giant stomach. The surprise ending is great fun!

McDermott, Gerald. *The Stonecutter: A Japanese Folktale.* Viking, 1975. KP
The theme of this folktale is the foolish longing for power. The story is illustrated in vivid color and appeals to children.

Mizumura, Kazue. *If I Built a Village.* Crowell, 1971. K-3
The author attempts to show how harmony between homes in towns and nature can be accomplished for protection of the environment.

_____. *Flower Moon, A Book of Haiku.* Crowell, 1977. 2-5
Thirty haiku selected to read to young children; includes information about the writing of Haiku.

Mosel, Arlene. *The Funny Little Woman.* Dutton, 1972. K-3
Americans delight in this retelling of the adventures of the little woman and the wicked one and its scary illustrations. Children enjoy dramatizing this story.

Newton, Patricia Montgomery. *The Five Sparrows.* McClelland and Stewart, Ltd., 1982. KP
This Japanese folktale reminds children to be kind to helpless creatures. Compare this tale with *India's Magic Cooking Pot* by Faith Towle.

Nikly, Michelle. *The Emperor's Plum Tree.* Greenwillow Books, 1982. NK
The Emperor learns a lesson in wisdom from a small boy, a nightingale, and a plum tree in this appealing Japanese folktale. Delicate drawings complement the story.

Paterson, Katherine. *The Tale of the Mandarin Ducks.* Lodestar Books, 1990. KP
The famous Dillons illustrate another fine adventure that provides an entertaining learning experience for children.

Pittman, Helina Clare. *The Gift of the Willows.* Carolrhoda Books, Inc., 1988. KPI
A hard-working Japanese couple learn a valuable lesson about survival and gratitude.

Pratt, Davis. *Magic Animals of Japan.* Parnassus, 1967. K-3.
Twelve tales from Japanese folk literature are about animals brought to life for young children through the illustrations.

Sakade, Florence. *Japanese Children's Favorite Stories.* Charles E. Tuttle Company, 1988. P
Twenty favorite stories, each illustrated in the typical Japanese style, treat children everywhere to a glimpse into the lifestyle and traditions of this ancient culture. Tales of bravery, magic, and cunning delight young readers, just as fairy tales have done through the ages.

Sasaki, Jeannie and F. Oyeda. *Chocho Is For Butterfly: A Japanese-English Primer.* Seattle: Uyeda Sauki Art, 1975. K-1

This book introduces Japanese-American children to oral Japanese language with illustrations.

Say, Allen. *The Bicycle Man.* Parnassus Press, 1982. KP
A mountain schoolhouse in Southern Japan is the setting for Sportsday, as recalled by the author. Americans surprise the Japanese children by participating in the events. The action is depicted in pen-and-ink drawings.

Snyder, Dianne. *The Boy of the Three Year Nap.* Houghton Mifflin Company, 1988. P
A trickster tale from Japan, illustrated by Allen Say, a Japanese American. This humorous story about a lazy boy is a Caldecott Honor book.

Soya, Kujoshi. *A House of Leaves.* Philomel Books, 1986. KP
This book encourages a young child to experience a home in the garden with a roof of leaves. Subtle watercolors by Japanese artists complement this sensitive story.

Tompert, Ann. *Will You Come Back for Me?* Albert Whitman and Co., 1988. NK
Children can identify with four-year-old Suki as she is left in a day care center for the first time. Illustrations by Robin Kramer add to the appeal of this book. The biographies of the author and artist are written on an elementary level so that children can understand them.

Wisniewski, David. *The Warrior and the Wise Men.* Lothrop, Lee & Shepard Books, 1989. KP

Intricate paper-cuts strikingly illustrate the triumph of gentle reason over force as twin brothers compete for the Emperor's throne.

Yashima, Taro (author, illus.) *Crow Boy*. Viking 1955.   NK
The story depicts a teacher's sensitivity to a child who is considered "different." Yashima's books are illustrated in soft pastel colors. The books reflect universal themes popular with children today. Japanese characters appear in some of his books. Also available in libraries are *Plenty to Watch* (1954), *Momo's Kitten* (1961), and *Umbrella* (1958).

Yoshi. *Who's Hiding Here?* Picture Book Studio, 1987.   NK
Batik paintings with cut-outs capture children's curiosity about nature's camouflage. This book is this Japanese artist and author's first book for children.

Children will also enjoy the following books. Look for them in your library.

Baker, Keith. *The Magic Fan*.
Haskins, Jim. *Count Your Way through Japan*.
Glubok, Shirley. *The Art of Japan*.
Matsuno, Masako. *A Pair of Red Clogs*.
_____. *Taro and the Bamboo Shoot*.
Mizumaru, Kazue. *If I Were a Cricket*.
_____. *If I Built a Village*.
Matsutani, Miyoko. *The Crane Maiden*.

Resources for Adults

Books

Aoki, Michiko Y., and Margaret B. Dardess. *As the Japanese See It*. The University of Hawaii, 1981.
Background information for teachers interested in marriage customs and childbearing practices. Helps in appreciating Japanese-American families.

Berger, Donald P., *Folk Songs of Japanese Children*. Charles E. Tuttle, Company, Inc., 1969.
Kindergarten and older.
Includes information about the source, meaning and use of each song.

Bucklay, Roger. *Japan Today*. Cambridge University Press, 1985.
Contemporary political system and economic advances are surveyed in this concise edition. Japanese attitudes toward nuclear installations and toward the U.S. are explained.

Grilli, Susan. *Preschool in the Suzuki Spirit*. Distributed by Olive Press, 1987.
Adults who often wonder how children come to love the violin at such an early age will find all the answers in this book. The author, a contemporary of Dr. Suzuki in Japan, demonstrates how she adapted the method in a preschool setting.

Hirai, Bernice K., and Yuriko Tcheou. *Japanese Resource Book for Teachers*. Department of Education, Honolulu, Hawaii, 1980.
A variety of activities in English and Japanese help Japanese immigrant children learn about their language and cultural heritage.

Jackson, Paul. *The Complete Origami Course*. Gallery Books, 1989.
This gorgeous book introduces the art of paper folding. Decorative boxes and jewelry, which are made using basic techniques and new ideas, are only two of the myriad projects in this book. Some of the less-complicated ideas could be adapted for use with children.

Kitano, Harry. *The Japanese Americans*. Chelsea House Publishers, 1987.   Intermediate
From the series "The People of North America," this book uses detailed pictures and text to describe the immigration of Japanese people to America, their struggles and adjustment and their present-day status.

A Look into Japan. Tokyo: Japan Travel Bureau, 1984.
Even though Japan has become Westernized, almost all aspects of traditional Japanese life remain. This brief reference book describes a great deal about the cultural aspects of this society.

Makino, Yasuko, Compiler. *Japan Through Children's Literature: An Annotated Bibliography*. Westport, Conn., Greenwood Press, 1985.
This bibliography includes books available in English. Topics are art, drama, fiction, poetry, folklore and legend, and social studies.

Nakans, Ichiro (trans.) *101 Favorite Songs Taught in*

Japanese Schools. Tokyo, The Japanese Times, 1983. K-12
Includes popular tunes and nursery songs, songs influenced by Western music and songs of modern Japan. A bilingual book with piano accompaniment.

Palate Pleasers. Published in English semi-annually by APCON International, Inc., 420 Boyd St., Suite. 502, Los Angeles, CA 90013.
A magazine of Japanese cuisine and culture. Includes art, food and recipes, homes, life in the country, Japanese language expressions, and many related topics accompanied by color photographs. Advertisements with addresses for Japanese products are included.

Sato, Esther, and L. Shisido. *Japanese Children's Songs.* Honolulu Department of Education, 1980. K-6
Audiotapes accompany the book. Songs are in English and Japanese.

Smolen, Rick, and David Cohen, Producers and Directors. *A Day in the Life of Japan.* New York, Collin Publishers, 1985.
Large color photographs taken by one hundred of the world's foremost photo-journalists record ordinary events of a typical day.

Takahama, Toshie. *The Joy of Origami.* Tokyo: Shufunotomo/Japan Publications. Order from Kodansha International/USA Ltd. through Harper & Row Publishers, Inc., 10 E. 53rd St., New York, NY 10022.

This excellent work has large color illustrations and step-by-step instructions in English for traditional and new models that range from easy to difficult.

_____. *Origami Toys.* Tokyo: Shufunotomo/Japan Publications, 1973. Order from address above.
Instructions for fifteen simple models are included in this book.

Welch, T. G., and K. Hiroki. *Japan Today!* Passport Books, 1990.
This guide was written for Western visitors to Japan who want to become familiar with the basic language and culture. The wide range of topics covers the principal facts about the country. The descriptions are brief but comprehensive and are arranged alphabetically for quick, easy reference.

White, Merry. *The Japanese Educational Challenge.* Distributed by Olive Press, 1987.
Through observations and interviews, the author traces the lives of Japanese children and writes about their school experiences and home relationships, including a mother's role and the teacher's part in learning. This up-to-date information is essential for all adults planning a multicultural approach to education.

Yasuo, Aoto, et al., eds. *Nippon, the Land and Its People.* Nippon Steel Corporation, Personnel Development Division, 1984.
This information was compiled to contribute to mutual understanding between the Japanese

and people of other countries. Answers to questions frequently asked by non-Japanese are given. Brief sections on all aspects of Japanese society are included. This book is very helpful in understanding this unique culture.

Films, Filmstrips and Videos
Children of Japan. Coronet Film and Video, 1987.
This documentary, appropriate for school-age children, focuses on the life of Makoto as he relates to an American pen pal by emphasizing "learning the new, remembering the old." Children become aware of cultural differences and similarities between the United States and Japan as they view the scenes with a parade, a basketball game, calligraphy class, and a traditional Japanese home.

The Emperor and the Nightingale. Distributed by Music for Little People, 1988.
In this video, actress Glenn Close relates this tale of the difference between the genuine and the fake. Also available in cassette.

Festival in Japan. English version. Sakura Motion Picture Company, Ltd. Distributed by Japan National Tourist Organization, 45 Rockefeller Plaza, New York, NY 10020, 1968. Film No. 67. 21 minutes.
Scenes showing migrating birds, kite flying, farming, fishing, and ice skating are entertaining for children.

McDermott, Gerald. *The Stonecutter.* Distributed by Weston Woods, 1965.

Graphically interpreted in vivid color, this Japanese myth's theme is the foolish longing for money. Available as filmstrip, film, or video.

Stories from Many Lands. Distributed by Weston Woods, 1981 This video, filmstrip and cassette kit, or 16-mm film contains many of children's favorite tales.

Unlearning Asian American Stereotypes. Produced and distributed by Council on Interracial Books for Children, 1982. Insensitivity to Asian culture is dramatized in this film, with children providing the primary voices of concern.

Yashima, Taro. *Umbrella*. Distributed by Weston Woods, 1959.
Japanese-American Momo wants to use her new umbrella and boots. She learns patience and self-confidence in this sensitively written story.

Materials and Experiences
Dolls—Asian Boy, Asian Girl. Claudia's Caravan, Nos. 19G, 18G.
Thirteen-inch vinyl Asian dolls.

Ethnic Dolls. Child Craft, Nos. 182758, 182774.
Asian Boy and Asian Girl dolls promote ethnic pride.

Mien Dolls. Claudia's Caravan, No. 31G.
Handcrafted cloth doll in traditional dress.

Asian Girl Body Puzzle. Educational Teaching Aids, No. 8779D-E9.

Accurately proportioned, this puzzle is 3 3/4 inches long when assembled.

Asian Personalities. Kaplan, No. 1791.
Four full-color prints in 11 1/2-by-16-inch size.

Asian American Posters. Educational Teaching Aids, No. 2725-99.
Fourteen color posters with information on each.

Records and Audiocassettes
Berger, Donald P. *Folk Songs of Japanese Children*. Tuttle, 1969. K-12
Includes information about the source, meaning and use of each song.

Japanese Children's Songs. Claudia's Caravan, No. 18H2.
Thirty Japanese songs for children are presented on this bilingual audiocassette with a book that is recommended for all ages.

Jenkins, Ella. *I Know the Colors of the Rainbow*. Educational Activities, Inc., 1981.
Song "Chotto Matte Kudasai" has call and response using Japanese words. Children enjoy singing it again and again.

Koto Music of Japan with the Ensemble Nipponia. Distributed by Music for Little People, Box 1460, Redway, CA 95560.
Traditional instruments—the Koto, Shakuhachi and transverse Japanese flutes —create soothing melodies.

Margaret Marks, *Making Music Your Own* six record album set. Silver Burdett Company. Dis-tributed by General Learning Corporation, 8301 Ambassador Rd., Dallas, TX 75247. Album 75180.
Have you ever heard about a school for birds? "Chi Chi Pa Pa" tells about one. "Empress" provides Asian sounds for listening music that encourages children to create and dramatize stories. The "Japanese Rain Song" listens to a rainy day in Japan, prompting gestures and movement.

Oriental Sunrise. Distributed by Music for Little People.
Japanese flutist offers peaceful, serene sounds.

Raffi. *Everything Grows*. A and M Records, Inc.
Raffi sings "Haru Ga Kita," a Japanese version of "Springtime Is Coming," from the *Making Music Your Own* album.

Sato, Esther and L. Shishido. *Japanese Children's Songs*. Honolulu, Department of Education, 1980. K-6 with audiotapes.
Fifteen songs, in English and Japanese, are about animals, insects, flowers and seasons.

KOREAN AND KOREAN-AMERICAN CULTURES

Numerous Korean families have settled in America in the past years, and many Americans have contact with Koreans every day, especially in the cities. Korean children attend public schools, and many Korean students are enrolled in American colleges. Because their numbers are increasing in the United States, an effort to increase understanding of their culture is important.

Korea has a very long history, but many dramatic changes have taken place in the country over the last 25 years, including widespread industrialization. The world learned more about the Korean culture during the 1988 Olympics in Seoul. As in other countries today, many urban Koreans live and dress in Western style, while in the rural areas, they live more traditionally.

Dr. Ye-Hwa Jun, graduate in Early Childhood Education at the University of North Texas, professor in Seoul; and Jong-Eun Choi, doctoral student in Early Childhood Education at the University of North Texas, were valuable consultants in validating the contents of this unit and interpreting Korean culture.

Dr. Jun also provided the photographs in this section, which were taken in Seoul.

FAMILY LIVING

HOMES

Many years ago farmers in Korea lived in L-or U-shaped one-story houses that had enough rooms for the extended family. The curved roof was made of black tile, and the house was surrounded by a wall. Today, many Koreans live in Western-style homes or apartments.

Make a traditional house (*jip*) using a large refrigerator box turned on its side. Cut out windows and a door. To simulate the tile roof, cut two pieces of butcher paper to fit the length and width of the box. Staple the two pieces together lengthwise, and attach them to the top of the box. Turn the corners up slightly to make the curved eaves. Paint the roof black to give a clay-tile effect. Children can build a wall with blocks around the house to make a courtyard.

Some teachers prefer to build the house for the children, while others involve the children in planning and executing the activity. Show pictures of Korean houses to children and discuss what the house should look like. Solicit the children's ideas on how to make the house and determine what materials are needed. Let children help measure, cut, paint and attach the roof, and discover how to curve the eaves.

Bed (*Chim-dae*)

In the past, Koreans slept on a quilt on the floor or on a low bed. The quilt was folded up and stored during the day. Many Koreans use Western-style beds today.

Talk about how space in a room can be used when the bed is put away during the day, how the floor must be kept clean, and how comfortable a quilt on the floor is compared to a bed. Invite quilters to demonstrate how quilts are made, or bring examples to class for children to examine.

Children who are interested in sewing may wish to make a quilt as a group project and use it in the home center. An adult who sews may be willing to supervise the children's work. Children can also participate in making a collage quilt. Provide construction paper, scissors, and glue. Let children cut and glue small colored squares of paper on an 8-1/2-by-11-inch sheet of paper. After they glue on the squares, suggest attaching all the sheets together to make a large community quilt. Wallpaper samples or fabric may be substituted for paper.

Older children may create individual patches from fabric to make a large quilt for the classroom.

Cushions (Bang-sak)

Families use Western-style furniture or sit on cushions on the floor. In the summer, they sit on straw mats. The cushions are covered with fabric such as cotton or silk. Some of them are embroidered with beautiful designs.

Buy or make four cushions, about 10 to 12 inches square, each large enough for one child. The cushions are flat but have sufficient padding to be comfortable. Any kind of fabric may be used. Parents or others who sew may be willing to make them for classroom use.

Home Decorations

Koreans show their appreciation for the arts in the way they decorate their homes. Wall decorations include scrolls of paintings or calligraphy; folding screens made of embroidered silk or paintings on paper are placed in the corners of rooms (see Creative Art Expression in the Japanese and Japanese-American Cultures unit for painting and calligraphy).

Potted green plants beautify rooms. Potted plants may be placed in the classroom. Have a parent or nursery grower discuss types of indoor plants that are easy to grow.

Gardens

Koreans recreate the natural environment in the area around their homes. They plant flower beds and build Oriental rock gardens that remind them of the mountains and valleys of the countryside, as well as cultivating trees, bushes, and plants in containers.

Let children make a rock garden outdoors, including mountains, valleys, and some stones in their designs. Branches and twigs may be used for plants and trees if actual plantings are not possible, or children may make plants and flowers as an art activity.

Discuss how the natural environment is often changed by people: large trees are bulldozed to make room for a building, and hills are flattened and trees removed to make a playground. Think of other examples in your area. Talk about how buildings and playgrounds can be built without changing the land.

DRAMATIC PLAY

The following articles may be provided for dramatic play:
—chopsticks
—doll quilts for beds
—floor cushions
—Korean and American —dolls
—marbles
—straw mats, which are used on the floor in summer
—a low, round table
—tablespoons
—teacups
—traditional and Western-style clothing

CLOTHING (EUI-BOK)

One of the first things young children want to do when exploring a culture is to try on traditional clothing. Have clothing available for children to examine, or have them make their own by adding a creative touch to an existing garment or using a pattern and starting from scratch. Involve the children in determining what tools are needed, selecting materials, and deciding where to cut.

Traditional style clothing has been worn for more than 2000 years. Ask a Korean family in your community to show examples of traditional garments to the class.

Men wore wide trousers (baji), which were tied at the waist and at the ankles with a cloth draw string. The jackets were short and loose and were fastened by a tie with a single bow. Children can make these items from fabric or paper, decorating them with marking pens or crayons to make Korean designs. Women wore very full, long skirts (*chima*), which were gathered under the arms and tied with a cloth string. A short jacket with full sleeves (*chogori*) was worn over the skirt. It was fastened with a bow on one side. The dresses were made of brightly colored satin fabric.

Today, traditional clothing is most often worn for special holidays such as New Year's Day, Chusok, and Korean Thanksgiving Day; and western-style dress is used for everyday wear. Men may wear trousers and a short-sleeved shirt over a long-sleeved shirt; women may wear slacks or a skirt with a blouse, or a simple dress. An excellent resource for clothing and customs is *Korean Ways* by Eileen Moffett.

Korean and American children wear the same styles of clothing to school. Private schools and some public ones require uniforms. Generally, girls wear black skirts and boys wear black trousers. Kindergarten children wear a hat, the style and color of which is selected by the school.

All children use school bags with handles to carry their papers and lunches. All children begin homework in the first grade.

Ethnic Dolls and Clothing

When selecting ethnic dolls, look for authentic features. Be careful not to stereotype the Korean culture in the style and selection of clothing for dramatic play. See Resources for places to find Asian dolls.

A New Baby (*Kumjal*)

In the past, when a Korean baby was born, a small straw rope was hung across the gatepost. If the baby was a boy, pieces of charcoal and red peppers were fastened to it; if it was a girl, pieces of charcoal and green pine branches were fastened to it.

When a child in the class announces the arrival of a new sibling, hang a small rope above the door frame. Let children decide what to hang on it. They may decide to hang the name of the child on the rope.

Infant Carriers (*Podaegi*)

Mothers carried their babies on their backs, using a piece of cloth wrapped around the mother and infant. The baby's head was behind the mother's to help the infant control the neck muscles. This practice continues today in rural areas of Korea; in cities, Korean mothers use infant carriers similar to those used in America.

To make the podaegi, cut fabric about 12 inches wide and long enough to fit over the child and cover the mother's back. Attach two ties or strips of fabric on each end of the cloth as illustrated. Lay the fabric across the child's back; place the doll inside the fabric, leaving its head visible; knot the ties in front.

Have a baby carrier available so that children can practice the traditional and modern ways of carrying infants. Compare the American Indian, African, Chinese, Korean, and Mexican ways of carrying infants.

First Birthday

A big party is planned for a child's first birthday. The child is dressed in traditional clothes. Special foods are served, includ-

ing rice, rice cakes, and seaweed soup. Symbolic items are placed in front of the child, such as yarn, symbolizing a long life; money, symbolizing wealth; and a writing brush, symbolizing scholarly talent. The child's future is predicted according to which item the child picks up.

Korean children in the classroom may appreciate a traditional birthday celebration with customary foods. Show the other children how to make a birthday greeting with Korean designs from nature for the honored child. As the children gather, each makes a wish for the child and presents the greeting.

FOOD (EUM-SIK)

Korea has a great many varieties of food, including the following common ones: fruits (*gwail*) such as berries, melons, oranges; vegetables (*chae-soh*) such as Korean cabbage, large Korean white radishes, spinach, red and green peppers, bean sprouts, onions, carrots, and squash; *kimchi*—pickled vegetables eaten with every meal; mushrooms; edible greens, such as watercress, roots of water lily and lotus, dandelions; seaweed mixed with noodles or rice (obtained at a health-food store); chicken, pork, beef, and fish; barbecued beef (*bulgogi*) called "fire beef" because it is spicy; *kalbi*—short ribs cut into small pieces; soups, such as bean sprout, beef and radish, and pollack (fish); eggrolls (*mandu*); chestnuts, walnuts, pine nuts, ginkgo nuts. Foods are prepared using strong, hot spices—red pepper, garlic, and sesame oil, sesame seeds, soy sauce, green onions, and salt.

Acquaint children with some of the common foods eaten in Korea. If the school has a lunch program or serves snacks, include these foods in the menus. Most of them are available in grocery stores. Some stores place them in the Asian food section of the produce department.

At snack time, discuss the size, shape, color, taste, and texture of the foods they are eating and how they are grown. Some children will only smell foods they are reluctant to try, and many do not like strong spices. This activity combines language development with science.

(Safety Note: Be sure to obtain parental permission before allowing children to eat anything in case of allergies or diet restrictions.)

Meals

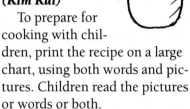

The traditional setting for meals is a low table, with each person sitting on a cushion on the floor. Families today may use a western-style table and chairs. They may also sit on cushions on a large, straw mat (*dot ja lee*), with the serving dishes placed in the center.

The menus for the three meals a day are similar. The main meal of the day is served in the evening. Each meal consists of rice, soup, kimchi, and several side dishes of meat and vegetables.

In the home center, arrange a low table with individual cushions or mats around it. For role-playing a meal, each child needs chopsticks, a tablespoon, and a plate. Food is served from bowls placed in the middle of the table.

Toasted Seaweed (Kim Kui)

To prepare for cooking with children, print the recipe on a large chart, using both words and pictures. Children read the pictures or words or both.

10 sheets seaweed (1 package)

2 T sesame seed oil

Salt to taste (optional)

Brush seaweed with sesame seed oil. Sprinkle with salt.

Toast over open flame in a hot frying pan or under a broiler until the seaweed turns green.

Cut into fourths or smaller pieces to serve.

Koreans eat enormous amounts of edible seaweed.

Egg Rolls (*Mandu*)

Mandu are similar to egg rolls. Chopped meat and vegetables are lightly sauteed, then rolled in a thin piece of dough or in an egg roll wrapper. Steam over water until done (approximately 15 min.).

Dessert (*hoo-sik*) and Beverages

Koreans often have fruit and a cold drink for dessert. Fresh fruit is preferred to cooked or canned. Tomatoes are eaten as fruit.

Tell the children that a special Korean dessert—a surprise—will be served. Prepare bite-sized tomato pieces and explain that these are eaten as a dessert in Korea. Or cut several kinds of fruit into small pieces, add water and sugar, and serve.

For a drink (*shikhye*), mix cooked rice and pine nuts in water, or make a fruit punch (*sujonggwa*), by soaking dried persimmon in ginger water for two or three days. Add honey, spiced cinnamon, and pine nuts before serving. Limit the amount of ginger for children. All these ingredients can be purchased at Asian stores.

Serve the beverages and desserts at snack or lunch time on different days. Tasting new foods gives children an opportunity to develop vocabulary as they use a variety of words to describe the tastes and textures.

Rice Cakes (*Ttok*)

Rice cakes are a special food in Korea. They are always served at birthdays of young children. Women get together to shape each rice cake into a half-moon by hand. Dyes from plants are used to make them different colors.

Rice Cake (*Ttok*)—from Ye-Hwa's mother

4 C rice flour
1/2 t salt
1/2 T sugar
1 T baked sesame seeds
1/2 t sesame oil

Mix sugar and sesame seeds and set aside. Mix rice flour and salt. Knead the flour mixture with hot water. Cut a small piece of dough and roll it into a ball. Put a small amount of sugar mixture inside the ball. Shape the ball into a half moon. Put the rice cakes into a steamer and steam. Rinse them in cool water for a short time. Spread sesame oil on each cake.

Make rice cakes for a Korean birthday party. Children enjoy shaping rice cakes. They can also be purchased in grocery stores.

Tea (*Cha*)

Scorched rice tea is used daily by many families. Other kinds of tea are served at special occasions. The accepted way to drink tea is to sip it slowly in silence.

To prepare scorched rice tea, cook rice in water. Take most of the rice out of the steamer, then scorch the remainder. Add water and serve.

Ginseng tea grows in the mountains of Korea. It is an important ingredient in Oriental medicine.

Plan to serve rice for a snack or lunch. Make weak scorched rice tea for the beverage. Serve it in small cups for a tasting experience. Talk about how the taste of this tea compares to other beverages they enjoy.

School Lunch (*Jeom-sim-sik-sa*)

Children take their lunch to school. A typical lunch is rice, side dishes, kimchi, and eggs (fried, boiled, or scrambled). The school serves water or milk.

Designate one day as Korean school lunch day. Serve plain rice; a side dish of chicken, pork, or beef; vegetables, and eggs. Children may wish to taste the hot and spicy kimchi. Some children may wish to try eating with chopsticks; others will use a spoon.

Snacks at School

Snacks are raw or cooked vegetables, cookies, fruit, and beverages such as milk, water, or juice—similar to the snacks American children eat. Very few sweet snacks are served.

Discuss the fact that Korean and other Asian children eat fewer sweet foods than American children. Their desserts contain less sugar than American desserts.

MARKETS (SI-JANG)

In the rural areas, farmers sell their products in open-air markets that are open several days a week. Buyers can find anything they need, including food and fabrics. Common foods in these markets are rice, edible seaweed, pork, beef, and vegetables.

In the cities, stores are very modern. Travelers can find dessert shops and street vendors selling food.

To make a market, you will need a table or blocks and boards. Set up an open-air market and have children stock it with nonperishable items—dry beans, rice, canned goods, and things they have made.

Ask children to make play money, price their items, and bring bags. A box with divided sections is provided for play money. Encourage practice in the process of buying and selling.

Older children may price items according to the prices of goods in stores and ads in newspapers. Addition and subtraction can be practiced, depending on developmental levels.

TRANS-PORTATION

Koreans have many ways to travel. Trains (*gi-cha*) take people all over the country. The modern subway (*ji-ha-cheol*) in Seoul is a rapid way to travel. In the cities, some drive to work and others ride the subway or bus. Rural Koreans ride their bicycles (*ja-jeon-geo*) or walk.

Talk with children about the subway. Include how it is built underground, the difficulty of building below the streets, and the reason the subway can travel fast. Compare riding the subway to traveling by car and bicycle. Discuss safety, travel time, and cost.

A train can be made out of large boxes that are painted to resemble a train, with an engine, one or two cars, and a caboose. Let the children make the tickets and role-play taking a trip. An electric train may be used instead of the box train.

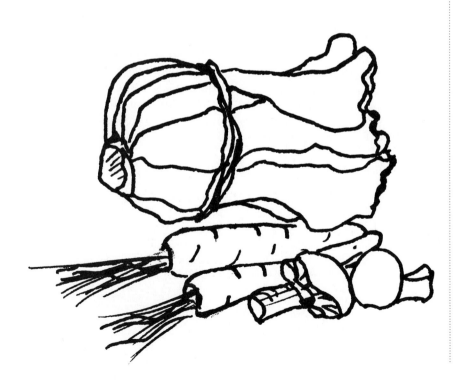

CREATIVE ART EXPRESSION

Creativity means to begin with ideas generated by children. The role of the adult is to foster creativity by asking questions, supervising the projects and providing reinforcement. Provide many choices of materials.

KOREAN ARTISTS

Famous Korean painters of the past were Kim Hong-do, who portrayed many different subjects that showed Western influence; Chang Sung-op; and An Kyon, who was famous for his landscapes in the Northern Chinese style. Well-known painters of today are Yi Sang-bom, who paints in the style of the old school; and Kim In-sung and Yi In-song, who are noted for their modern realism.

Kim Chong-hui was known as a great calligrapher; O Se-chang is a prominent figure in calligraphy today.

Two famous sculptors today are Kim Pok-chin, pioneer of modern sculpture, and Chong-yong, who has won recognition in Korea and other countries for abstract representations. Twentieth-century novelists are Yi-In-Jik, Yi Kwang-su, Kim Tong-in, and Pak Chong-hwa. A famous Korean poet today is Kim So-wol.

DECORATIVE ART

Flags (*Taeguk*)

The flag of the Republic of Korea (South Korea) symbolizes the land, people, and the government. White represents the land; the red and blue circle, the people; and the black bars, the government.

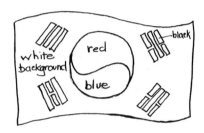

The flag of North Korea is red with a red star in a white circle in the middle, with a light blue border at the top and bottom.

To make a flag, cut a sheet of white fabric or strong white paper, such as butcher paper, any size the child desires. Let the child use paint, crayons, or marking pens to make the flag as illustrated. Attach the flag to a paper stick made of rolled newspaper. Let children use their creativity in figuring out how to fasten the flag to the stick. Children can have a parade of flags or display them in the classroom.

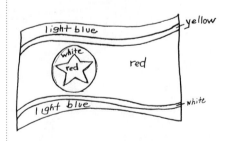

Pottery (Do-gi-ru)

Ceramic pottery is one of the most famous art objects in Korea today. The inlay celadon pottery, created about 700 years ago, is one of the most well-known types. Green and brown tones are favored. Nature provides the designs on the pottery—cranes, clouds, orchids, willow trees, fish, ducks. White or blue and white porcelain were used by many Koreans in the past.

Kim Chong-ho is a famous potter who is following in his father and grandfather's footsteps in recapturing the celadon porcelain created in the 12th century.

Bring pictures of Korean pottery from the library to help children understand the inlay process. Show the children an object that has an inlay design, and let them shape a vase out of potter's clay. Older children cut designs on the outside of the vase, being careful not to cut through the clay, and insert colored objects, such as buttons, sequins, or small colored pieces of plastic or paper, into the design. Younger children may press small objects into the clay. Dry the vases in the sun.

Painting (Geu-rim)
—Brushwork

The colors of traditional paintings were pale gray, pale green, brown, and tan. The themes of most paintings were landscapes with mountains, rivers, clouds, willow trees, and other designs from nature.

Show pictures of traditional paintings. Point out the subdued colors, simple lines, and light strokes, which in some paintings only suggest the shape of trees or scenes. If you have modern Korean paintings, contrast the two styles.

Calligraphy (Seo-yae)

Calligraphy is a form of writing with a brush. The letters are large and are written on special paper with black ink. The artists place the paper on the floor and paint basic forms of the letters in different styles. The long, narrow paper, hung vertically or horizontally, may reach from the ceiling to the floor.

Give children an opportunity to experiment with calligraphy on 12-inch wide rolls of computer paper cut to appropriate lengths. Supply black Chinese ink sticks, which are available at office and art supply stores. Black tempera paint mixed to the consistency of cream may also be used. Let children use easel and watercolor brushes in a variety of thicknesses to create sizes of letters and shades of black that are pleasing to them. Have them copy Korean or American letters (see Language Development).

Embroidery

Korean embroidery is a work of art that is very colorful. It is used today to decorate objects in the home.

For embroidered pillows, provide 12-by-12-inch squares of loosely woven fabric, large plastic embroidery needles, and several colors of embroidery floss. Let children draw designs on the fabric and then sew or glue the floss onto the design to give an embroidery effect. Some children may wish to use an embroidery stitch. Two squares of fabric may be sewn together and stuffed to make a pillow.

Work hard

Su-pok

A well-known Korean symbol is *su-pok*, made up of two Korean letters. It is used on clothing, furniture, standing screens, and home decorations. The first letter, *su*, means "long life." The second letter, *pok*, means "happiness."

Print the letters for *su-pok* on several cards children can refer to when making designs for calligraphy or embroidery. Indicate the bottom of the cards so that children use them right side up. Explain that items with the su-pok design are given to express best wishes to another person. Children may wish to exchange su-pok cards or make them to give to their parents.

Bells

Large bronze bells, some as much as ten feet high, were made many years ago and are one of the best-known metal crafts in Korea. The sound these bells make is deep and rich. The Emille bell, made in about 900, is the largest example and is seen by many visitors each year. The bells were decorated with lotus flowers, birds, plants, and animals. Temples still use the large bells. Town bells are rung by the mayor on the last day of the year.

Display several kinds of bells. Hold them at the top and ring them one by one. Then ask children to describe and compare the sounds—high or low, loud or soft, clear or muted.

Jade Jewelry

Jade is used to make jewelry and is worn with traditional colthing for special occasions. (See the Creative Art Expression section in the Chinese and Chinese-American unit.) Rings, pendants, pins, and hair ornaments are typical. Jade shaped to look like the claw of a tiger, symbolizing its most powerful weapon, has been found on the crowns of rulers of long ago. Some children may choose to make claw shapes out of clay to put on their crowns in the following activity.

Gold Crowns

Gold crowns decorated with jade and glass beads were worn by the Korean kings years ago. Children delight in making and wearing these beautiful crowns. Inexpensive gold paper crowns are available at party supply stores. Let children decorate them with sequins, glitter, small glass beads, and tiger claws made from clay. Also provide colored telephone cable wire for children to use to create the drops on these crowns that hang over the ears. Children can also cut crowns from tagboard and decorate them with designs cut from colored paper.

Kites (*Yeon*)

Flying kites is a favorite pastime for children and young people. Kites are flown during the first lunar month of the year. On the last day of the month, children draw a flag or picture on a piece of paper and attach it to the kite string; they also may write "Away evil, come good luck" on the paper.

Sometimes boys have contests between two kites by coating the strings with powdered glass. The strings are then crossed in flight, and after a few minutes of pulling and releasing the kites, the string of the better kite flyer will cut through the string of the other kite.

The size of Korean kites is about 15 by 20 inches. Fathers

often make kites for their children, though today they can also be purchased.

Children can make kites, shaped as illustrated, out of heavy paper. Have them draw the Korean flag or their initials on top of the kite and attach a streamer to each of the four corners. A string is then attached to the middle of the bottom of the kite as shown.

Children and the Arts

The purpose of introducing the arts in the schools is to teach children to appreciate and create the arts, to enjoy the beauty of nature, and to use leisure effectively.

Korean children create with colored paper, watercolors, clay, and crayons. In the art program in the schools, they paint outdoor scenes about once a month in the spring and fall. Children make pottery of clay, painting their works after they dry. They can visit one of the factories where pottery is made in Seoul to watch the artists and learn how pottery is made.

On a warm, quiet day, plan to take children outdoors to paint with watercolors as Korean children do. Explain that in the past most Korean paintings depicted scenes from nature. Ask children to find something from nature in the area and paint it.

NATURE AND SCIENCE

Koreans respect their natural environment. Their pride is evident in their use of the wooded mountains, rivers, flowers, and animals in designs and decorations. They try to preserve the path of the rivers, shapes of the mountains, and natural landscape when they construct buildings, bridges, and roads.

ANIMALS (DONG-MOOL)

Oxen (*Soo-soh*)

Oxen are treated with great respect because they help and work for the farmer. In the past, oxen carried heavy loads and pulled carts and plows in the rural areas. Today many farmers also use machines.

In Asian countries, animals that help people are treated very gently. Some Asians do not eat beef because of their respect for the oxen that help them. Share with children that in America in the past, horses were used to help rural people and that today machines have replaced most of the horses. Have pictures and books available for children about the work done by oxen and horses.

For information on the tiger, turtle, and fox, see Language Development.

Pets (*Ae-wan-dong-mool*)

A special breed of dog (*gae*), the chindo (*jindo*), originated in Korea. It is a middle-sized dog. Dogs and cats (*go-yang-i*) are the favorite pets of Korean children. Goldfish and birds are kept in schools.

Discuss pets, especially cats and dogs, with children, describing their appearance, how they should be cared for and treated, and why they are fun to have. Exhibit photographs of pets on the bulletin board.

Older children can write and illustrate a small book about pets to share with the class. To make the book, children take two or more 8-1/2-by-11-inch sheets of white paper and one sheet of colored paper for the cover. They fold the sheets in half and fasten them together. They may write one or two sentences on each page. If younger children want to make a book, they can dictate the story to an adult, who prints it in the book or on another paper for children to copy.

PLANTS

Flowers (*Ggot*)

Korea has numerous flowers, including azaleas, magnolias, lilacs, and cosmos. Lilies, roses, carnations, and chrysanthemums are favorite flowers to give as gifts. Some Korean kindergartens plant flower gardens.

Identify the flowers listed above that bloom in your community. Bring some of them to show the children.

Make a window box for your room, involving the children in the planning and planting as much as possible. If help is needed, invite a horticulturist from the county, or city, to suggest where to put the window box, how to prepare the soil, what to plant, and how to take care of the plants selected.

Older children may choose to write a story or make a poster about the sequence of growth in the flowers. As a group project, make a poster illustrating each step in the process, from planting the seeds to cutting the flowers. Children can keep individual or class diaries, measuring and recording the amount of growth day by day. Some children may wish to record the information on a graph.

National Flower (*Mugunghwa*)

The Rose of Sharon is a symbol of the Republic of South Korea. It blooms in light pink, purple, and white in all parts of the country. The flower's design is on all government medals.

Show pictures of the Rose of Sharon and talk about its importance to Koreans. Also show pictures of your state flower, talking about where and when it blooms. Bring your state flower to show children when it is in bloom.

Pine Tree (*Sona moo*)

Koreans enjoy many kinds of trees, but the most important one is the pine. The mountains are covered with them, and they are mentioned in many songs and poems. The pine is noted for its color, shape, resistance to lightning, and perfume. It also provides food for wild animals and birds.

Bring books with pictures and information about pine trees. Share some facts and guide children in finding out more about them. Older children can find and share information. For younger children, adults can model how information is found in books. During the holiday season, bring a pine branch into the room. If there is a pine tree nearby, take a walking trip to see it.

Willow Tree (*Be-deu-na-muo*)

The willow tree is a symbol of the peace and beauty of women. Because the wood is light and flexible, it is used in making wooden shoes, chests, baskets, and furniture.

Willow trees also grow in many sections of the United States. Show pictures of them in Korean paintings and in America. Go to see willow trees if they grow in your community. Elicit children's responses as they view the tree or pictures. What makes this tree so unique and beautiful?

Bamboo (*Dae-na-moo*)

Bamboo is used to make hats, fans, screens, pens, paper, flutes, and a hundred other useful articles. It grows in all Asian countries. Asians make many useful items of bamboo. See the Nature and Science sections in the other Asian units for more information.

Bamboo grows as a bush in some countries, while in others it becomes a very tall tree. Its growth pattern depends on climatic conditions.

Arrange to bring in a bamboo for discussion. You may want to buy a plant for the room so that children can observe its growth and keep a record of it. Invite a nursery grower to talk to the children about the care of the plant.

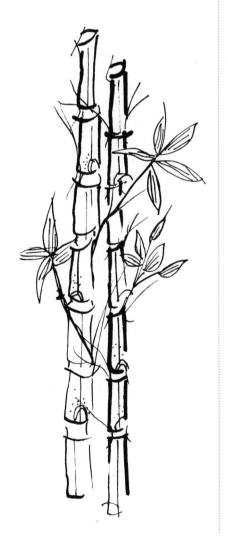

GEOGRAPHY AND ECOLOGY

Peninsula

Korea is a peninsula; it has water on three sides. Because of its shape, it has a coastline where many fish and pearl oysters are found. Fish are also plentiful in the inland lakes and rivers. Locate this peninsula on a globe.

Conservation

Conservation means taking care of the land, water, and other natural resources so that people will always have them for their use.

Korea and many other countries cut so many trees that many hills become bare. Korea has a reforestation program to plant trees on these hills each year. Only a certain number of trees can be cut annually. When new trees are planted, they are cared for, and big trees are protected because more trees cause less soil to erode when it rains or the wind blows. Koreans are developing trees that better resist pests and diseases.

The Han-gang River, which runs through Korea, became polluted as industries increased. A river development project was undertaken to clean up the water, and efforts are being made to eliminate air pollution.

Planting trees and bushes is important to conserve soil. Plant a tree or bush around the center or in the nearest park. Check periodically to see if it is getting sufficient water.

Excursions

Korean children frequently take excursions, such as going to special outdoor places to paint, touring factories, or visiting farms, where they can see animals, vegetable gardens, and other crops.

Plan nature trips to see animals, trees, farms, flowers, or other nature places of interest. Some school districts have special nature centers. Before the trip, discuss the things you hope the children will observe. Have someone along to take photographs of the trip. A class book of these photos, with typed statements or responses by individual children, is of great interest to children all year. Walking nature trips are also valuable learning experiences.

LANGUAGE DEVELOPMENT

Language skills are among the most important that children develop in group settings as they work freely with each other, and learn to listen, talk, write, and read. Learning words from another culture helps children understand that people communicate in many languages.

The literacy rate in Korea is 99.8%. The Korean alphabet has ten vowels and fourteen consonants. Koreans say it is easy to learn and print their alphabet.

Vocabulary

The following words may be used in labeling pictures and objects in the room.

bang suk—cushion
chima—woman's traditional skirt
chogori—woman's traditional jacket
dot-ja-lee—straw mat
ggot—flower
gom—bear
gu-sul—marbles
ho-rang-ee—tiger
in-hyung—doll
jip—house
jup-shi—dishes
jut-ga-lak—chopsticks

kang-a-zi—puppy
kang—river
kimchi—pickled vegetables
mul—water
na-moo—tree
sal—rice
san—mountain
sang—table
sut-ga-lak—spoons

Additional words and terms may be found in the various sections of the unit.

Symbols

Use the Korean alphabet (below, left) along with books, pictures, and posters to introduce children to Korean letters and numbers. Children may copy them or use them as labels.

Korean Words and Phrases

An nung haseyo—Hello.
An nung hee gaseyo—Goodbye.
Gam sa hamnida—Thank you.
Chun maneyo—You're welcome.
Na nundang sin eul sarang hamnida—I love you.
Shille-hamnida—Excuse me.
Ye—Yes.
Anio—No.
Mian-hamnida—I'm sorry.
Towa-juseyo—Please help me.

Korean Vocabulary

abuzi—father 아버지

awmoni—mother 어머니

jakeun—small 작은

keun—big 큰

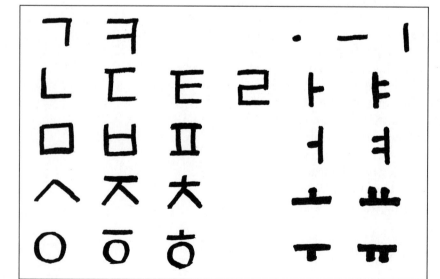

namoo—tree

나무

sonyon—boy

소년

sonyo—girl

소녀

Korean Numbers

hana—one 하나

dul—two 둘

set—three 셋

net—four 넷

dasut—five 다섯

yusut—six 여섯

llgop—seven 일곱

yudul—eight 여덟

ahop—nine 아홉

yul—ten 열

Children's Literature

Few Korean children's stories have been translated into English, and few books have been written about Korean American children. *Soon-Hu in America,* by Schi-Zhin (1977), for kindergarten through second grade, tells the story of a five-year-old girl who learns to appreciate Korean and American cultures.

Stories

The literature of a country expresses its culture. Stories, especially those written by authors who are natives of the country, provide authentic information about the culture. Stories are powerful sources of vocabulary and language development. They also provide many ideas for creative expression.

Story time can take place several times a day, either with individuals or with small groups. A child asks an adult to read a book brought from home or selected from the library or book center in the room. The book is often read to one child or a small group. Sometimes all of children will be interested in hearing the story.

Animals in Stories

In some Korean stories, animals such as the sparrow, toad, hare, and tiger have human characteristics. In others, an evil person turns out to be a fox, an animal that is not well liked.

The tiger is the leading animal in Korea. In the past, many tigers lived in the mountains. The tiger is used in many children's stories, which focus on this animal's positive traits, such as kindness and helpfulness. The tiger is a symbol that protects Korea from the West. Legend has it that the tiger is fun-loving and respected and feared but quiet. After the tiger is 500 years old, it turns white. It is believed to be the bright star in the Milky Way. The tiger is a character in some trickster tales, sometimes playing the trickster, other times the one who is tricked. Sometimes the tiger is a person in disguise, but more often it is an animal.

Many turtles are found in Korea and are important in legends and fairy tales. The turtle represents a healthy way of life because it is never in a hurry and always thinks things through. The turtle is one of ten symbols of long life and is included as a decoration on folding screens with other such symbols. The hexagonal design on the turtle shell has fascinated artists for years. The largest granite sculpture of a turtle, carved long ago, measures 13 feet long and 10 feet wide. Many visitors travel to see it in Chik-chi-sa, Korea.

Symbols in Korean Legends

In ancient days, Korea adopted four mythical symbols to protect its people from evil, one for each direction on the compass:

A blue-green dragon protects from the east and is the most powerful of the four symbols.

A red phoenix protects from the south.

A white tiger protects from the west and is the second most powerful symbol.

A black turtle protects from the north.

These symbols have been used in art and legends for centuries.

Folktales

Exposing children to folktales gives them insight into the thinking of a culture. Folktales reflect the fundamental beliefs of a culture. Young children become familiar with folktales through listening and dramatizing. Korean folktales include the best-loved nursery tales, folk history, and animal heroes such as tigers and foxes.

In the past, storytelling was a folk tradition in Korea. After supper, the family gathered to listen to grandparents and parents tell folktales. Children learned much about the world, life, nature, and what they should and should not do.

Dramatization

After children know and enjoy a story, plan its dramatization with them. Ask questions to help them decide what characters and props they need. Then let children act out the roles, using the dialogue in their own words and with their own interpretation.

Children may dramatize *Korean Cinderella,* from a book edited by Edward B. Adams, or *The Chinese Mirror,* by Mirra Ginsburg.

Sijo Poetry

Poetry has always been a part of Korean life. Koreans write poetry for special occasions. Sijo is a three-line poem, usually unrhymed, with fourteen to sixteen syllables per line. Korean children six and seven years old begin writing sijo poetry. Read sijo poetry to children.

Proverbs

Proverbs reveal the characteristics, customs, feelings, and humor of a culture and share a common spirit of imagination and hope with people in other parts of the world. Every area of human experience is covered by Korean proverbs. Talk with older children about the meaning of the following proverbs:

Five pennies make a nickel. (saving)

Even a sheet of paper is lighter when two people lift it. (cooperation)

When nice words go, nice words come. (kindness)

Too many captains steer a boat up a mountainside. (too many leaders)

A quarrel is to be stopped. (intervention)

Work like a dog, eat like a king. (success)

Stick to one well when you are digging. (perseverance)

Don't start up a tree you cannot climb. (goals)

References for information on Language Development: *Literature for Children about Asians and Asian-Americans,* by E.C. Jenkins and M.C. Austin, pp. 150-151; *Korea's Cultural Roots,* by J.C. Covell, pp. 33, 41, and 46-49; and *Korean Folk Tales,* by Yong Chun Shin (ed.), pp. 9-11.

MUSIC (EUM-AK), DANCE (CHOOM), AND DRAMA (YEON-GEUK)

Some traditional dramatic arts were created for ceremonies, for entertaining rulers, and for holidays. Folk music and dance were created in the villages and in rural areas. Today, traditional as well as Western music, dance, and drama are enjoyed, giving Koreans a great variety of entertainment.

Many Koreans who attend American colleges are able to play some of the instruments described below. Contact the music or International Studies department to locate them. Invite them to demonstrate their instruments at your school. American musicians who play instruments and music from other countries may also be available.

Four traditional instruments still played today are described below.

Zither (*Komungo*)

Many different kinds of zithers were made and used in Korea. A classical orchestra of more than fifty musicians consisted only of zithers and two sets of bells. A small zither was popular in early America and has been revived in recent years. The autoharp, a small stringed instrument similar to a zither, is played to accompany children's singing in many classrooms in America.

To make a zither, obtain a long, flat piece of cardboard, the kind used to hold bolts of fabric, from a fabric shop. Let children paint it with metallic gold tempera paint. String large rubber bands across the board lengthwise. Put a small wedge of folded cardboard across the middle, under the rubber bands, to serve as a bridge to keep them from touching the board. To play, pluck the stretched rubber bands with the fingertips.

Flute (*Tanso*)

The Korean flute is made of bamboo. It has a mellow tone and is used either as a solo instrument or to accompany songs and dances. In some schools in America, children learn to play the recorder, an instrument similar to the bamboo flute in Korea.

Korean instruments may be purchased in school supply and Asian stores. If you have some of these in the room, encourage children to experiment with them. With some guidance, most children will be able to produce sounds, and some children may learn to play a simple melody.

Listen to classical music that features the flute and ask children to identify its sound.

Bells (*P'yonjong*)

Bronze bells are hung in two rows, eight in a row, on a wooden stand and are struck with a

hammer made of horn. All the bells are the same size, but their sounds differ because of differences in the thickness of the metal. Bells on a stand can be found in many school supply stores.

A musical scale can be made with graduated lengths of steel. These can be difficult to locate. One can also be made using quart jars filled with varying amounts of water. Children may experiment in preparing this scale. Or clay pots, gradually increasing in size from tiny to large, may be used. Tie a string to a small washer, pull it through the bottom hole, and tie it to a frame. Use a wooden mallet to tap the pots.

Some children discover how to play simple tunes on the bells. Colors or numbers corresponding to each bell may be used to guide other children in playing familiar melodies.

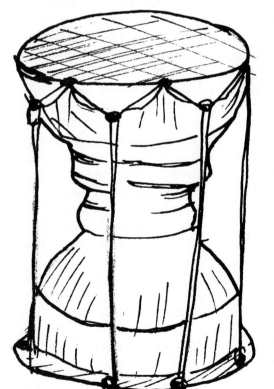

Hourglass-Shaped Drum (*Changgo*)

One of the most popular traditional instruments is the two-headed hourglass drum. It is played either with other instruments or separately to accompany a singer. It also may be carried by dancers. The skin of the left drum is thick and is struck with the palm of the hand; the skin of the right drum is thin and is struck with a stick. Drumming, even on the round drum, is basic to Korean music and dance.

Two types of dance began years ago. One dance was connected with farming, while the other was used in ceremonies and rituals. Koreans enjoy traditional folk dances and modern dance, drama, and ballet today. Korean and Asian music tapes are available in Asian stores and also in some music stores.

Farmer's Dance (*Nong-boo-choom*)

This dance is a celebration of planting, harvesting, and other farm events. It is the most popular of all Korean dances. The performers dress in white and wear brightly colored sashes and headdresses. They play drums and gongs, trumpets, and oboes while they dance. The dance is fast and lively. The dancers have a long white paper streamer attached to the top of their hats, and they twirl it in big loops and figure eights.

Give each child a brightly colored sash, three to six inches wide, or a large colorful scarf to tie around the waist. Sashes can be cut from used fabric. Show children how to make colored hats with high crowns and attach a long white paper streamer of crepe paper. To make the hats, roll a 12-by-18-inch sheet of colored construction paper and staple the 12-inch sides together to form the crown. Cut an oval-shaped brim from another sheet the same size. Cut slits around one end of the stapled roll. Fold tabs up and attach the crown to the brim as illustrated on page 161.

Arrange the children in a line. Play Korean music (or some other fast, lively music), and have several children accompany it with drums and gongs. Let the other children swirl the streamers in big loops and figure eights to the rhythm of the music.

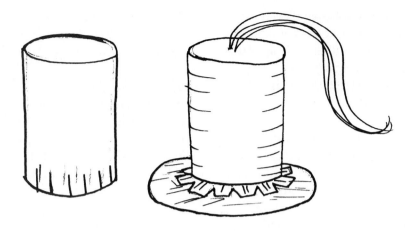

Folk Dance (*Min-sok-moo-yong*)

One folk dance features a woman who wears a red stovepipe hat with a feather and carries two fans. It is a fast, acrobatic, humorous dance. The dance was created to chase away evil, cure disease, or bring good luck.

One person dances at a time. Make a high red stovepipe hat with a brim and a feather on it for the dancer. The hat can be made using the instructions in the previous activity. The dancer carries one or two fans. Children can volunteer to be the dancer. Suggest to them that this is a fast, acrobatic, funny dance. Each dancer creates her own movements.

Circle Dance

This dance is slow at the beginning and very fast at the end. The women dancers sing while circling around, hand in hand. This dance began during the wars. Women danced around a bonfire near the coast to frighten the enemy. Compare the American Indian Round Dance with this Korean dance.

Use Korean or Asian music. If this is not available, use music that suggests dancing in a circle, begins slowly, and gradually goes faster. Have children hold hands and walk or dance around the circle.

Mask Play

The mask play is presented at farm festivals in the villages. The actors wear masks and play and dance to music based on folk songs.

Masks with holes for eyes and mouth and a small one for the nose may be plain white orcolorful papier-mache masks; they may be elaborate or plain, and they may depict animal or human heads. A hat or a cloth wrapped around the head hides the edge of the mask, and costumes that match the theme of the mask may be worn.

One way to make a simple mask is to cut holes in paper plates, then let children decorate the plates to portray a familiar character in a story. Fasten a string on each side of the plate or let children discover their own way to hold the mask on their heads. Have each child wear the mask and give a few clues so that the others can guess the character portrayed.

To make a colorful mask, children cover a blown-up balloon with papier-mache. (Adults should blow up the balloons and tie them securely.) Show children how to tear newspapers into narrow strips and dip the strips into a mixture of white glue and water, covering the balloon with five or six layers of paper strips to make papier-mache. Allow the balloons to dry overnight or longer. When dry, puncture the balloon with a pin and cut the papier-mache ball in half to make two masks. Let children paint the masks with bright colors of tempera paint.

Books describing how to decorate masks can be found in your library.

GAMES AND MANIPULATIVES

Games have been played for many years at festivals and by families. Interest in individual and team sports has increased, due in part to the medals Koreans have won at the Olympics.

Jump the Rubber (*Go-moo-jool-nol-i*)

Koreans use a rubber string, the thickness of a large rubber band, to play this game. Chinese jump ropes purchased in toy stores may be substituted. Whatever is used, it must stretch. Lengths of rubber string are tied together to make a long rope, long enough to allow two or three children to jump over it at a time. While children sing, two children hold the stretched rubber string tight at a low height. Children jump over the string. It is moved a little higher for each round of jumps. A child who misses a jump takes a turn holding one end of the string. Children create many variations of this game.

Yutnori

Yutnori is one of the most popular games played by families and older children on New Year's Day. Four wooden sticks, called yuts, each measuring 1 by 6 inches and having a flat side and a round side, are needed. A yutnori game board, or a 12-to-15-inch square piece of cardboard or wood—marked as illustrated—is used for scoring. In the illustration, a player may take any route with the team's marker as long as it is continuous. Players sit on the floor around a mat and the board. They divide into two teams. Each player throws the four yuts in the air with a yell, letting them fall on the mat. A marker is placed on the board as follows:

1 flat side up and 3 round sides up—1 point.

2 flat sides up and 2 round sides up—2 points.

3 flat sides up and 1 round side up—3 points.

4 flat sides up—4 points.

4 round sides up—5 points.

The winning team is the one who reaches home first.

Any small object can be used as a marker—pebbles, pieces of plastic, small wooden or plastic beads. Cut 3/4-inch-wide strips of molding with a round and a flat side into 6-inch lengths for yuts and sand the two ends. Molding can be purchased at lumber and hardware stores.

Older children can play the game according to the rules; younger children may manipulate the wooden sticks, count the dots, and play the game according to their own rules.

Shuttlecock (*Jei-gi*)

(See the Games section in the Chinese unit.) An old coin with a hole in the middle is sometimes used to hold the feathers. Korean boys play this game.

Hopscotch

This game is a favorite of Korean girls. It is played the same way as hopscotch is played in America.

Marbles (*Gu-sul*)

Marble games are played by boys in Korea. The same rules apply as in America. The goal of the game is to hit someone else's marble.

Jackstones

Jackstones is a pebble game similar to the American game of jacks. Each child takes five small pebbles. Substitute jacks for pebbles for safety. The goal is to throw the jacks in the air and catch them as they fall. In the first round, one jack is thrown; in the next round, two jacks, and so on. A point is scored for each successful catch until a jack is dropped, and then the next child has a turn.

Physical Education in the Schools

Elementary school children learn volleyball and basketball. In the track program, they practice running and jumping. Gymnastics is included in all Korean schools.

Modern playgrounds are equipped with swings, see-saws, slides, ladders for climbing, and horizontal bars for gymnastics.

Martial Arts

Koreans excel in the martial arts. *Tae kwon do* is a self-defense martial art that began 2000 years ago. It began as a protective skill during the wars. Today it is a national sport taught in 100 countries. Primary-age children begin to learn tae kwon do under the supervision of a trained expert.

Classes for training young children in tae kwon do, beginning at about age five, are available in many American communities. Invite a tae kwon do instructor to demonstrate various movements. Ask the instructor to dress in the official tae kwon do suit and explain its significance. Children may be able to imitate a few of the motions under the supervision of the instructor.

Judo emphasizes throwing the other person and is studied throughout Korea. Judo can be learned from judo experts.

Abacus (*Joo-pan*)

Korean children learn how to solve mathematical problems using the abacus. Using the abacus, they can compute answers about as fast as they can using a calculator. Koreans believe that using an abacus helps the development of a child's intelligence. The abacus may be used to add prices and compute change in stores, but clerks are not required to use it. Children attend private institutes for one or two hours a week to learn how to use the abacus. Contests are held each year.

Have an abacus available for children to manipulate. Some children may discover how to use it for mathematical calculations. Try to locate a Korean or other Asian who can demonstrate calculations on the abacus.

SPECIAL EVENTS

Involving parents in some of their children's learning experiences promotes understanding and extends communication.

Parents, Children, and Teachers Together

Thousands of Koreans have settled all over America. Invite a family to a school get-together to share their culture with children. A menu for a meal would include plain rice, bean sprout soup, kimchi, several meat-with-vegetable side dishes, and fruit. (See the Food section in this unit).

Cultural Events

Check your community's cultural calendar for museum exhibits and dance and music programs. Cultural exchanges are increasing and local Koreans may sponsor programs. Arrange a visit to a Korean restaurant where adults and children can talk to the personnel and experience the atmosphere.

Teacher's Day

In the spring in Korea, a day is designated as Teacher's Day. Children give their teachers a corsage of flowers with another gift. They write notes thanking the teacher for their education.

Designate a teacher's day for your classroom or school. A vase with one flower may be placed on the teacher's desk. Children write thank-you notes to the teachers. Older children write and perhaps decorate their notes; younger children may dictate their messages to an adult or older child or scribble and tell the adult what their note says.

CELEBRATIONS

Korean holidays are times for celebrations with the extended family. Holidays include wearing traditional costumes, conducting memorial ceremonies to remember ancestors, eating special foods, and playing traditional games. The three major festivals are New Year's, Tano, and Chusok. Contact the Korean families in your school or Koreans in your community and plan to celebrate some festivals with them. Invite them to talk to the children about their holidays.

New Year's Day—First day of the first lunar month of the lunar year

One of the most important festivals of the year occurs when plum blossoms bloom and snowflakes whirl in the air. The family is dressed in traditional clothes early in the day. The memorial ceremony, held in the home, is a major solemn observance for the year. The younger members of the family show respect to their parents and grandparents by bowing to them and giving them wishes for the new year. They may say, "I hope you live a long and healthy life," or "I hope you have many blessings in the new year." Family members visit neighbors to offer greetings. Children receive money gifts from their elders. Special food at the feast is rice cake soup (*ttokkuk*). The family plays traditional games such as yutnori and see-sawing. Flying kites is a favorite activity during this month.

Arbor Day—April 5

Government officials, teachers, and children throughout Korea plant trees on this day as part of the government's reforestation program. Arbor Day in the U.S. is generally between late April and early May, the specific date determined by each state. Join Koreans in planting trees on Arbor Day.

Children's Day—May 5

On this day, excited and colorfully dressed children enjoy playing in the parks with their parents. Special programs are held in children's centers, recreation centers begun in the 1970s. Children also receive gifts.

Memorial Day—June 6

The nation pays tribute to the soldiers who defended Korea in the wars. Memorial services are held at the National Cemetery in Seoul, as well as in all national cemeteries in the country.

Constitution Day—July 17

The adoption of the constitution of the Republic of Korea in 1948 is commemorated on this date.

Harvest Moon (*Chusok*)—Fifteenth day of the eighth lunar month of the lunar year

Harvest Moon, the Korean Thanksgiving, is a major festival. The feast is cooked with newly harvested grains. Rice cakes, taro soup, and fresh fruits are part of the menu. Families have a memorial ceremony for their ancestors at the family grave site, usually in the mountains. Festivities include visiting relatives and viewing the full moon in the evening. The women perform the traditional Circle Dance, while men perform the Farmer's Dance.

Armed Forces Day—October 1

This day commemorates the armed forces with military parades, honor guards, ceremonies, and other martial activities.

National Foundation Day—October 3

The traditional founding of Korean nations by Tan-gun in 2333 B.C., during the Choson Dynasty, is celebrated.

Korean Alphabet Day—October 9

This is the celebration of the anniversary of the alphabet (*han-gul*) by the Choson Dynasty in 1448. The written alphabet was created by decree of the king.

Christmas Day—December 25

This day is celebrated in a way similar to Christmas in Western countries, especially by middle-aged and younger families. The focus is on the children and creating a day of enjoyment for them.

Full Moon Day—Fifteenth day of the first month of the lunar year

The first full moon of the year is observed on this day.

Firecrackers are lit and traditional games are played, such as tug-of-war. The game juggernaut is played by young men. It represents a fight with torches that occurred years ago between two villages. Today, two huge, connecting, rope-covered frames are built. The two teams try to bump each other off the juggernaut. They believe that the winning village will have a very good crop during the year, or that good luck will visit the winning team all year. A substitute game is a dragon fight, using paper dragons instead of the juggernaut.

Tano—Fifth day of the fifth lunar month of the lunar year—early June

The full moon night is celebrated. New summer food is offered for the ancestors at the family shrine. The family is dressed in new clothes. Men engage in wrestling. Years ago, the winner was given a bull for a prize. Women engage in a swinging competition. The winner receives a gold ring.

Winter Solstice (*Tongji*)—December

The longest night of the year is observed in December. Rice cakes and rice with red beans are served. The traditional purpose of this observance was to rid the home of evil spirits. As a symbol of the past, a ritual of prayers is observed in front of the kitchen at a table on which rice cakes have been placed, and in front of the house.

RESOURCES

N Nursery
K Kindergarten
P Primary
I Intermediate

Books for Children

Adams, Edward B., ed. *Korean Cinderella.* Seoul International Publishing House, 1983.   P
This bilingual book introduces children of the Western world to Korea's cultural past. Children can compare folktales that feature a stepmother, jealous sisters, and a lost slipper.

Adams, Edward B., and Dong Ho Choi. *Blindman's Daughter.* Charles E. Tuttle Company, Inc., 1981.   P
This Korean folktale for children relates a daughter's sacrifice for her father as fulfilling a basic duty children have to their parents. Korean traditions and culture are explored. Phonetic Korean words with the English translation and finely detailed drawings enchance the text.

Ashley, Gwynneth. *A Family in South Korea.* Lerner Publications Company, 1987.   P
Eating dinner in the family room and getting up early to harvest rice or work in the coal mines are part of the life of the Chuns in a village in the Republic of Korea. The full pages of color photographs interest children of all ages and adults too.

Choi, Dong-ho. *Learning About Korea.* Seoul International Publishing House, 1983.   KP
Traditional ways and modern lifestyles are illustrated in this large-format coloring book about Korea.

Gerard, Linda Walvoord. *We Adopted You, Benjamin Koo.* Albert Whitman and Company, 1989.   P
A story about adoption told through the eyes of a nine-year-old, a lovable Korean refugee boy.

Han, Suzanne Crowder. *Let's Color Korea. Traditional Lifestyles.* Hollym Corp., 1989.   KP
The four-stick game, kicking the jaegi, and the fox game are favorite traditional games included in this bilingual edition. Use as a resource, not a coloring book.

Haskins, James. *Count Your Way Through Korea.* Carolrhoda Books, Inc., 1989.   KP
Did you know that Koreans use two different numbering systems? Sino-Korean numbers count minutes and money; Korean numbers count people and things. Through color-filled illustrations, numbers introduce children to many aspects of

Korean culture. One book in a series of eight.

Lye, Keith. *Take a Trip to South Korea*. Franklin Watts, Inc., 1985. KP
An excellent reference to use when describing some Asian meals. American children love dramatizing eating with chopsticks on a low table. Children also gain from knowing that there are other ways to do things.

Moffett, Eileen F. *Korean Ways*. Seoul International Publishing House, 1987. KP
Traditional and modern cultural experiences of Korean families are explored in this colorful edition. It is a helpful book for all libraries serving children and also for adults who seek to enrich their awareness about Korean culture.

Mueller, Mark. *Let's Color Korea. Traditional Games*. Hollym Corp., 1989. KP
Use this beautiful book as a delightful resource for learning about games children play in Korea. Many of the games are familiar to American children; some will be new; all are to be enjoyed. This is a quality publication with excellent art and design.

Rhie, Schi-Zhin. *Soon-Hee in America*. Hollym, 1977. KP
A five-year-old girl learns to appreciate her Korean and American backgrounds. The illustrations are black and white photographs.

Seros, Kathleen (adap.). *Sun and Moon: Fairy Tales From Korea*. Hollym, 1982. PI

A collection of Korean fairy tales for young children with large boldly colored illustrations.

Locate new books for children about the Korean culture from the book review section in the following publications:
Children's Books in Print
Horn Book Magazine
School Library Journal
Young Children

Resources for Adults
Books and Periodicals
Adams, Edward B. *Art Treasures of Seoul*. Samheva Printing, 1980.
Photographs in full color reveal traditional and modern national treasures.

Asian Culture Center for UNESCO. *Folk Tales From Asia For Children Everywhere, Book Four*. Weatherhill, 1976. I
A fourth volume of Asian folk tales; includes Korean literature. Useful for understanding Korean folk tales and telling and reading them to children.

Baron, Virginia (adap.) Trans. by S.P. Chung. *Sunset in a Spider Web*. Holt, Rinehart, and Winston, 1974. I
Collection of sijo poetry, portraying the Koreans' love of nature.

Facts About Korea 1988. Korean Overseas Information Center (230 North Michigan Ave., Suite 1500, Chicago 60601), 1988.
Current information about Korea: its land, people, history, culture, society, traditions and modern achievements.

Five Thousand Years of Korean Art. Asian Art Museum of San Francisco, 1979.
Black and white and color photographs of the exhibition of Korean art which toured the United States for two years beginning May, 1979.

Hurh, Won Mov, and Kwang Chung Kim. *Korean Immigrants in America*. Associated University Presses, Inc., 440 Forsgate Dr., Cranbury, NJ 08512
A scholarly book that includes an historical overview of Korean immigration. Others books in this series cover dance, music, and painting.

Lee, Chong-Sik. *Korea, Land of the Morning Calm*. Universe, 1988. A Korean author and New Zealand illustrator team up to present an attactive and sensitive volume. Much more than a coffee table book, this text, with its large, beautifully printed pages and photographic genius, beckons the interested student.

McHugh, Elizabeth. *Raising a Mother Isn't Easy*. Greenwillow Books, 1983. Grades 4-6
The first of three books by this author about the adoption of two Korean orphan girls. A warm positive picture of a bicultural family.

Popham, Peter. *Korea*. Hunter Publishing Co, 1987.
More than a guide book, this informative text has a wealth of photographs of costumes, traditional houses, and a meal in a bowl.

Seoul. HEK COMMUNICATIONS, 1-12 Hoehyon-dong 3-ga, Chung-ku, Seoul, Korea.

This monthly periodical is written in English to increase understanding of Korea and to let others experience the culture and customs of the country. Articles cover many topics and include large, colorful photos.

Shin-Yong, Chun, ed. *Korean Folk Tales.* International Cultural Foundation, 979.
One is able to understand a culture in a deeper sense by reading its folk tales. This book is one in a series about Korean culture.

Winchester, Simon. *Korea, A Walk Through the Land of Miracles.* Prentice-Hall, 1988.
The author presents a survey of Korea's lifestyle and culture that helps others have a more sympathetic understanding of this beautiful land.

Yoo, Yushin. *Korea the Beautiful: Treasures of the Hermit Kingdom.* The Golden Pond Press, 1987.
Art, calligraphy, music, dance, food, and homes are only a small part of this splendid book, which is embellished with large color photographs.

Filmstrips
The Republic of Korea: Geography; Resources and Industry; Customs and Culture; Korea Today. Distributed by the Society for Visual Education, Inc., 1988. 60 min. Four filmstrip/cassette sets with guide.
Recommended for use at seventh-grade level, these filmstrips could also serve as a review or overview. They provide an excellent way to gain an understanding of the diversity in Korean lifestyles.

Program 1: Korea—Geography. This typical presentation of the geographical features of the Republic of Korea makes this filmstrip a necessity when learning about the regions and their resources in order to determine what to present to children. The vivid photographs of the rice fields, rocky inlets, sheer cliffs, Taebalk Mountains, Yellow Sea, drying peppers, and the Korean people make this an excellent resource. Background music sets the perfect mood for viewing.
Program 2: Korea—Resources and Industry. This overview of major industries and natural resources enlightens teachers about Korea's resources. Farming methods, such as mini-plows, are fascinating to children, as are the heavier, four-legged variety. You could present the sections of the filmstrip that show firs, oaks, maples, citrus, and bamboo trees, and scenes of the fishing industry.
Program 3: Korea—Customs and Culture. Learning about customs is important for preparing a plan for children. This filmstrip explains religions and philosophies to help you discern what is appropriate for children. Discussion about the emphasis on *kongbu haera* (study) helps children understand why many Korean Americans are very successful in school. Learning the traditional and contemporary ways is especially important when evaluating stereotypes.
Program 4: Korea Today. This filmstrip enables you to determine similarities and differences between urban and rural life.

Manipulatives
Language Lotto—Korean.
Claudia's Caravan.
Lotto set with cards and cassette tape teaches basic vocabulary.

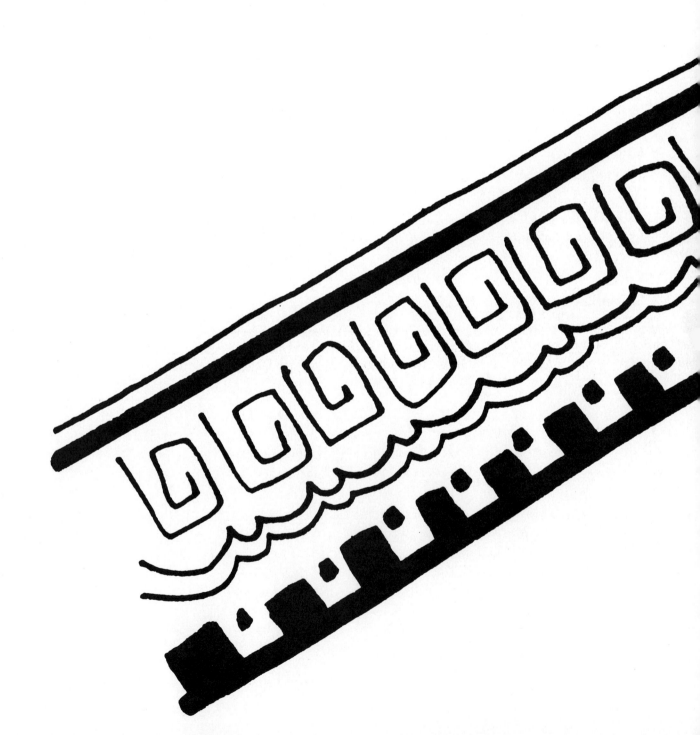

MEXICAN AND MEXICAN-AMERICAN CULTURES

Mexican Americans were among the first cultures to settle in the Southwestern United States. They brought with them customs and traditions from the varied cultures in the six main regions of Mexico. At the same time, they adapted Mexican customs and traditions to this environment and began some new customs of their own. Today, some Mexican-American families have lived in the United States for several generations. Some see themselves as mestizos, descendants of Spanish and Indian people; some are of Spanish ancestry; most see themselves as Americans. Become acquainted with Mexican Americans and people from other Hispanic cultures in your community. Learn about the traditions and customs these families observe and practice. Children see, hear, and taste the influences of Mexico every day as they experience Mexican music and dance, foods, games, colorful artifacts, crafts, and special events.

Becoming aware of the Mexican and Mexican-American cultures exposes children to the rich heritage of Mexico and fosters an appreciation for the vivid quality and variety of the Mexican and Mexican-American lifestyles.

People in the U.S. population who are of Hispanic descent include Mexicans, Puerto Ricans (who have dual citizenship—U.S. and Puerto Rico), Cubans, Dominicans, and Central and South Americans. Each of the groups comes to the United States with varied cultural patterns. The authors' study for this book includes only a part of the Hispanic family—the Mexican and Mexican-American cultures.

The authors are grateful to Josefina Concha, El Paso, Texas, for her expertise in translating English into Spanish in this unit. She worked with her daughter, Dr. Elva Allie, to clarify and make suggestions. Dr. Allie received her doctorate from the University of North Texas in Early Childhood Education. She is the chairperson of the Child Development Program at Tarrant County Junior College in Fort Worth, Texas.

FAMILY LIVING

HOMES

Homes in Mexico are interesting and varied, from elegant, sprawling haciendas to compact functional adobe houses. Today, many Mexicans live in modern housing that often has been remodeled to reflect a blending of the traditional and the modern.

Traditional homes are constructed of adobe bricks and have several rooms built around a central patio. Plastered walls and thatched or tile roofs are a trademark of rural homes.

CLOTHING

Today, many Mexican Americans and Mexicans wear clothes similar to the styles worn in North America and Europe. In the various regions of Mexico, traditional clothing is worn for work and play, for dances or fiestas, or for religious occasions. Provide examples of traditional clothing for children, available at Mexican import shops or borrowed from Mexican-American parents or friends in the community who have traveled in Mexico.

DRAMATIC PLAY

Children especially enjoy wearing the following articles of clothing:

chaleco—vest made from woven fabric that is like a blanket
falda—long full colorful skirt worn by some women, such as the Tehuanas in the state of Oaxaca, Mexico
guayabera—men's dressy cotton shirt
huaraches—leather sandals
huipil—long or short tunic dress, shift, or blouse that is decorated with colorful embroidery
mantilla—a large lace head scarf worn by some Mexican women
pantalones—trousers for men
rebozo—colorful shawl worn by some Mexican women to cover their heads or for carrying a baby or supplies
sarape—a blanket used for a wrap in cold weather

The following items are useful for dramatic play:
bandera mexicana—red, green, and white Mexican flag
canastas de paja—straw baskets
castañuelas (castanets), *maracas*—rhythm instruments

jarrones y floreros—flower vases
joyas mexicanas—Mexican jewelry
marionetas—traditional string puppets
metate—stone (with a concave surface) used for grinding corn, other vegetables, and seeds
molinillo—wooden beater used for breaking up and stirring chocolate bars used to make hot chocolate
muñecas—dolls
piñatas—papier-mache containers shaped and decorated like animals or other characters or shapes and filled with candy and small gifts
pottery—pots and clay figures
prensa de tortillas—tortilla press
sillas pequeñas—small chairs

sombreros—hats; try to find the type made of straw and also those worn by the *charro* (Mexican cowboy). These are large-brimmed, velvet hats decorated with silver sequins and trim.
straw dolls and animals

Families Celebrate—Fiesta

Different communities celebrate various fiestas or holidays, both Mexican and American. Find out which holidays are celebrated by Mexican Americans in your community. The way holidays are celebrated in the United States by Mexican Americans is similar in many ways to the way Mexicans celebrate. The celebrations may include wearing special folk clothing, playing games, dancing, breaking piñatas, and eating traditional foods. Mexican Americans in each community may make some changes, adding some activities and omitting others. Many other ethnic groups join the Mexican families in their love of and participation in the celebrations, which are enjoyed in many areas of this country. "Cinco de mayo" (Fifth of May) and "El día de independencia" (Mexican Independence Day—September 16) are two popular celebrations.

Books describing these celebrations are *Fiesta: Cinco de mayo*, by June Behrens, (also available in a filmstrip), *The Mexican Americans*, by Julie Catalano, and *The Toy Trumpet*, by Ann Grifalconi.

FOOD

The foods of Mexico and ways of cooking them vary in different regions of the United States. Meat, corn, chilis, tomatoes, beans *(frijoles)*, and tortillas are basic to the Mexican diet.

(Safety Note: Be sure to obtain parental permission before allowing children to eat anything, in case of allergies or diet restrictions.)

Print recipe directions on a poster board in both English and Spanish to introduce children to the idea that words can be read and directions followed.

Memela
1 corn tortilla

2 T refried beans

1 t chili sauce

Shredded cheese

Put 2 tablespoons refried beans in center of heated corn tortilla. Add 1 teaspoon of chili sauce. Sprinkle with shredded cheese. Roll up. Makes one serving. Enjoy!

Beans
1 pound dried pinto beans
water
Add 2 quarts of water,
a piece of salt pork, and
salt to taste
Cook beans until tender, about 2 1/2 hrs.
Serve with tortillas.

Frijoles
1 libra de frijol pinto
agua
Se agregan 2 cuartos de agua, un pedazo pequeño de puerco salado, y sal al gusto

*Se cuecen los frijoles
hasta que se ablanden, approxi-
madamente 2 y 1/2 horas.
Se sirven con tortillas.*

Bread *(Tortillas)*

Tortillas are the basic bread of Mexico. They are round and thin and are made of corn flour or wheat flour. *Masa harina,* a fine corn flour, is sold in many grocery stores. Children can make tortillas with the tortilla press or they can shape them with their hands. Here is a corn tortilla recipe:

Mix 2 cups of masa harina with 1 cup of water. Make small balls and press them flat until they are thin and round. To cook, heat a large ungreased skillet or griddle. Drop tortillas one at a time onto the skillet. Brown on one side, then turn and brown on the other. Serve with butter or beans. (See previous recipe for Beans.)

Chili *(Carne con chile)*

4 lbs ground beef
2 t chopped garlic
2 T shortening
4 t ground *cominos* (cumin)
1/2 C chili powder
4 T flour
2 T salt
2 t pepper
6 C water

Lightly brown ground beef and garlic in hot fat, stirring with fork to crumble beef. Cover and cook on low heat for 15 minutes. Combine ground cominos, chili powder, flour, salt, and pepper; add to cooked meat and stir well. Add water and cook over low heat for 1 hour. Serves 12.

Enchiladas

48 tortillas
4 T shortening
4 lbs. natural cheddar cheese, grated
6 onions, chopped
3 10-oz. cans enchilada sauce

Dip tortillas in heated oil. Place 1 T cheese and 1 t onion in the center of each tortilla. Roll tortilla and place in large baking dish, seam side down. Cover with sauce. Top with cheese and onions. Bake at 350° for 15-20 minutes or until cheese melts. Serves 24.

Tacos

This recipe comes from a Mexican-American grandmother who makes tacos with the children at the Learning Tree.

1 lb ground meat
1 pkg. taco seasoning mix
taco shells
grated cheese, chopped lettuce, diced tomatoes

Brown the ground meat in a frying pan. Mix 1 package taco seasoning mix with the cooked meat and cook as package directs. Fill taco shells with the meat mixture—about 2 T per shell. Prepared taco shells can be purchased or tortillas can be made from scratch, cooked, and folded in half while they are being fried. Top the meat with grated cheese, chopped lettuce, and diced tomatoes.

***Pan Dulce*—a sweet bread for supper**

1 box hot roll mix
For glaze:
2 C powdered sugar
3 T milk
1 t vanilla

Prepare the hot roll mix according to the package directions. Knead the dough and then give each child enough for one roll. Each child kneads the dough and forms a ball. Bake rolls as directed on package. Prepare a glaze by mixing the powdered sugar, milk, and vanilla. Spread on rolls when they are removed from the oven, then cool to set. Pan dulce may also be purchased at some grocery stores and at Mexican bakeries.

Mexican Hot Chocolate

While making hot chocolate, children will enjoy learning the following chant that has been passed from generation to generation in Mexico. As they stir their hot chocolate, they will love using a *molinillo,* or a little mill—a wooden beater that is twirled between the palms to break up the Mexican chocolate.

Rima de chocolate

Uno, dos, tres, cho-
Uno, dos, tres, co-
Uno, dos, tres, la-
Uno, dos, tres, te.
Cho-co-la-te, cho-co-la-te
Bate, bate el chocolate.

Chocolate Rhyme

One, two, three, cho-
One, two, three, co-
One, two, three, la-
One, two, three, te.
Cho-co-la-te, cho-co-la-te
Beat, beat the chocolate.

Mexican hot chocolate and cookies may be served to celebrate Independence Day on September 16. The cookies are called *galletas* and are available

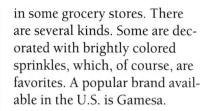

in some grocery stores. There are several kinds. Some are decorated with brightly colored sprinkles, which, of course, are favorites. A popular brand available in the U.S. is Gamesa.

Mexican Hot Chocolate

Mix these in a cup:
1 t cocoa
3 t sugar
1/3 cup powdered milk
1/2 t cinnamon
Fill cup with hot water and stir. Top with 1 T whipped cream.

Chocolate caliente mexicano

Mezcle en una taza:
1 cucharadita de cacao
3 cucharaditas de azúcar
1/3 taza de leche en polvo
1/2 cucharadita de canela
Llene la taza de agua caliente y mezcle bien. Ponga encima una cucharada de crema batida.

Note: Bars of chocolate for making Mexican hot chocolate are available in many grocery stores.

Lemonade (*Limonada*)

Another favorite beverage is lemonade. Provide lemon squeezers, plastic knives, lemons, sugar, and water. Children cut 8 lemons in half, squeeze, and then add 1 gallon of water. Stir in 2 cups of sugar. Children like mixing the ingredients, pouring the lemonade into cups, and serving it. If you think more will be needed, have a can of frozen lemonade handy!

CREATIVE ART EXPRESSION

Creativity means beginning with ideas generated by children. The role of the adult is to foster creativity by asking questions, supervising the projects, and providing reinforcement. Provide many choices of materials.

CLOTHING

One of the first things a young child wants to do when exploring a culture is to try on traditional clothing. Have clothing available for children to examine, or let them make their own by adding a creative touch to an existing garment or using a pattern and starting from scratch. Involve the children in determining what tools are needed, selecting materials, and deciding where to cut.

Sarape
(Blanket or Heavy Shawl)

Sarapes are light-weight blankets, worn like shawls over the shoulders. They are brightly colored, sometimes fringed, and were once worn with the charro or horseman's costume. Children make sarapes using a 12-by-36-inch piece of colored burlap. With large-eyed plastic needles, they create their own designs on the burlap with multicolored yarn.

You may also use the valance part of brightly colored cafe curtains to make sarapes for small children.

Poncho

A *poncho* is worn by a man, a woman, or child. It is a blanket with a slit in the middle for the head. Provide an 18-by-36-inch piece of fabric. Fold it in half

diagonally, and cut a slit in the middle that is large enough to go over a child's head. Children can fringe the bottom of the poncho by cutting vertical slits all the way around the edge. Let them use fabric crayons and marking pens to create designs on the poncho. Display a poncho with designs for ideas.

Rebozo (Shawl)

A rebozo is a fringed, woven shawl worn by a Mexican woman. It may be plain or brightly colored. Provide 36-inch triangles of fabric for children to make rebozos, which they can decorate with marking pens and fabric crayons. Display a rebozo or pictures for children to examine.

Skirt and Blouse —Poblana Style

This distinctive dress for women is usually worn for the *Jarabe Tapatío*, the Mexican Hat Dance. The two-piece poblana costume is a red and green full skirt decorated with beads and sequins, worn with a white blouse that has been embroidered with bright silk threads or glass beads in flowered designs.

Children can make the poblana skirt from red and green crepe paper, a material they can easily manage. Teachers or parents sew the gathered skirts, and children decorate

them with colored glue and glitter designs. Older children can manage sequins, the authentic material for designs.

Sashes

Wide, colorful, handwoven sashes are worn by Mexican women and men. Let children draw animals, plants, and other designs with fabric crayons on a 3-by-36-inch piece of unbleached cotton fabric or old sheet. Adults iron over the drawings and then children tie this sash around their waists or heads.

DECORATIVE ART

Jewelry

Mexico is known for its beautiful handcrafted silver jewelry. A display of pieces and pictures of jewelry will help the children appreciate the artistry and skill of the Mexican craftspeople. Mexican silver rings, pins, necklaces, and bracelets should be available for children to wear and examine.

Necklaces and Bracelets

Children can make imitations of silver jewelry in several ways. They can string balls of foil and metal disks on yarn or colored pipe cleaners to make necklaces and bracelets, punching holes in the caps and the disks with a hammer and nail. Or they may make rings and bracelets out of strips of foil or silver ribbons.

Clay Beads

Semi-precious stones and other natural materials are used by Mexicans to make pieces of jewelry. The stones are polished and strung to make beads. A recipe for clay beads follows:

Soda-Cornstarch Clay
1 C cornstarch
2 C baking soda
1 1/4 C cold water

Mix the cornstarch and baking soda together. Add the water and cook and stir over medium heat about 4 minutes; consistency will be that of mashed potatoes. Cover with a damp cloth and cool. Knead like a yeast dough. Several drops of food coloring may be added to make different colors of beads. Children also enjoy adding colored glitter for special effects when they mix the clay. Let children form marble-sized balls from the clay and suggest ways to punch holes in the center of each ball. Bake for 1 hour at 200°. Children spend a great deal of time checking on the drying beads. Discuss and examine beads removed too soon. This is all part of the creative process. If an oven is not available, clay beads will dry in the sun in about 24 hours. String the dried beads on colored pipe cleaners to make bracelets and necklaces. Connect several pipe cleaners for longer necklaces.

Passport to Mexico, by Carmen Inizarry, *A Family in Mexico,* by Tom Moran, and *We Live in Mexico,* by Carlos Somonte are helpful resources when searching for the proper way to make and wear folk clothing and modern dress.

Fiesta Decorations

Some religious and patriotic fiestas have regional themes and ties and so are celebrated only in certain parts of Mexico; others are observed throughout the country and in many parts of the United States. Children decorate the classroom for a celebration such as Cinco de mayo or Las Posadas by making tissue paper flowers, hanging a piñata, and displaying the flags they have made.
(See Holidays and Celebrations.)

Cascarones

One of the spring traditions of Mexico is the breaking of *cascarones*. The literal translation of this word is "eggshells." A cascarón is an empty eggshell that has been painted and filled with colorful confetti. The hole is sealed by gluing tissue paper over it.

Europeans brought this tradition of the cascarones to Mexico many, many years ago; Mexicans and Mexican Americans have kept it alive. The colors of the confetti inside the eggs represent the colors of the spring. In freeing the confetti, the children release the seasonal colors, much as spring releases us from the bleakness of winter.

To make cascarones, a small piece from the end of the shells of raw eggs must be carefully removed and the contents gently shaken out. The shells should then be washed out and left to dry. Let children decorate them with marking pens, glitter, or watercolors, and then fill them with confetti. Parents hide the cascarones. As the children find them, they crack the shells over the heads of their friends to release the confetti. Don't worry—it doesn't hurt!

Yarn Painting

In the region of Nayarit, beautiful pictures are made from brillantly colored woolen yarn, which is used to create the pictures on boards covered with sticky beeswax. The yarn is pressed into the wax in a design.

Provide heavy cardboard, white glue, and an assortment of lengths of brightly-colored yarn, and let children experiment with making yarn pictures, a unique art form of Mexico.

Bark Painting

A rough textured paper is made from the bark of the Amate tree in the state of Puebla in Mexico. The paper is made by boiling the bark and then pounding it with stones, much like papyrus was made in Egypt.

Clothes were first made from this material, but now it is used for painting colorful pictures. Fluorescent shades of paint are used to paint birds, flowers, and animals.

Display bark paintings and pictures of them in books for children to examine. Children can use heavy brown butcher paper or grocery bags and fluorescent tempera paints to imitate these beautiful bark paintings. They begin by cutting the paper into rectangles and crumpling it to soften it. Then they paint the paper with brown tempera. After the brown paint is dry, children can paint designs of flowers, birds, butterflies, and animals on the "Amate" paper using fluorescent tempera paint.

An excellent resource for the art of Mexico is *The Popular Arts of Mexico* by Kojin Toneyama.

Mantelitos (Place Mats)

Mexicans typically use tablecloths, but place mats are used by some families in Mexico as they are in this country.

Children delight in drawing pictures or designs on a paper towel or on a plain paper place mat, available at grocery stores. Use water-base marking pens to make the design. Drip or sprinkle water on the drawings. Watch the colors bleed and run together.

Place mats can also be made by weaving strips of paper of different colors, and widths.

The woven paper mats look like the Mexican mats. Cut slits across the length of a piece of construction paper, one or two inches apart. Cut narrow and wide colored strips for weaving. Show children how to weave the strips over and under through the slits in the large piece of paper. Staple the ends of the strips to hold them in place.

Canastas (Baskets)

Baskets are an artistic contribution from many Mexican cultures. Mexicans weave beautiful designs into their baskets. Baskets are used in everyday life— for carrying food, clothing, and other things. The baskets are important to Mexicans because of their utilitarian and aesthetic qualities.

To make baskets, children can wrap strong twine or heavy string around a bottle, can, or jar until it is covered. An adult then sprays or paints with varnish or liquid plastic to give a finish that looks like wicker. Older children can also make baskets by coiling heavy twine into a bowl or basket shape, gluing each coiled row to the next and then letting the basket dry.

Mosaics

Display books with pictures of the mosaic art of Mexico.

Show the bold and brilliant style of Mexican artists such as Alfaro Sequeiros, Diego Rivera, and Rufino Tamayo. Borrow works of Mexican artists from friends or families in your school to share with the children. Local museums and libraries may loan pictures. Talk about these works with children, asking questions about colors, shapes, and designs to spark interest.

To make mosaics, children use small pieces of different colors and shapes of construction paper, gluing the pieces close together on a sheet of brightly colored construction paper to form a design.

A different effect can be achieved by painting over the whole mosaic with a solution of one half water and one half white glue. Place a sheet of colored or white tissue paper on top of the glue before it dries.

Mexican-American artists specializing in mosaics include Michael López, Luis Jiménez, Antonio García, Eduardo Carrillo, Mel Casas, and Chelo González Amerzcua.

Murals

Mural painting has been revived by modern Mexican artists, including Diego Rivera, David Sequeiros, and José Orozco. Many murals can be found in Los Angeles and other U.S. cities, in addition to the numerous ones on buildings in Mexico.

Provide pictures, posters, and illustrated stories of the plants and animals of Mexico. Study the landscape. Children delight in drawing and painting anteaters, giant spiders, parrots, flamingos, and snakes in mural format. Older children can examine the information and then paint Popocatepetl, "The Smoking Mountain." Don't be surprised when younger children want to take "their part" of a mural home! *The Mexican Americans* by Julie Catalano is an excellent reference.

Tissue Paper Flowers

Paper flowers from Mexico can be purchased in import shops, but children can also make them. Invite children to analyze a paper flower to see how it is made. Discuss the process with children and encourage their suggestions. One excellent way to make a flower is to cut four 6-by-10-inch pieces of brightly colored tissue paper into rectangles or circles. Lay the four pieces on top of each other. Gather tissue paper together in the center for a bow-tie effect. Wrap a colored pipe cleaner around the center. Then pull each layer apart to make the flower. These paper flowers may be used to decorate the room or adorn the girls' hair.

Piñatas

Piñatas are used on Halloween, for birthdays, and during other festive occasions, such as Las Posadas. The piñata is a decorated container, often in the shape of an animal, that is filled with candies and toys. Traditionally, piñatas were made of clay; piñatas of papier mache, which can be purchased at import shops and variety stores in the U.S., are now often substituted. The piñata is decorated with crepe paper to make colorful Mexican designs.

Making piñatas is fun for young children. They can stuff a large grocery sack with crum-pled newspaper and then paint the sack with bright colors of tempera paint. When the paint is dry, let children decorate the bag by taping crepe paper streamers of assorted colors and lengths around the sides and on the bottom. Have goodies available for filling the piñatas. Place a wire coat hanger inside the top of the bag so that only the hook is sticking out of the top. Fold the top of the bag over the hanger and staple securely across the top. Bend the hook and tie a strong string through it. Children take this home and have a piñata party with friends and family. A stick for hitting the piñata can be decorated with crepe paper streamers. An interesting reference describing the piñata is *Hello, Amigos* by Tricia Brown.

The piñata is the center of a popular activity at children's birthday parties in the United States. (See Games and Manipulatives)

Flags

The Mexican flag, with its symbol of an eagle with a snake in its mouth, fascinates children. Display a Mexican flag along with pictures of the flag. Talk about the colors, the symbol, and the folklore concerning the flag. Most children are eager to make them.

To make flags, use fabric or strong white paper such as butcher paper. Children can make flags any size they desire. Let them use marking pens or crayons to draw and color the symbols. Attach flags to paper sticks. To make sticks, children can roll newspaper into cylinders and tape them. Encourage children to use their creativity in figuring out how to fasten the stick to the flag.

LANGUAGE DEVELOPMENT

Spanish is the official language of nineteen countries. Approximately 12 million persons in the United States are Spanish-speaking, and nearly 700 Spanish words are accepted as standard English terms, giving the Spanish-language experience a greater dimension.

For young children, sharing the language of a Spanish-speaking friend promotes a feeling of kinship and encourages understanding of the multilingual nature of our world. Building self-esteem in both the English-speaking and bilingual child is another important benefit. Children gain command of another's language if the bilingual experience is continued.

For the young child, a primary goal is to become aware that others speak a different language—that there are other ways to talk. Children may learn just a few words, or they may have enough exposure to begin to converse in Spanish.

Some concerns for educators searching for language models are in the area of recruitment. Employ Spanish-speaking persons as classroom teachers so that they can provide role and language models for the children. College students with Hispanic background could be invited to become involved as aides and resource people.

Be informed about the closeness of the Hispanic family, and invite grandparents to the classroom to teach a song, help with a cooking experience, read a book, or tell a story. Be aware of the tendency to stereotype Mexican cultures. Books, pictures, songs, and advertisements often present an image of a person or group that does not allow for individuality. Discourage the use of slang terms. Invite Mexican American parents, grandparents, and others from the community who are bilingual to talk with children about how they use two languages. Posters, pictures, and books in Spanish and English enhance the environment and foster language and literacy.

Vocabulary

adobe (ah-DOH-bay)—clay brick
amiga (ah-MEE-gah)—friend (female)
amigo (ah-MEE-goh)—friend (male)
atole (ah-TOH-lay)—a mush made of cornmeal
cabeza (kah-BAY-sah)—head
casa (KAH-sah)—house
corazon (coh-rah-SOHN)—heart
familia (fah-MEEL-yah)—family
fiesta (fee-ESS-tah)—party
frijoles (free-HOHL-ace)—beans
grande (GRAHN-day)—large
huaraches (wah-RAH-chase)—woven sandals
libro (LEE-broh)—book
mantilla (mahn-TEE-yah)—head scarf, often of lace
masa (MAH-sah)—corn flour
niña (NEEN-yah)—girl
niño (NEEN-yoh)—boy
rebozo (ray-BOH-soh)—shawl
sarape (sah-RAH-pay)—blanket worn over clothing
sombrero (sohm-BREH-roh)—hat
tortillas (tor-TEE-yahs)—flat pan bread made of corn or flour
zapatos (sah-PAH-tohs)—shoes

Additional words and terms may be found in the various sections of the unit.

Colors

amarillo (ah-mah-REE-yoh)—yellow
azul (ah-SOOL)—blue
blanco (BLAHN-koh)—white
negro (NAY-groh)—black
rojo (ROH-hoh)—red
verde (BEHR-day)—green

Words and Phrases

sí (see)—yes
muchas gracias (MOO-chahs GRAH-see-ahs)—thank you
buenos días (BWAY-nohs DEE-ahs)—good morning
adiós (ah-dee-OHS)—good-bye
hola (OH-lah)—hello
¿Cómo está usted? ((COH-moh ehss-TAH oo-STEHD?)—How are you?
Me gusta (may GOOS-tah)—I like
Quiero (KEE-EH roh)—I want
Me llamo (may YAH-moh)—My name is ("I call myself")
¿Qué? (kay?)—What?
¿Por qué? (pohr-KAY?)—Why?
¿Dónde está? (DOHN-day ehs-TAH?)—Where is it/he/she?

Labeling

Label objects in the room in Spanish and English.

la mesa (lah MAY-sah)—the table
la puerta (lah PWEHR-tah)—the door
la silla (lah SEE-yah)—the chair
la ventana (lah vehn-TAH-nah)—the window
los libros (lohs LEE-brohs)—the books

Make word cards with both English and Spanish words on each card. Select words that children use often. The child may copy the word from the word card or have an adult print it.

If a child draws a picture of a family in a house, it could be labeled in both Spanish and English.

Numbers

uno (OOH-noh)—one
dos (DOHSS)—two
tres (TRACE)—three
cuatro (KWAH-troh)—four
cinco (SEEN-koh)—five
seis (SACE)—six
siete (see-EH-tay)—seven
ocho (OH-choh)—eight
nueve (NWAY-bay)—nine
diez (DEE-ACE)—ten

Names

Discourage the use of nicknames in place of Spanish names unless a child expresses a desire to use a name other than his or her given name. Have classmates learn to pronounce names correctly, being tutored by the parents of the child if necessary.

Dramatization

Most of the time children can find props they need for their roles in dramatizing stories. Some children need help from adults to find props that satisfy them. Provide a variety of items to accommodate the spontaneous needs of the children.

A Chair for My Mother by Vera Williams is available in both Spanish and English. Children like to dramatize this story over and over again. Sequels to this book are *Something Special for Me* and *Music, Music for Everyone*.

Another favorite is *The Toy Trumpet* by Ann Grifalconi, and "The Three Bears" is also popular. Children dramatize as a bilingual teacher tells the story in Spanish. Adults are amazed at how easily non-Spanish-speaking children are able to follow the story as it is told in Spanish.

Language Games

Mexican bingo games (*lotería*) can be purchased in Mexico or in some Mexican import shops and also from educational supply companies. You can make the game, using a picture lotto or bingo game, and labeling the pictures with Spanish and English words.

Adapt favorite children's games such as "Duck, Duck, Goose," using other animal names to broaden vocabulary. For example, instead of a duck and goose, use a mouse and cat ("*ratón, ratón, gato*") or elephant and tiger ("*elefante, elefante, tigre*"). Other games to adapt are "Hokey Pokey," using the Spanish names for body parts, and "Colored Eggs," using the Spanish color names.

Stories

Experience with the Mexican cultures gives children many ideas for creating their own stories. A child may dictate a story to an adult, who prints it on paper while the child watches. Some children need encouragement, while others will ask for assistance. Children take pride in seeing their own ideas on paper. Many children also like to draw illustrations for their stories. Compile the stories into a class book to be enjoyed over and over.

NATURE AND SCIENCE

Exploring the natural resources of Mexico interests children. Many birds and insects found in the United States migrate to the tropical forests of Mexico for the winter.

The monarch butterfly stops in the west and southwest on its journey from Canada to Mexico. The second week of October can be a time to celebrate this migration. Books, pictures, and other reference materials can be put to good use as questions about the butterfly are posed. This event sparks the creativity of many children for writing stories and poetry and creating paintings.

In the spring, bags of live ladybugs may be purchased from nurseries and released by the children. Through books, children discover that these beetles spend their winter vacation in Mexico.

Mexico is a land of many topographies and climates—deserts, mountains, and tropical forests. It is also the home of many animals that fascinate children. Coyotes, rattlesnakes, and lizards live in the Mexican deserts. The mountains provide a habitat for bears and mountain lions. Alligators, anteaters, jaguars, and ocelots live in the forests.

Two books that add to a nature study of Mexico, are *We Live in Mexico* by Carlos Somote and *Focus on Mexico* by Louis Casagrande.

PLANTS

Limes, papayas, mangoes, oranges, avocados, sugar cane, melons, tomatoes, squash, and beans are some of the plants native to Mexico. Children may not be familiar with some of them. Bring them into the classroom and let the children use their senses to explore the foods. Sensory learning adds to the interest. Discuss the names of the foods and describe how they grow.

Tropical fruits are often a new experience for children. Bring a papaya to school and have children cut, examine, and eat it. Talk about how the papaya grows. Show children the interesting seeds of the papaya and compare them to the seeds of other, more familiar fruits.

Avocado

Another interesting fruit is the avocado. Peel a ripe avocado, cut it into sections, sprinkle the sections with lime juice, and invite the children to eat them.

A guacamole dip or salad dressing can be made from mashed avocado.

1 avocado
Lemon or lime juice
1 tomato, chopped
Salt to taste
Tortilla chips and/or raw vegetables

Cut the avocado in half and remove the seed. Scoop the avocado meat from the shell. Mash the avocado meat and add the lemon or lime juice, the chopped tomato, and salt to taste. Mix well. Return the seed to the guacamole mixture to prevent discoloration. Serve as a dip with crisp tortilla chips or use it as a salad dressing over raw vegetables.

Plant the avocado seed. Place it in a small jar of water; stick toothpicks into the side of the seed to hold it so that only the bottom part of the seed is in the water. Watch the roots and avocado leaves grow!

Gum Tree (*Arbol Gomífero*)

Sapodilla trees grow in the forests of Mexico. These trees contain chicle, which is used to make chewing gum.

Sugar cane (*Caña de Azúcar*)

Buy sugar cane at a produce market when it is in season. Children can peel off the outer skin and chew the sugar cane. Talk about how sugar and syrup are made from sugar cane.

Jumping Beans (*Frijoles Saltadores*)

The Mexican jumping bean received its name from the way it jumps from side to side. Its movement is caused by the full-grown larva of the moth that lives inside the bean. These beans have value only as a novelty. They are known in Mexico as "leapers."

Break open one or two beans to see the worm inside. Children enjoy playing with the jumping beans, which can occasionally, be purchased at variety stores. Use the book *Jumping Bean,* by Edna Miller, and an encyclopedia to find out more information about jumping beans.

Cacti (*Nopales*)

Display several different kinds of cacti, along with books that describe different types and their uses.

The fruit and leaves of the prickly pear cactus are boiled, fried, or stewed, and then eaten. The water stored in the maguey cactus is used by some Mexicans as a drink.

Grow a cactus in your room. Observe the small amount of water it takes to keep the cactus alive. Talk about the places in America where cacti grow.

In the Southwest, candied cactus is available and provides a special treat for children. Prickly pear is available in some grocery stores in the produce section, and it can be made into jam.

CLAY (ARCILLA)

Mexico is noted for terracotta—baked clay. It is used to make dishes and pots. Bring examples of authentic Mexican pottery into the classroom for children to examine. Buy Mexican red clay from an art supply store to make pots and other dishes. Children decorate the moist clay with a sharp object, making flower and animal designs on their creations. Clay can also

be dug from a creek bed. For a description of how to prepare clay from a creek bed, see the Creative Art Expression section in the American Indian unit.

Adobe Houses or Mexican Pyramids

A wonderful clay for building adobe houses or the pyramids of the Zapotecan Indian civilization is sand clay. It can also be used for making animals. Sand clay can be made in advance or in the classroom in an electric skillet:

Sand Clay
1 C cornstarch
2 C sifted dry sand
1 1/2 C cold water

Stir together the cornstarch and and the sifted dry sand in an old electric skillet. Add 1 1/2 C cold water all at once and stir until smooth. Stirring constantly, cook over medium heat until the mixture is very thick and holds its shape—5-10 minutes. Turn the clay onto a plate and cover with a damp cloth; cool. When it is cool enough to handle, knead thoroughly until pliable.

This recipe makes about 2 1/2 pounds of clay; two batches make enough for about 15 children. If you are not using the clay immediately, cool it completely and store it in a tightly covered container. Use within several days. Knead before using.

Older children can locate information about Popocatepetl, the "Smoking Mountain." They can then construct and paint the volcano from sand clay.

MUSIC AND DANCE (MUSICA Y BAILE)

The music of Mexico has a distinctive sound and tempo. A strolling guitarist, a mariachi band, the rhythms of castanets, maracas, and claves sticks are all a part of this lively sound. After listening to Mexican music, children are soon able to identify the distinct sounds and rhythms. Provide authentic instruments for children to use.

The folk songs and dances of Mexico vary by region. The country's national dance, the "Jarabe Tapatío," originated in Jalisco. Folk songs (*canciones folklóricas*) are an important part of fiestas and fairs.

Children enjoy listening to

music from these tapes and records:

El Mariachi, Vol. 1, Silvestre Vargas

A Journey around the World, Time Records

Cha Cha Cha—Merengue and Mambos, Pupi López and Orchestra, Design Records

A Taste of Education, Eddie Cano

An important reference for music is *Arroz con Leche: Popular Songs and Rhymes from Latin America* by Lulu Delacre and *Canciones de Compañeros* by Ruth Schoenbach.

Famous Mexican-American musicians include Joan Baez, Jose Feliciano, and Herb Alpert.

Mariachi

Today *mariachi* bands, groups of strolling musicians, are part of the festivities at national holidays and other special occasions. Let children choose instruments for a mariachi band and play for a group of friends. Popular instruments typically included in such a band are trumpets, marimbas, violins, guitars, and maracas.

Guitar (*Guitarra*)

The guitar is a popular instrument in Mexico. Make a guitar by nailing a wooden cigar box or a foil pan to one end of a 3-by-24-inch board. Hammer the same number of nails on each end of the board. String rubber bands across the length of the guitar, fastening them to the nails. Children can strum on the guitar, accompanied by recorded music. Include recordings by Spanish classical guitarist Andrés Segovia.

Castanets (*Castañuelas*)

In Mexico castanets are used in pairs, one set for each hand. They are clicked together to add lively rhythmic accompaniment to dancing. Most young children can manage only one hand at a time!

Children can make castanets to wear while they dance "La Raspa." Let children use a hammer and nail to make a hole in the center of metal lids from frozen juice cans. Then show them how to stick a pipe cleaner through the hole in the lid and through a pea-sized wooden or plastic bead, then back through the hole. They twist the ends of the pipe cleaner together and make a loop for holding the castanets onto the fingers, then repeat the process with the other lid. Children wear one castanet on the thumb and the other on the index finger. Play the music and listen to the sound of castanets!

hands high. Then everyone turns and dances the other way, forming a big circle again and bending low. Repeat three times.

La Raspa (Danced to "La Raspa" music)

Slide your foot this way,
One two, and three.
And now the other foot,
One, two, and three. (Repeat)
To the right, to the right
To the right, to the right
To the left, to the left
To the left, to the left.

Resbale así su pie,
Uno, dos, y tres.
Y ahora el otro pie,
Uno, dos, y tres.
A la derecha, a la derecha
A la derecha, a la derecha
A la izquierda, a la izquierda
A la izquierda, a la izquierda.

See the Resources section for a description of recordings of popular and familiar children's song that are in Spanish or are bilingual.

Children enjoy doing traditional dances as a group or individually. The steps and movements are simple.

Mexican Hat Dance

The "Jarabe Tapatío" is the national dance of Mexico. Invite children to form a large circle, and show them how to put the heel of one foot forward and then the other, following the rhythm of the music. First everyone dances to the right in a circle. When the music changes, everyone turns and dances to the left. The heel step is repeated to the rhythm of the music. Next everyone joins hands and dances to the center of the circle, raising joined

GAMES AND MANIPULATIVES

Soccer (*fútbol*), baseball (*béisbol*), and handball (*jai alai*) are popular sports in Mexico, as well as in the United States.

Tag (known by many different names in Spanish-speaking countries), hopscotch (*bebeleche*), handball, and soccer can be adapted for younger children.

Other games for outdoors or a circle time are suggested in *Nuevo Amanecer: An Early Childhood Resource Program,* by Gloria Rodríguez Zamora and Rebecca Barrera. "Old Aunt Claire," a traditional game, is played like the popular "Colored Eggs." Other games described in this book are a Spanish version of "London Bridge" and "La Piñata." *Games, Games, Games: Juegos, juegos, juegos,* by Ruben Sandoval, is a book about the play and games of Mexican children.

La Piñata

The piñata is hung up high so that it hangs above the children's heads. One child at a time is blindfolded and takes a turn trying to break the piñata with a stick. Older children can be turned around a few times before trying to hit the piñata; younger children may not want to be blindfolded. When the piñata is broken, all the children scramble to grab the goodies.

This game can be adapted for young children. Give them a choice about being blindfolded. Then give each child three chances to strike the piñata. Count in Spanish, "Uno, dos tres." Keep other children behind a barrier, well away from the stick. When the piñata is finally broken, children are allowed to scramble for the

goodies. Extras are saved and put aside for the less aggressive children. Be aware that papier mache piñatas are very difficult to break in damp, rainy weather. A strong adult arm is usually needed after everyone has had a turn.

Bingo

Use a color bingo game and call the colors in Spanish. (See the Language Development section for the names of colors in Spanish.) Mexican bingo and lotto games are found in specialty stores.

Lotto

Play picture lotto and number games using Spanish and English vocabulary. (See the Language Development section for numbers in Spanish.) "Lingo" is a UNICEF game, played like bingo, that teaches the names of foods from around the world in English, French, and Spanish.

Puzzles

Playskool "Wood Board Matchups" are wooden matching puzzles using Spanish words. They include "People and Their Jobs," "Animals and Their Homes," and "Foods and Colors."

SPECIAL EVENTS

Interest Trips
• Tortilla factory
• Mexican bakery and market
• Mexican restaurant
• Mexican import shop
• Trip to a farmer's market or grocery store to buy avocados, papayas, pineapples, and sugar cane
• Local cultural exhibits, Mexican-American programs, and fiestas in your community

Parents' Visit

Invite Mexican-American parents and grandparents to visit and help children make tortillas, tacos, frijoles, and guacamole. (See Food.) They may also be willing to share crafts and customs from their culture.

Mexican Dinner

A dinner for the school's children and their families is a social and cultural experience. The food is prepared by the teachers, parents, and friends. Decorations from Mexican cultures are planned, created, and arranged by the children. Teachers and parents plan the Mexican menu, which might include enchiladas, tacos, frijoles refritos (refried beans), rice, guacamole, and pan dulce. Let children suggest their favorites.

CELEBRATIONS

Some holidays celebrated in Mexico are observed by Mexican Americans in the U.S. Look for announcements in the newspaper of Mexican-American holidays celebrated in your community. Take children to these celebrations, or invite some of the parents or leaders of these celebrations to talk to children about the meaning of the holidays. The following holidays are celebrated in some areas:

El cinco de mayo (The Fifth of May)—May 5, 1862

This is remembered as the day Mexican soldiers were victorious over the French army in the Battle of Puebla.

El día de independencia (Mexican Independence Day)—September 16

This is a celebration of independence from Spain, which was won in 1821. On September 15, the mayor of every town in

Mexico reads the Declaration of Independence. On the 16th, people celebrate with parades, patriotic speeches, and evening fireworks.

El día de la raza (Day of the Race)—October 12

This fall holiday is observed by Spanish-speaking people all over the world, especially in Latin America, as a day to remember their common heritage in language and traditions.

Las posadas (The Inns)— Christmas season

From December 16th through the 24th, groups of Mexican Americans dramatize the story of Mary and Joseph's traveling from inn to inn to find a place to sleep. Activities during this season include special songs, piñatas, games, and refreshments. Christmas is celebrated differently among Mexicans and Mexican Americans in different parts of the country, but one celebration that seems to be the most common is "Las posadas." *Nine Days to Christmas* by Marie Ets and Aurora Labastida, describes this pilgrimage.

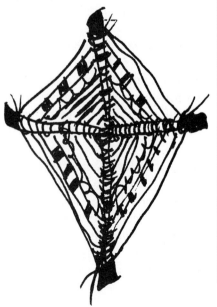

RESOURCES

N Nursery
K Kindergarten
P Primary

Books for Children

Aardema, Verna. Pedro and the Padre: A Tale from Jalisco, Mexico. Dial Books for Young Readers, 1991. KP
Young children think it's fun to read about a boy who is sometimes in trouble with adults. Pedro's imaginative ways and wit add a cheerful note to this tale about learning responsibility.

Alexander, Frances. *Mother Goose on the Rio Grande.* National Textbook Company, 1977. NKP
This authentic bilingual volume includes nursery and nonsense rhymes, riddles, and games. Unfortunately, some illustrations are stereotypical.

Alvarado, Manuel. *Mexican Food and Drink.* Bookwright Press, 1988. P
Favorite foods of Mexico are explored. The production, preparation, and enjoyment of various specialties are presented in detailed pictures using appropriate vocabulary. P

Behrens, June. *Fiesta! Cinco de mayo.* Children's Press. 1978. KP
An excellent description of one way to celebrate, with colorful photographs to document this annual event.

Bishop, Dorothy Sword. *Había una vez.* National Textbook Company, 1985. NK
Contains simple versions of three well-known tales, "The Little Red Hen," "Goldilocks and the Three Bears," and "The Boy and the Donkey." Illustrated with simple, colorful line drawings.

Brown, Tricia. *Hello, Amigos!* Henry Holt & Company, 1986. P
It's Frankie Valdez's birthday, and for this Mexican-American boy that means a day with friends and family wishing him "Feliz cumpleaños," wearing a corona at school, watching Mother mash the avocados with her molcajete, eating frijoles refritos, singing songs with

Father's mariachi friend, and at long last, breaking the piñata.

Casagrande, Louis B., and Sylvia A. Johnson. *Focus on Mexico.* Lerner Publishing Company, 1986. P
This book describes the ancient land of Mexico as a modern developing nation. Introducing four young Mexicans who face new opportunities, it makes the point that most Mexicans today do not live as Indians but are proud of their country's Indian heritage.

Chlad, Dorothy. *Safety Town Series.* Children's Press, 1980. P
Several of the Safety Town books are available in Spanish, including *Cuando cruzo la calle (When I Cross the Street), Cuando hay un incendio...sal para afuera (When There's a Fire...Go Outside), Es divertido andar en bicicleta (It's Fun to Go Bicycling),* and *Los venenos to hacen dano (Poisons Hurt You).* Large print and drawings are identical to English editions.

Coronado, Rosa. *Cooking the Mexican Way.* Lerner Publications Company, 1982. P
Authentic Mexican specialties are vividly illustrated and clearly written to encourage children to explore this ethnic cooking experience. A full day's menu is included, written in both English and Spanish, with pronunciation guides.

Delacre, Lele. *Arroz con leche: Popular Songs and Rhymes from Latin America.* Scholastic, Inc., 1989. KP

Children's songs, games, and rhymes are collected in this volume of traditional Hispanic verse.

Eastman, P.D. *Are You My Mother? ¿Eres tú mi mamá?* Beginner Books Division of Random House, 1960. NK
The bilingual version of this most popular children's "beginner books" story is widely available. It provides lots of repetitive Spanish practice.

Ets, Mary Hall and Aurora Labastida. *Nine Days to Christmas.* Viking Press, 1956. KP
An explanation of "Las posadas" is beautifully told in this enduring book.

Fife, Dale H. *Rosa's Special Garden.* Albert Whitman Company, 1985. NK
Young children identify with Rosa as she feels left out of things. Even though her family believes she is too little to have a garden, she proves that the best garden of all may differ from what others plan for you.

Griego, Margot C., et al. *Tortillitas para mamá.* Holt, Rinehart, and Winston, 1981. NKP
The oral tradition of Latin American cultures has preserved songs of childhood for Spanish-speaking children. Bright paintings by Barbara Cooney present a pictorial essay of Hispanic family life, accompanied by bilingual text. To dispel the false image created by some of the stereotypical illustrations, discuss long-ago folk clothing and traditions with the children.

Hall, Barbara J. *Mexico...in Pictures.* Lerner Publications Company, 1987. P
Photographs, maps and clear illustrations invite children to conduct informal research about Mexico, its land, and its people.

Haskins, Jim. *Count Your Way Through Mexico.* Carolrhoda Books, Inc., 1988. KP
Through numbers, a part of Mexican culture is introduced to children.

Hill, Eric. *Spot Series in Spanish.* G.P. Putnam's Sons, 1980 and later.
Several of these popular "pop-up" books are available in Spanish hardcover.

Inizarry, Carmen. *Passport to Mexico.* Franklin Watts, Inc., 1987. KP
This is an excellent resource for young children as they learn about Mexico through colorful photographs and descriptive drawings.

Jacobsen, Karen. *Así es mi mundo: México.* Children's Press, 1982. P
This large print book, completely in Spanish, familiarizes children with the land of Mexico, its homes, food, clothing, and diverse ethnic groups.

James, Betsy. *The Dream Stair.* Harper & Row Publishers, Inc., 1990. NK
Children enjoy the improbable bedtime adventures, the imaginative descriptions, and the detailed illustrations in this book. Glimpses of cultural artifacts add an important dimension.

Jernigan, Gisela. *One Green Mesquite Tree*. Harbinger, 1988. NK
The desert Southwest is a stage for counting wildlife.

Lewis, Richard. *All of You Was Singing*. Atheneum, 1991. KP
Illustrated in brilliant design and color, this Mexican myth describes how the sky sends the wind to steal music away from the sun.

McNaught, Harry. *500 palabras nuevas para tí/500 Words to Grow On*. Random House, Inc., 1982. KP
This is a good, well-illustrated children's thematic dictionary.

Manley, Deborah. *Es divertido descubrir gentes y lugares* and *Es divertido descubrir cosas*. Plaza & Janés, S.A., 1983, 1981. P
These colorful books each have short sections on many different themes. Labeled pictures and brief text in each section make them particularly appropriate and interesting to early elementary-age children.

Miller, Edna. *The Jumping Bean*. Prentice Hall, 1979. NK
Beautiful illustrations trace the life cycle of a jumping bean.

Moran, Tom. *A Family in Mexico*. Lerner Publications Company, 1987. P
The full-page photographs in bright colors, and the text for older children reveal a modern society with a richness of traditions.

Rohmer, Harriet, and Mary Anchondo. *How We Came to the Fifth World*. Children's Book Press, 1988. P

Bold, bright colors illustrate this lively story about wishes fulfilled. The text is written in English and Spanish and provides a clever way to present a myth recounting creation and destruction.

Rohmer, Harriet, and Jesús Guerrero Rea. *The Treasure of Guatavita/El tesoro de Guatavita*. Children's Book Press, 1978. P
One in a series of bilingual myths and legends from the different Spanish-speaking cultures. "The real story of treasure in the Columbian highlands."

Rolans, Donna. *Grandfather's Stories from Mexico*. Educational Activities, Inc., 1986. KP
In this volume from a series of ten stories for young children, many cultural traditions are told to grandchildren by their grandfather. American children are introduced to customs of their ethnically diverse playmates.

Scarry, Richard. *Mi primer gran libro para reír*. Western Publishing Company, Inc./Spanish edition published by Editorial Brugera, S.A., 1981. NKP
Spanish edition of Best Word Book Ever, with the usual delightful Scarry illustrations. Most of the other Richard Scarry books are available in Spanish.

Seuss, Dr. *The Cat in the Hat Beginner Dictionary in Spanish*. Random House, 1966. KP
This excellent reference book can be found in almost any bookstore that carries Spanish materials for children, even though the copyright date is old.

Somonte, Carlos. *We Live in Mexico*. The Bookwright Press, 1985. P
A wonderful way to present the diversity of Mexico, using color photographs and individual stories about children and adults from all areas in this southern part of the North American continent.

Stanek, Muriel. *I Speak English for My Mom*. Albert Whitman and Company, 1989. NK
The desire for a better job inspires Mrs. Gomez to learn English, to the delight of Lupe, her daughter and translator.

Tompert, Ann. *The Silver Whistle*. MacMillan Publishing Company, 1988. KP
Children learn about a holiday festival in Mexico. The watercolor and pen-and-ink illustrations add another dimension of pleasure for the reader.

Watson, Carol, and Dolores Bereijo. *Round the World in Spanish*. Hayes Books, 1980. KP
This colorful book is a good way for children to review topical vocabulary. There is an extensive pronunciation guide at the end.

Williams, Vera B. *Music, Music for Everyone*. Greenwillow Books, 1984. NK
More adventures for Rosa's family as she and her friends organize a four-friends band. Delightful illustrations are found throughout this clever series!

_____. *Something Special for Me*. Greenwillow Books, 1983. NK

This sequel to *A Chair for My Mother* finds Rosa's family still squeezing into the chair together and making plans for a money jar adventure. The long search for the perfect birthday present ends with something special for the reader.

Children will also enjoy these books. Look for them in your library.
  Baylor, Byrd. *Amigo.*
  Grifalconi, Ann. *The Toy Trumpet.*
  Vavra, Robert. *Pizarro.*
  Weissman, Anne. *Castle of Chuckurumbel.*

Resources for Adults

Books and Articles
Allie, Elva. *Childrearing Attitudes of Mexican-American Mothers: Effects of Education of Mother.* Denton, Texas. University of North Texas, 1986, Doctoral Dissertation. Order No. DA8705114.
An important finding in this study was that Mexican-American mothers with eleven years or more of education have more positive childrearing attitudes than mothers with ten or fewer years. Includes an extensive review of related literature.

Catalano, Julie. *The Mexican Americans.* Chelsea House Publishers, 1988.
This useful book of facts about culture and history for adults as well as older children is an excellent reference when compiling a list of famous people, popular celebrations, and historical facts.

Clay and Weaving: A Child's Experience/La experiencia de un niño con la cerámica y los tejidos. National Dissemination and Assessment Center for Bilingual Education, 1980.
The artistic techniques that began years ago and have remained a tradition are presented. A history is included, along with bilingual text.

Dale, Doris Cruger. *Bilingual Books in Spanish and English for Children.* Libraries Unlimited, Inc., 1985.
A compilation of bilingual books in Spanish and English for children from 1940-1982.

Duran, Helen. *Blonde Chicana Bride's Mexican Cookbook.* Filter Press, 1981.
Here's that authentic recipe, prepared in a traditional way with a contemporary twist—"whirl it in a blender"—for the quick atole. Traditional atole is also described. Sopapillas, little tacos, corn tortillas, are simple recipes that children can make. In 1983, this author added "Mexican Recipe Shortcuts." This quick and easy cookbook includes favorites such as pizza and tacos.

Hall, Suzanne, and Carleen Peck. *Integral Education: A Response to the Hispanic Presence.* National Catholic Educational Association, 1987.
Based on a desire that their children be given the best possible education, Hispanic parents and educators shared their views at a series of national hearings. Published information from these hearings about family patterns, language, racial compositions, and celebrations educates non-Hispanics about areas that are critical to understanding.

Linse, Barbara. *Mexican Heritage Through Arts and Crafts: Art of the Folk for Boys and Girls.* Distributed by Arts' Books, 1980. KP
An authentic guide for making crafts from all parts of Mexico, including a guide for cooking in the classroom and a good resource bibliography.

Perl, Lila, and Alma Flor Ada. *Piñatas and Paper Flowers/Piñatas y flores de papel: Holidays of the Americas in English and Spanish.* (Bilingual) Clarion Books, Houghton Mifflin Company, 1983. P
A terrific resource, especially for non-Hispanic educators and parents who want to help children celebrate U.S. and Hispanic holidays "a la española."

Sandoval, Ruben, and David Strick. *Games, Games, Games—Juegos, juegos, juegos.* Doubleday and Company, Inc., 1977.
Informative text and lively photographs explore the special world of Chicano children at play in the barrios, with many suggestions for formal and informal games.

Wymar, Lubomyr, and Lou Buttlar. *Ethnic Film and Filmstrip Guide for Libraries and Media Centers: A Selected Filmography.* Libraries Unlimited, Inc., 1980.
This reference to audiovisual ethnic sources assists media specialists, librarians, teachers, and educators "who are responsible for the development of well-balanced ethnic collections and curricula at their institutions and library media centers."

Film, Filmstrips, and Videos

Cinco de mayo. Produced and distributed by Society for Visual Education, Inc., 1987. Photographs and colorful illustrations dramatize this event in history and its celebration through "festivity, parades, good food, and relaxing with family" scenes. An activity for intermediate junior high school or adult students is included with permission to copy. Very useful on May 5, a historic date in Mexico and in the United States, in developing an awareness of history, traditions, and social values of the Mexican people.

Mexico: The Land and The People, Third edition. Encyclopedia Britannica Educational Corporation, 1986.
Informative videotape covers all the geographical aspects of this country—mountains, deserts, plateaus, volcanoes, rain forests, and beaches—in addition to modern shopping centers and skyscrapers. A guide suggests questions for discussion after viewing.

Williams, Vera B. *A Chair for My Mother.* Distributed by Educational Record Center, Inc. NP Another way to enjoy this heartwarming story about a loving family.

Your Child's Language and Culture. Produced and distributed by High Scope Educational Research Foundation, 1979. A Describes the basic tenets of an environment that fosters language development.

Materials and Experiences

Baby Dolls. Child Craft, No. 172718.
Hispanic baby doll with layette set.

Dolls—Hispanic Boy and Hispanic Girl. Claudia's Caravan, NOS. 21C & 20G.
Thirteen-inch washable dolls that are durable enough for the classroom.

Ethnic Dolls. Child Craft, Nos. 182766 & 182790.
Hispanic boy and girl dolls.

Hispanic Family. Preschool Source, No. 596-01493
Hispanic family set with five figures.

Multi-Ethnic Dolls. Child Craft, Nos. 152686 & 152769.
Hispanic boy doll and Hispanic girl doll are sixteen inches tall, with moveable heads and arms. A perfect way to introduce cultures and build healthy self-concepts.

Hand in Hand. Constructive Playthings, No. SEL3536L.
Thirty-six wooden tiles with multicultural pictures are the source of several games for young children.

Language Lotto—Spanish. Claudia's Caravan, No. 5E3.
The vocabulary for this game is recorded on a cassette tape, which is helpful for learning pronunciation.

Lotería Mexicana. Claudia's Caravan, No. 17D
This lotto game has been adapted to include Mexican crafts.

Spanish/English Vocabulary Matching Cards. Educational Teaching Aids.
English/Spanish alphabet set with colorful, puzzle-like pictures.

Spanish Flash Cards. Claudia's Caravan, No. 2E2.
Colored pictures with corresponding English and Spanish words spelled phonetically.

Rhythm Band Instruments. Oscar Schmidt International, 230 Lexington Dr., Buffalo Grove, IL 60089.
Instrument sets include bongos, drums, castanets, bells, flutes, and numerous others.

Hispanic Personalities. Claudia's Caravan, No. 17E3.
Fourteen full-color posters, 11-1/2 by 16 in., with information and a guide.

Spanish America. Educational Teaching Aids, No. 2985A-99.
Spanish influence is depicted in twenty prints.

Twentieth Century Spanish Americans. Distributed by Cole.
Twenty informative 11-by-16-inch brightly colored photographs with information describing each personality.

Records and Audiocassettes

Cabrera, Dogomar. *Arco iris de colores (Rainbow of Colors).* Melody House Publishing Company, 819 N.W. 92nd, Oklahoma City, OK 73114. No. MH-82.
This children's musician, originally from Uruguay, sings six "teaching songs" for kindergarten through early elementary-age children. One side of the album is in Spanish, and the other is in English; lyrics in both languages are included.

Cano, Eddy. *A Taste of Education, Vol. I & II,* and *Canasta Musical.* Educational Activities, Inc., 1975 and later.   KP
The bilingual Taste tapes/records help children practice thematic vocabulary to a Latin beat. Canasta has lively songs for children who are native speakers of Spanish and for advanced students.

Cruz, Ben. *Songs of Spanish America.* Bowmar Records, Inc., 4563 Colorado Blvd., Los Angeles, CA 90039, 1970.
This two-album set, in addition to its many good songs for children ages six and up, has a complete recording of Posadas music. Bilingual lyrics for all songs are included.

Glazer, Tom. *Children's Songs from Latin America.* CMS 659. CMS Records, Inc., 14 Warren Street, New York, NY 10007, 1973.
Traditional children's songs from across Latin America are sung in Spanish and in English.

Jenkins, Ella. *Little Johnny Brown.* Folkways Records. "Mexican-Hand Clapping Chant" and "La Raspa" are two songs included on this album that appeal to children.

_____.*You'll Sing a Song.* Folkways Records. This album includes "Dulce, Dulce," a Spanish song meaning "Sweet, Sweet."

Mi casa es su casa (My House Is Your House)—A Bilingual Journey Through Latin America. Performed by Michele Valeri. Rossinyol Records, 1980. Available through Caedmon.

On this lively audiocassette, Spanish is mixed in with the English songs as the performer "travels" through Latin America, introducing some geography along the way.

El Niño Bilingue/The Bilingual Child. Distributed by Kimbo Educational, LP record 7213. Animals, trains, food, time concepts, and other topics are explored. These Kimbo albums are bilingual, with Spanish on one side and English on the other.

El Niño Canta/The Singing Child. Distributed by Kimbo Educational, LP record 7211. Favorite songs about families, homes, and friends.

El Niño Creador/The Creative Child. Distributed by Kimbo Educational, LP record 7212. Songs about the five senses, toys, and other topics.

El Niño Sabio/The Knowing Child. Distributed by Kimbo Educational, LP record 7214. Spanish/English recording introducing the alphabet, numbers to ten, months of the year, and musical instruments.

Palmer, Hap. *Aprendizaje de conocimientos básicos através de la música, vol. I.;* adapted by Lourdes Serrano. Educational Activities, Inc.
The Spanish version of "Learning Basic Skills Through Music" featuring favorites such as "Colors," "The Numbers March," and "What Are You Wearing?"

_____.*Holiday Songs and Rhythms.* Educational Activities, Inc., Freeport, NY 11520, 1969.

"Cinco de mayo" is a favorite on this record of holiday songs.

Paz, Elena. *Songs in Spanish for Children.* Columbia Special Products, a service of Columbia Records, 1962 No. 91A 02029.
This lively album will help increase awareness of Spanish sounds and pronunciation among children in the early elementary grades.

Raffi. *One Light, One Sun.* Shoreline Records, 6043 Yonge St., Willowdale, Ontario, Canada M2M 3W3.
Includes "Tingalayo," a Mexican song about a donkey, and "De Colores," one about the colors of spring.

Rollings, Laurie M. *Mother Goose Rhymes: Vers D'Enfant, Versos Infantiles.* Matterplay. 1986.   NKP
Familiar Mother Goose rhymes in English and Spanish. The set includes two fifty-minute audiocassettes, one English-Spanish and one English-French, plus a sixty-four page book of twenty-six familiar rhymes.

Songs of Mexico (Sing Children Sing series). Performed by the "Niños cantores de la ciudad de méxico." Caedmon, 1980. (Produced by arrangement with the U.S. Committee for UNICEF.)
This wonderfully lively and joyful Mexican children's choir, accompanied by typical Mexican instruments, performs many of the traditional Mexican children's songs, including "Sandunga," "El florón," "La adelita," "La bamba," "Doña blanca," and "Las mañanitas."

Teach Me Spanish (1985) and *Teach Me More Spanish* (1989) with Mary Cronan and Judy Mahoney. Distributed by Teach-Me-Tapes, P.O. Box 35544, Minneapolis, MN 55435.
These songs in English and Spanish are all-time favorites such as "The More We Get Together," "Are You Sleeping?" "Hush, Little Baby," and many others that are popular with children.

Catalogs and Publishers

Fiesta Book Company, 6360 N. E. 4th Court, Miami, FL 33138-9937, (305) 751-1181.
Most selections are for adults, but they carry the "Barrio sésamo" (Sesame Street) comic-book style magazines.

Hispanic Books Distributor Catalog, Hispanic Books Distributor, Inc., 1665 W. Grant Rd., Tucson, AZ 85745.
Lists Spanish-language books for children and young adults. Selections are evaluated according to subject matter, literacy quality, and format. Sections include materials for preschoolers, beginning readers, better readers, and middle readers, as well as resource books. Subscribe to Hispanic Books Bulletin.

The Kiosk, 19223 DeHavilland Dr., Saratoga, CA 95070. (408) 996-0667.
This company markets games, posters, diplomas, stickers, bookmarks, puzzles, coloring books, and stationery in several languages. Write for a catalog.

Mariuccia Iaconi Book Imports, 1110 Mariposa, San Francisco, CA 94107. (415) 285-7393.
Spanish-language records and books for children, including a learning-to-read "big book" series.

Santillana Publishing Company, Inc., 901 W. Walnut St., Compton, CA 90220. (800) 245-8584. A tremendous resource for the teacher or parent seeking children's books—paperback and hardback—for all ages. All listings are annotated, and information and much guidance is provided to help with selection.

World Wide Games: Exceptional Handcrafted Games, Colchester, CT 06415.
A selection of beautiful games from all over the world.

THAI CULTURE

Thailand is a country of traditions. Thais in cities such as Bangkok have adopted some Western customs, but most Thais live in rural villages, and make their living as farmers or fishermen. Their lifestyles vary depending upon the climate, the land, and the crops in each of the five regions of the country.

Traditional crafts, handmade by farmers and their families in their spare time, are created from materials found in each region. They show Thai artistic skill and their love of vivid colors. The Creative Art Expression section illustrates some of these crafts.

The environment in the villages provides almost all of the things families need—food, clothing, and household items. Products derived from forests, farms, and animals are sufficient to meet people's basic needs.

As you become familiar with the beautiful country of Thailand, you will discover its unique and interesting heritage and how people have adapted to their environment. Locate Thais in your community who can serve as resources. Many Thais live in America today, and Thai students attend colleges in various areas of the U.S.

Dr. Songsri Virojphan Davis of Dallas, who holds a doctorate in Educational Administration from Kensington University and taught in the graduate psychology program at Bansomdej Teachers College, Bangkok, and other Thai doctoral students at the University of North Texas, were valuable consultants in validating the contents of this section and in interpreting their culture.

Dr. Davis also contributed the photographs for this section, which were taken in Thai schools.

FAMILY LIVING

HOMES

Village families live in small wooden or brick houses (*ban*) with roofs covered with palm leaves. Homes may have only one or several rooms. They are elevated on stilts or posts for protection from floods and wild animals, and are entered by means of a ladder. In the cities, the homes and apartment buildings are as modern as in America.

At the Learning Tree the children use a wooden tree house to recreate this palm-leaf-covered dwelling.

Floor Mat (*Sue*)

The *sue* is a tan mat, woven from reeds in different sizes, that is laid on wooden floors. Sandals are removed in the house to keep the sue clean. The family sits on the sue for meals and for socializing.

Provide a straw mat for children to use as a sue in the family living center.

Beds (*Tiang*)

A thin mattress, folded and stored during the day, is laid on the sue for sleeping. Many Thais use Western-style beds today.

Provide a thin mattress or quilt for the family living center. Decide with the children where to store it. A sleeping bag may be substituted.

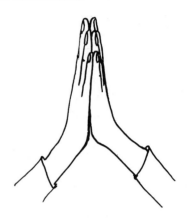

Wai (*Wi*)

Children learn the proper way to greet others in Thai style called *wai*. Show them how to press the palms of their hands together in front of their bodies to anyone in authority. To make a formal greeting, they press their hands together at chin level and bow from the waist. They then press their hands together at a lower or higher level, depending upon the rank of the person they are greeting.

During the time children experience the Thai culture, encourage them to greet each other and visitors using the wai as illustrated.

Bathing Thai Style

Thais have high standards of personal cleanliness and neatness. Each family member has an aluminum bowl that looks like silver to wash the face and to pour water over the body when bathing twice a day.

These inexpensive bowls and pitchers are available at many Asian stores. Children enjoy this method of washing hands, pouring the water, and refilling the pitcher.

Young Children

When young children are old enough to play with other village children, they engage in a great deal of make-believe play. Girls take care of their dolls, make mud pies to sell in the market, cook meals in clay pots, and imitate buyers and sellers in the market. Boys imitate plowing fields, flying kites, and teaching crickets and tiny fish to fight.

Talk with the children about the similarities and differences in play, comparing Thai and American children. Discuss how the environment influences play.

Infants and Toddlers

Infants in the villages are placed in oval-shaped bamboo or rattan baskets used as cradles. When infants are a little older, mothers carry them straddled on their hips, supported by one hand. When the children can walk and run, they are taught to climb the ladder into the house. Parents also may teach young children to swim if the homes are near the river bank.

Provide a basket with blankets for dolls in the home center. Demonstrate how Thai mothers carry their infants.

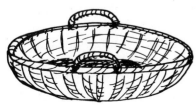

Children's Work

In the villages, children help the family, beginning at about age eight. Girls help mothers and care for the younger children, while boys watch the family buffalo and feed the livestock. Older children take the livestock to a field to graze before they bathe and go to school. If families live near the rivers, children help row the boats, using one oar, beginning at about age ten.

Discuss the responsibilities children in the class have at home. They may talk about doing household chores, keeping their bedrooms neat, and caring for pets. Guide them to think about how well they perform these tasks and how they help the family.

CUSTOMS

American teachers of Thai children who have recently arrived in the United States should be aware of the following behaviors which are not acceptable in Thailand:

The sole of the foot should never be pointed upward since it is considered to be the least clean part of the body, or the lowest part of the body.

Never pat adults on the head. Adults may pat young children on the head if they are relatives or students. The top of the head is considered to be the most sacred part of the body.

Never stand over someone who is sitting down during a conversation. Proper respect is shown by sitting alongside the person.

Shoes are never worn inside the house so that the floor is kept clean for sitting or sleeping.

DRAMATIC PLAY

Have some of these items available for role-playing the Thai culture:
Boats—various kinds (see Transportation)
Bowl for bathing (see the section on bathing Thai style)
—oval basket for infant cradle
—children's clothing
—clay pot for water
—coconut—remains fresh until opened
—farmer's straw or bamboo hats
—plastic or real fruits and vegetables
—plastic toys—cartoon characters, cars, trucks
—rice—uncooked
—small plates—salad size
—small serving bowls with a spoon for each
—straw mat large enough for several children
—stuffed or plastic animals—water buffalo, elephant, pig, chicken, dog, cat, small fish, bird
—tablespoons and forks
—Thai dolls (both boys and girls play with dolls)
—umbrella—parasol type made of paper and bamboo frame

CLOTHING

One of the first things young children want to do when exploring a culture is to try on traditional clothing. Have clothing available for children to examine, or have them make their own by adding a creative touch to an existing garment or using a pattern and starting from scratch. Involve the children in determining what tools are needed, selecting materials, and deciding where to cut.

Most Thais in the cities wear Western-style clothing. Traditional clothing is worn for festivals and ceremonies. Thais in the villages wear clothing of cotton, which is grown in Thailand. White is a popular color, suitable for every occasion.

Women

Women wear a blouse with a *phasin,* an ankle-length skirt. It is a long length of fabric with the ends sewn together. Women buy or weave the fabric. It is fastened by pulling it together at the waist and folding it over on one side, or by gathering it at the waist and using a belt. Phasins are made in solid colors or may have an intricate design woven into the fabric.

Men

Men in the villages wear khaki or dark blue knee-length or shorter pants with a white, khaki, or light-blue shirt. A checkered strip of cloth, a *phakhoma,* two to three feet wide and about two yards long is worn loosely around the waist. It may also serve other purposes—as a turban for protection from the sun, as a sweat-absorbing towel, or as a hammock.

Children

Children's clothing is the same as adult styles. Girls wear shorter skirts and colored blouses. The boys' short pants are khaki color and are worn with a shirt. Boys generally do not like to wear brightly colored clothing.

If the children in your class wish to role-play a Thai woman, village farmer, or a child, add a phasin, phakhoma, and children's clothing to the dramatic play center.

Clothes for School

School uniforms for boys are khaki shorts and white shirts. Girls wear a navy blue skirt and a white blouse with a navy blue collar and tie.

The uniforms for kindergarten children consist of a white blouse and blue skirt for girls and a white shirt and short blue pants for boys.

FOOD

Due to the tropical climate, many varieties of fruits, vegetables, and fish are available in Thailand, and a traditional Thai saying expresses the abundance of resources: "Because of the prosperity of the land, we have fish in the water and rice in the field."

(Safety Note: Be sure to obtain parental permission before allowing children to eat anything, in case of allergies or diet restrictions.)

Fruit *(Pol mai)*

In the villages, Thais get most of their food from the trees and gardens around them.

Common fruits include coconuts; twenty-eight varieties of bananas, from small to very large; citrus fruits, including

oranges, grapefruit, and limes; papayas; large pineapples; grapes; guava; durians; jack fruit; watermelons; apples; and twenty kinds of mangoes.

Vegetables

Common vegetables include corn that is roasted or steamed in its shuck; green and napa cabbage; turnips; tomatoes; eggplant; cucumbers; green onions; celery; spinach; and boiled peanuts.

Introduce children to foods that are new to them, as well as some favorite fruits and vegetables. Discuss sizes, colors, shapes, smells, tastes, and textures; as well as how the foods are grown, for valuable vocabulary development.

Fish (*Pla*)

Fish is the main source of protein, and both freshwater and saltwater varieties are available. Fresh fish may be curried or barbecued and dried or salted to preserve them. If they live near the water, Thais catch their own fish, including mackerel, grouper, perch, white promfret, tuna, shrimp, and lobster. Fish are boiled in a ginger liquid to take away the fishy taste.

Buy and steam one kind of fish for a snack. Show the children the whole fish first. Discuss their observations. Provide several kinds of sauces for dipping.

Meat

Meat is boiled, roasted, fried in batter, barbecued, or cut into small pieces and cooked with vegetables. Pork and chicken are eaten often. Beef is enjoyed in the cities, but less beef is eaten in the rural areas because the cow, ox, and buffalo are work animals that are treated with respect.

Select meat and vegetables for a stew. Involve the children in making choices and in washing and cutting the vegetables. Serve it for lunch or a snack.

Family Meals

In the villages, family members sit in a circle on a sue to eat a meal. The fork is held in the left hand and the spoon in the right. The food is served from bowls placed in the middle of the mat.

Provide the appropriate items in the dramatic play center so that children may role-play a family meal.

Menu for Meals

Rice is served at each meal. A typical meal includes soup; curry with meat and vegetables; fried meat, fish or chicken with vegetables; and water. Thais eat noodles with chopsticks or spoons.

Lunch at School (*Ahr han klang wan trong rian*)

Thai children take their lunch to school. It may include noodle soup with pork and bean sprouts, rice and curry with meat fish or chicken, and fried or boiled eggs. Fruit may be a banana, papaya, mango, or orange. Dessert may be fruit or another item. The drink may be water, iced tea, or water flavored with orange juice or sugar cane. The lunch for kindergarten children is served by the school.

Plan a school lunch day when children bring a typical Thai lunch in a school bag or other type of bag.

Water Jars (*Dtoom*)

Large jars with lids are used to store many things. The main use of the jar is to store water (*nam*). (See Creative Art Expression.) Water is stored for cooking. Villagers have several jars— separate ones for drinking, cooking, bathing, and other uses. Some villages get their water from wells. The Thais in the cities use tap water.

Large clay jars are available at many nursery and garden shops. Clay pot saucers may be used for lids. Place these in the dramatic play center.

Milk (*Nom*)

Milk is plentiful in cities but not in villages. It is expensive and some families lack refrigerators. Some Thais drink soy or evaporated milk; condensed milk is also available.

Provide an assortment of milks—soy, evaporated, condensed, and whole milk for children to taste and compare. Print their comments on a chart.

Herbs (*Kruang tate*)

Thais grow and use fresh herbs. They use a pestle and mortar to grind them to a fine consistency and then mix them with other spices.

The mortar is a shallow, round bowl with a thick, flat bottom. A pestle is a round, thick stick of wood, about four to six inches long. The bottom of the pestle is thicker than the top. Chili peppers, lemon grass, garlic, curry paste, and other herbs are finely ground.

A mortar and pestle can be found in many department stores in the cooking or housewares sections. Encourage children to experiment grinding things such as whole cloves, rock salt, or sugar cubes.

Fish Sauce (*Nampla*)

Fish sauce, served at every meal, is a popular liquid seasoning made from fermented fish, chili peppers, and other spices. It can be purchased in Chinese or Asian stores around the world.

Buy a jar of fish sauce for children to taste. Encourage them to use their imaginations to describe the taste.

RECIPES

Some typical Thai recipes follow. Look in bookstores for Thai recipe books. Involve the children in planning and preparing the foods for snacks or for lunch. Print the recipe on a chart in words and pictures so that children can follow it. An example is given below.

Coconut Pudding

Mix:
2 T instant coconut pudding and

1/3 C cold milk.

Stir until thick.

Sticky Rice

Sticky rice is popular in northern Thailand and is eaten for every meal. Rice is soaked in water for six to eight hours and then steamed until done.

For a dessert, add coconut milk and sugar to the hot rice. Cover and let it stand a while. Serve with ripe sliced mangoes, bananas, jack fruit (available in cans), or durians. Sometimes Asian custard is put on top.

Soup (*Kweng jood*)

Add fish, meat, or chicken to a thin chicken broth or water. Add celery, green onions, and other vegetables as desired. Use fish or soy sauce, pepper, and fresh mint to taste. For hot and spicy soup (*tom yum*), add

lemon grass, tomatoes, lemons, and chilis.

Pork and Vegetable Soup

2 C chicken or beef broth
1/2 lb ground pork
1 t soybean sauce
Spinach leaves, bean sprouts, or other vegetables
Pepper and garlic (optional)

Prepare a broth, add salt, and heat. Roll the 1/2 lb ground pork into small balls. Boil them in the broth until tender. Add 1 t soybean sauce. Cut washed spinach leaves into fourths and add to the soup. Bean spouts or other vegetables may be substituted. Sprinkle with pepper and garlic that has been chopped and saute in 1 T vegetable oil until yellow.

Papaya Salad

Peel and grate the fresh meat of a papaya. Add sugar, lime or lemon juice, and salt or fish sauce to taste. Add one medium diced tomato. Mix. Serve with barbecued chicken and sticky rice.

Green cabbage may be substituted for the papaya. This is a very popular dish!

Coconuts (*Ma praw*)

Coconuts are plentiful in Thailand. The coconut shell is used to make long-handled dippers for water, soup, and other liquids. The meat of the coconut is used to make milk, which is added to many desserts. Canned coconut milk is sold in many Asian stores.

Bring a fresh coconut to the classroom. Let children shake it and listen to the liquid inside. They can use a hammer and a large nail to put a hole into the

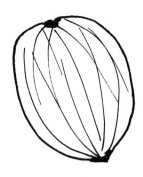

coconut. Pour the liquid or milk from the coconut into a cup. Then let children take turns hitting the coconut with the hammer until it cracks open.

To make coconut milk, scrape the coconut meat into a bowl with a rough-edged spoon. Add one cup water for thick milk or about two cups for thin milk. Thick milk is used more often. Let children mix the coconut and water. Squeeze the mixture to make more milk. Use to make the desserts described below.

Desserts (Kha-nhom)

The basic ingredients for making desserts are flour, sugar, egg, and coconut milk. Fruit, sweet potato, pumpkin, or tapioca may be added. These foods are also eaten with plain coconut milk or cooked in a syrup. Sweet potatoes are eaten as a dessert or as a vegetable in Thailand. (See the Food section of the African unit for yam and sweet potato recipes.)

Sweet Potato Dessert

Raw sweet potatoes
1 to 2 C coconut milk
Sugar
1/4 t salt

Cut raw sweet potatoes diagonally into small strips. Boil the strips in water until done; drain. Pour 1 to 2 C coconut milk into a pan. Add sugar, 1/4 t salt, and sweet potatoes. Heat until the sugar is dissolved and serve. Bananas may be substituted for the potatoes.

Coconut Custard

1 3/4 C thick coconut milk
3 eggs
3 egg yolks
1/2 C palm or brown sugar
2 t cornstarch

Bring coconut milk to a boil and remove from heat. Combine eggs, egg yolks, sugar and cornstarch. Beat until thick and creamy. Add the mixture to the hot coconut milk. Set the pan over low heat, and stirring well, bring to a low boil. Immediately place custard into a steamer to steam for approximately 30 minutes. Serve hot or cold.

Instant coconut pudding may be substituted for the Thai recipe above. Let each child make a cup of pudding by mixing 2 T instant coconut pudding and 1/3 C cold milk and stirring until thick.

MARKETS (TA LAAD)

Fruits and vegetables are arranged in the markets to make an eye-catching, artistic display.

Floating Markets

Floating markets are set up on boats where people who live on or near the water buy or sell goods all day. The farmers and traders, many of them women wearing straw or bamboo hats, bring their products in sampans and other boats. They announce their arrival by tooting a horn.

People can buy almost everything they need—food and household goods—at these markets.

Farmer's Market

In Thai villages, open-air markets are set up by the farmers. They buy and sell the foods they grow and the crafts they make. See the Market section in the Chinese unit for ideas on making an outdoor store market. Role-play buying and selling goods.

Vendors

Thais enjoy eating snacks. Some vendors on the street find a space, set up a small table and chairs, and sell snacks. Others pedal a tricycle with cart and umbrella attached. A special bell made from two pieces of bamboo announces the vendor's arrival. Some vendors have pushcarts. They sell rice and curry, chicken with noodles and

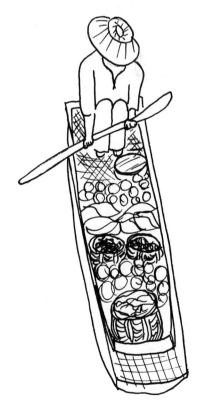

vegetables, chili peppers, fruit, meat and fish, and soft drinks.

Plan with children what items to sell and how to set up a place for a food vendor. Different foods may be sold on different days. Children may suggest baking cookies, bringing food from home, or selling vegetables from the school garden. Provide play money and have children alternate role-playing vendors and customers. Do the activity outdoors if the weather permits.

Shoulder Poles (*Hahp*)

A common scene is a vendor who carries a pole over the shoulders. The poles each have a triangular rattan basket that is filled with items to sell. The vendor may also carry a small stove.

Provide poles and baskets for children to role-play this vendor.

TRANS-PORTATION

Thais travel in many ways. They walk; drive cars and motorcycles; and ride bicycles; trains; and water taxis.

School Transportation

Some children travel to and from school in a mini-bus (*song-theaw*) that looks like a pickup truck. A roof over the back of the truck protects the children from the rain. Several benches are placed on the bed or back of the truck so that children can sit.

Some children walk or ride a bicycle to school. Kindergarten children ride on a school bus. In the cities, parents drive their children to and from school.

Canals (*Klongs*)

Unique in central Thailand is a network of canals called *klongs,* which are connected to the main rivers and canals around Bangkok. These klongs are used for traveling from place to place, for floating markets, for navigating water buses, and for sightseeing tours.

Children dig and build canals in the sand outdoors. Provide

different kinds of toy boats for children to use on the canals.

Long-tailed Boats (*Hang yaos*)

Long-tailed boats are about twenty-five feet long and five feet wide. They travel very fast in canals and rivers. Each boat has many rows of seats, with room for two people in each row. This boat is unique because the motor and propeller are on the stern, and it can travel in either deep or shallow water because the propeller can be raised or lowered.

Provide a variety of materials for children to use in making boats—wood scraps, styrofoam trays, straws, paper cups. Have books and pictures of Thai boats available for children to look at and discuss. Encourage their questions.

A large appliance box may be converted into a passenger boat. Cut panels out of the sides of the box as illustrated on page 207. Place small chairs inside the boat for seats. Children may role-play traveling to work on the long-tailed boat.

Boat Decorations

Traditionally, only royal boats were decorated on all sides with swans, snakes, and dragons

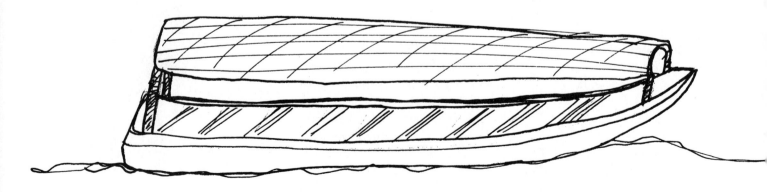

made with lacquer, gold, and pieces of glass.

Boat races, with twenty to thirty oarsmen, are held in the provinces in the fall. The boats are decorated in bright green, pink, and yellow, with garlands of flowers (*puang malai*) and candles. Special songs accompany the races.

In southern Thailand where men fish for a living, boats are decorated with very bright colors and designs.

Samlors

A *samlor* is a three-wheeled vehicle, with pedals or a motor, that has a coach to transport people in the cities and towns in the provinces. It is used for sightseeing, shopping, and taking children to school. It is a cheap and safe way to travel. The pedaler sits in the front of the coach, which is made of wood with a canvas or plastic hood. The coach is decorated in bright colors.

Find pictures of samlors in books about Thailand. Thai families in the community may share pictures or draw a samlor. Talk about the kind of ride one would have on a samlor in all kinds of weather.

CREATIVE ART EXPRESSION

Creativity means beginning with ideas generated by children. The role of the adult is to foster creativity by asking questions, supervising the project, and providing reinforcement. Provide many choices of materials.

DECORATIVE ART
••••••

The most beautiful art in Thailand is found in the temples. These arts include woodcarving, glass and porcelain mosaics, mural paintings, gold and black lacquerware, and mother-of-pearl inlays. After the harvest in the rural areas, in addition to enjoying festivals and social gatherings, families make crafts to use and sell. The crafts are different in each region, depending on the materials available.

This section has descriptions of some traditional crafts, many of which are still made today.

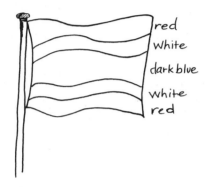

red
white
dark blue
white
red

Flag (Tong)

The flag of Thailand has five horizontal stripes: two red, two white, and a wide center stripe of dark blue. Red is the symbol of the country, white represents religion, and blue is the symbol of the king.

To make a flag, cut a sheet of white fabric or strong white paper, such as butcher paper, any size the child desires. Let children use paint, crayons, or marking pens to make the flag as illustrated. Attach the flag to paper sticks made of rolled newspaper. Let children use their creativity in figuring out how to fasten the flag to the stick.

Kites (Wow)

Great skill is required to make the men's and women's kites used for kite fighting. (See Games)

The *chula* (man's kite) is in the shape of a five-pointed star, which represents the five fingers and five senses.

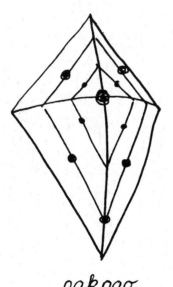

pakpao

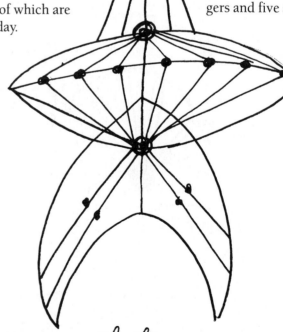

chula

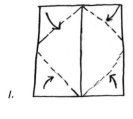

1.

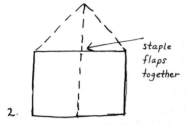

2.

staple flaps together

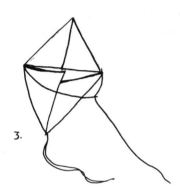

3.

The frame of the star is made of bamboo and is covered with paper. The chula is at least five feet long.

The *pakpao* (woman's kite) is a diamond-shaped kite that is from one to seven feet long. One end of the diamond is shorter than the other. A long, starched cloth tail is attached to the bottom of the diamond to maneuver the kite.

Toy kites can be purchased. They may be in the shape of snakes, dragons, frogs, or colored butterflies.

Children make the pakpao using a 24-by-20-inch piece of butcher paper. Fold the paper in half. Open it and fold the top corners over to the crease in the middle. Staple together.

Fold the bottom corners over to the crease and staple together. Attach a long string to the sides of the kite and a long cloth tail to the bottom.

Jars (*Dtoom ong*)

Rural Thais get water from wells or rivers. Plump jars with lids are made in all sizes to store water, including rainwater, and foods such as fish sauce, preserved fruits, garlic, onions, rice, and sugar.

These jars are made of a special red, sticky clay. The potter shapes the jars on the potter's wheel. They are then dried in the sun and fired in a kiln.

Provide Mexican red clay for children to mold pots or jars. Let the pots dry and then let children paint them with a mixture of red and brown tempera and white glue. When dry, this mixture gives a shiny finish that resembles the Thai dtoom-ong.

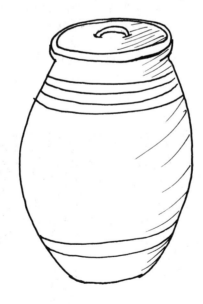

Silk Fabrics

For many years, after the rice harvest, women in villages have woven fabrics to sell at the market.

Breeding silk worms to produce high quality silk is an involved process. See the Nature and Science section of the Chinese unit for a description of how silk thread is made and how children can observe this process in the classroom. Thais dye the thread and weave it into cloth. The dyes are made from roots, berries, insects, and soil. Thais make all the colors they need from nature.

Children can experiment with berries, roots, and vegetables to make different colors of dye. See the Nature and Science section of the American Indian unit for additional information.

Cotton Fabric

Farmers grow cotton, which is dried in the sun. The seed is removed from the cotton boll. After the boll is spun into thread, it is woven into cloth on looms. (See the Nature and Science section of the Chinese unit for information about weaving.) Thais wear many cotton clothes because they are cooler in the hot climate.

Provide a cotton plant and bolls of cotton for children to examine. Children enjoy removing seeds from the cotton boll.

Paper Balls

A few Thai families developed the art of making honeycombed paper balls. They are about three inches in diameter and are used as decorations for Christmas and the New Year. The balls are brightly colored and creatively designed. Flowers are added to the top of the ball and streamers to the bottom. To make the ball, seventy-six layers of tissue paper are glued together in strips. These

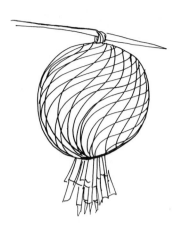

are then cut into a round shape and opened to make a ball.

Party supply stores sell honeycombed decorations at holiday times. Provide a honeycombed item so that children can examine the layers and the fragile paper.

Piggy Banks (Savings Banks)

Piggy banks have been a popular toy for years and were often the only colorful toy a child had. Piggy banks reflect the Thai twelve year cycle. Each year is represented by a different animal. A child is given a bank in the shape of its birth year animal. Papier-mache is put on a plaster of Paris mold to make the animal-shaped banks.

Older children are interested in making banks from papier-mache. (See the Masks section of the Korean unit for a description of this method.) Let children paint the piggy bank and put a slit in the top.

Mobiles (*Pla tapien*) for Infants

Mobiles hung above an infant's cradle are made from dried and painted palm leaves. Even though brightly colored fish mobiles are sold in the shops, those made from palm leaves are still appreciated. Children collect dried leaves and paint them. After the paint dries, they attach strings to the leaves. The strips are tied to a clothes hanger, which is hung from the ceiling.

Whirling Toys

The cicada or locust makes a shrill sound. Thai toy makers produce a cicada out of clay and bamboo, which is tied with cotton to a thin bamboo handle. When whirled around, the toys make the same shrill sound as the cicada. Toymakers also craft toy airplanes that make a similar sound when whirled around.

Show a whirling toy to the children. Compare its sound with the sound of the cicada if it lives in your community.

Look-choob

Look-choob is a sweetmeat, a dessert made in the shape of small fruits and vegetables. Skilled women copy these foods exactly, shaping every little detail by hand. It takes years to learn this art. Look-choob is given as gifts and used for special celebrations.

To make the dough, soybeans are soaked, skinned, and mashed. Sugar and coconut milk are added to taste. The ingredients are mixed, heated in a pan, and stirred with a bamboo stick until lumpy and sticky. After the dough is cool, it is shaped gently by hand into

tiny fruits and vegetables and painted with food coloring. When dry, the fruits and vegetables are dipped into a clear gelatin liquid that is not too thick. Experiment with creating look-choob; involve children in the process.

Carved Fruits and Vegetables

Thai mothers teach their high school daughters the art of carving designs and flowers in fruits and vegetables. A Thai buffet table with carved food is a work of art.

Look for a Thai woman in the community or contact a Thai restaurant to find a person who is skilled in carving foods. Invite her to demonstrate this art to the children.

The Umbrella Village

For 200 years in Bor Bang, hundreds of umbrellas of different sizes and colors have been dried in the sun every day.

The frame of the umbrella is made of bamboo covered with bright colored paper, cotton, or silk. The wafer-thin paper (*su*) is made from the bark of the paper mulberry or similar tree. (See the Creative Art Expression section in the Chinese unit for directions on making paper.) The paper is pasted onto the frame, layer upon layer, until it is thick and strong. The paper is smoothed by hand. When it is dry, artists paint designs of dragons or flowers on the umbrella.

These beautiful umbrellas, made in all sizes, are sold in import shops. Place one in the dramatic play center. Very small umbrellas are packaged for use at parties and can be used for counting and sorting.

Flower Arrangements

The art of traditional flower arranging is part of every Thai girl's education. They are expected to provide arrangements for special occasions. Two of the many styles of flower arrangements are described.

A *poom* is round and cone-shaped like a fir cone six to eight inches high. Flowers are fastened to a cone of plastic foam, earth, or sawdust that is soaked in water to keep the flowers fresh. This cone rests on a decorated bowl with a stand. Every bit of the cone is covered with flower petals that are arranged in a colored pattern. Each petal is pulled from a fresh flower, one by one, and fastened to the cone individually. The everlasting or straw flower is often used since it stays fresh for a long time. The bottom of the poom is arranged in the open lotus pattern.

poom

The *puang malai* is a garland—a ring of flowers—with a "ribbon" of flowers hanging from it. A needle with cotton thread is used to string the small white jasmine buds. Rose petals, purple orchids, red sage, and others are used to add color. A seven-color garland is favored.

Provide styrofoam cones and wreaths and plastic flowers for children to arrange their own poom and puang malai.

puang malai

Baskets (*Pakra*)

Baskets, usually woven by men, are made in many shapes and sizes. They are woven from a variety of dry grasses, especially bamboo and rattan. Specially shaped baskets are made for specific uses—for sticky rice; carrying a chicken, dry rice, or fresh fish; and other things.

Display pictures of the many kinds of Thai baskets. Invite someone from an import shop to show Thai baskets.

Invite a basket-maker to demonstrate the process. Contact art departments in high schools, colleges, and art organizations.

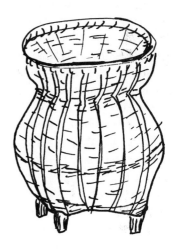

Wood Carving

Wood carving, especially on teak wood, is a very special skill. Carvers design elephants two feet high, wall plaques, tiny characters from Thai stories, furniture, and other decorative and utilitarian items.

Thais bring a plank or log of wood to the carver, who draws a design on the wood and then carves it with a chisel and mallet.

Many communities have wood carvers. Invite an artist to demonstrate this skill. Show carved wooden objects, especially of teakwood, and discuss the craft.

Banana Leaf Boats (*Krathong*)

Banana leaf boats, made in the shape of a lotus flower, are floated on the rivers at the Loi Krathong Festival. (See Celebrations for a description of this special boat.) Banana leaf containers are also used as dishes, especially for snacks.

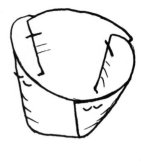

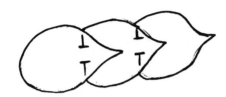

To make a banana leaf dish, cut a small circle out of a leaf. On each of the four sides of the circle, fold the leaf over about one half inch near the outer edge. Fasten the four folded parts. Thais use bamboo needles to fasten the folds. Children will figure out many ways to fasten them. Canna leaves can be substituted if banana leaves are not available. Crowns of leaves may be made from the leaves of the maple tree by attaching leaves together, end to end, with small twigs, as illustrated.

Farmer's Hats

Wide-brimmed hats worn by both men and women are woven of straw or palm leaves, lined with bamboo, and finished with a rattan edge. For women, the brim is a wide circle with a crown underneath that fits the head. Some men's hats are shaped like a cowboy hat with a narrow brim. Provide several of these hats in the dramatic play center so that children can examine and wear them.

Art in School

Kindergarten children draw with crayons; create objects with materials such as modeling clay, cloth, and paper; and learn how to fold paper to make boats, flowers, blouses, shirts, and other items.

Thai teachers must know all of these crafts in order to teach them. In the elementary grades, girls learn how to make pooms, carve fruits and vegetables, crochet, knit, sew, and make banana leaf boats. Boys learn to weave baskets and make trays and other useful items. Children go outdoors to paint landscapes on paper or canvas; they paint other items in the classroom. They are creative, expressing their own ideas. They make greeting cards, and also houses, airplanes, baskets, and other objects using recycled materials such as popsicle sticks.

NATURE AND SCIENCE

Thailand is a beautiful country of mountains, rivers, farms, and coastlines. The climate is tropical, so plants are lush year-round. Many varieties of trees, plants, and animals thrive there.

Thailand has had rubber plantations and pearl farms for a long time. Its newer crops are coffee, sugar cane, pineapples, and soybeans.

ANIMALS

Thai jungles and forests are inhabited by many kinds of animals. Tigers roam the woods, although many have been killed

for their valuable skins. Cows and goats provide milk for some villages.

Pets (*Sut liang*)

Middle-sized dogs and cats are the main pets in Thailand. Today many species of dogs are purchased from Western countries. In the villages these pets roam over the countryside.

Birds are also favorite pets. Parakeets, doves, parrots, and others are kept in bamboo cages shaped like those in America. The bird cages are decorated with small umbrellas with tassels that are placed over the top of the cage.

Plan with children to have a bird in the room. Suggest to children that they decorate the cage as Thais do. Invite an expert on birds to talk to the children about the bird's care. Then discuss how the responsibilities are to be shared.

Water Buffalo (*Quai*)

The water buffalo is the farmer's best helper. It is sociable, serene, gentle, and devoted to its master. When a buffalo dies, it is like the death of a beloved pet.

The buffalo is valuable because it is stronger than other animals. It is used in the rice fields and also protects the family.

Show pictures of the water buffalo. Elicit descriptions of it from children, including the hide, horns, and nostrils. Discuss how horses or similar animals worked for farmers and ranchers in early America.

Elephants (*Chang*)

Elephants have been important to Thais for hundreds of

years. Their main hard work is to pull the heavy teak logs from the forests into the rivers. The logs are then floated down the river to the lumber mills.

Elephants are trained in Elephant Training School. Some elephant owners give demonstrations to show how their animals have been trained.

In the autumn, about 100 elephants participate in an elephant roundup. Between folk dances and other events, they star in elephant hunts and show their intelligence, strength, gentleness, and obedience.

The royal "white elephants," named for their unique color, live on the grounds of the Royal Palace. They are a pinkish-brown color.

The elephant is an endangered species in Thailand and other parts of the world. People kill them for their ivory tusks, which are sold for high prices. All countries must protect the elephant so that future generations will be able to enjoy these animals.

Provide many books and pictures so that children can learn more about elephants.

Monkeys (*Ling*)

Many monkeys live in central Thailand. They are friendly to the villagers and are enjoyed as pets. They are trained to dance and entertain people on the streets when their masters play the mouth harp, and they perform in the circus.

Arrange with a school or city librarian for a classroom presentation on monkeys using books, pictures, poetry, and audiovisual materials. Inquire about checking out materials to your classroom.

Fishing

Thailand has water on three sides. The many kinds of fish in these waters are important for

Thais. Beautiful fish are seen in the clear waters. Older men and women weave fishing nets; others are made by machine.

When the fishing boats leave at night, they look like rows of fireflies as their navigation lights shine in the dark. The fishermen set off firecrackers as they leave to ensure a good catch of fish.

Bring in books about fish and guide children in comparing the different shapes and colors of the fish. Demonstrate how to find answers to the children's questions about fish. Older children could study one kind of fish and share their information.

If fishing is popular with parents in your school, invite them to talk about how they catch fish.

PLANTS AND TREES

Tapioca (*Mun sum pa lung*)

Cassava, the plant from which tapioca is made, is one of Thailand's major crops. The country exports a great deal of tapioca and its products. Tapioca flour is used in industries to make chips and pellets for animal feed and cooking starch.

Buy a box of tapioca and involve children in helping to prepare and serve it. Children enjoy measuring, pouring, and stirring. Talk about the consis-

tency of the mixture as it changes during cooking.

Many kinds of trees grow very large in Thailand because of its warm climate and plentiful rain. Thailand has very thick jungles and forests where animals live and trees grow untouched for many years.

Teak Forests (*Ton mai*)

Teakwood has been used for many years. It is a hard wood that lasts a long time. Some Thais beautify their homes with carved teakwood doors, figurines, window frames, and furniture. Teakwood bowls, breadboards, and other household items are sold in American stores.

Bring carved teakwood objects for children to touch and examine. Small teakwood animals are sold in import shops. Children can use them to inhabit the Thai jungles they create from blocks.

Banana Trees

The banana is an important food in the daily lives of Thais. The leaves are used for flower arrangements, krathong boats, small dishes, and bags used to steam food.

Coconut Palms

Coconuts grow at the top of tall palm trees. Dried coconut is used to make coconut oil; the bark is used for crafts and for the bow used to play stringed instruments.

Most plantations use monkeys to harvest coconuts. The Monkey Training School teaches monkeys to climb the coconut trees, select ripe nuts, and throw them down to a keeper below.

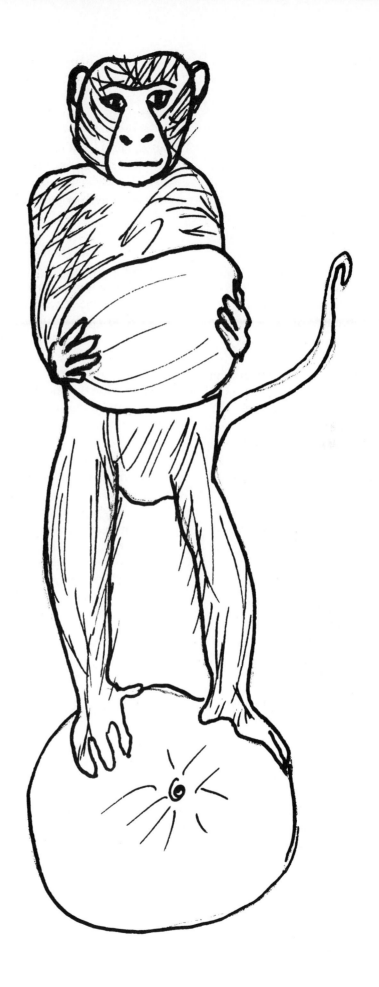

Bamboo

Many types of bamboo grass and trees grow all over Thailand. Houses and household goods and containers are among the hundreds of items made from bamboo. The shoots from young bamboo plants are eaten. Ask children to recall items made from bamboo from their experiences with other Asian cultures.

FLOWERS (DOG MAI)

Thai people love flowers and plants, which bloom all year. The air is filled with the fragrance of flowers. They are used for decorations and ceremonies, and their essence is used in desserts. A few of the many flowers are marigolds, zinnias, calendulas, hollyhocks, snapdragons, gardenias, and peonies. Many bushes, such as the bougainvillea and red sage, also bloom in Thailand.

Let children plant marigold, zinnia, and snapdragon seeds and share the job of watering them. Keep a daily class record of children's observations of the growth, recording the time it takes to sprout, to grow into a plant, to bud, and to bloom.

Lotus

The lotus is considered the national flower. It grows in the water and blooms in white, yellow, pink, red, and purple shades. It closes at night and opens in the morning. Stories and poems have been written about the lotus. Thais eat the pod, stems, and roots as a veg-

etable and also use parts of this plant as medicine.

Lilies

The royal lilies grow in the water. Thais cook the stems with shrimp or pork or add them to soup. The roots are used as an herb or medicine.

Jasmine

This small, fragrant, white flower is a symbol of purity. Jasmine is used to make pooms and puangs. (See Creative Art Expression.) The syrup made from jasmine is used in flavoring tea and desserts.

To make the syrup, soak the small jasmine flowers in water in a covered jar for twelve to fifteen hours. Add sugar, boil, and cool.

Show as many of these flowers to children as possible. Contact your florist for assistance. Make the syrup, then taste it. The scarcity of flowers and the possibility that children may be allergic to them may limit your use of this activity in the classroom.

FARMING

Rice Farming (Tam na)

Rice is the basic food in all Asian countries. The world's best rice grows in Thailand and is sold all over the world. A festival, the Plowing Ceremony, begins the planting season. (See Celebrations.)

Invite a county extension agent to talk about how rice is grown to help children appreciate the work required before it can be eaten. If rice grows in your community, plan an excursion to see it planted and later, to see how it is harvested.

Salt Farming (Tam na Klua)

Large areas of land along the coast south of Bangkok are used for salt farming during the dry season. A dike or hill of sand is built around a field to retain the salt water. The fields are then flooded with salty ocean water. The water evaporates in the sun, leaving the dry salt in the field. It takes from ten to thirty days for the water to evaporate. The salt is then packaged and taken to market.

To see this process, have children mix one cup salt and one quart water, stirring until the salt dissolves. Pour mixture into a shallow dish. Let children observe the daily, gradual evaporation of the water. They will be amazed to see what happens when all the water has evaporated.

Some younger children may wish to make a booklet about the changes, dictating their observations to an adult. Older children may want to keep a diary of their observations.

LANGUAGE DEVELOPMENT

ก ข ฃ ค ฅ ฆ ง จ ฉ ช ซ
ฌ ญ ฎ ฏ ฐ ฑ ฒ ณ ด ต ถ
ท ธ น บ ป ผ ฝ พ ฟ ภ ม
ย ร ล ว ศ ษ ส ห ฬ อ ฮ

The Thai language is spoken throughout the country. Exposure to Thai vocabulary will help children understand how languages differ. They will enjoy a visual comparison between Thai and American alphabets.

Most children in the world have learned several languages by the time they finish high school.

Vocabulary

The following words may be used in labeling pictures and objects created by children:

ban—house
bundai—ladder
chang—elephant
chula—man's kite
dek chai—boy
dek ying—girl
dtoom—large storage jar
hang yao—long-tailed boat
horp—farmer's hat
kai—chickens
khao—rice
leg—small
maa—mother
muu—pigs
pakpao—woman's kite
phakhoma—strip of cloth men wear around the waist
phasin—woman's skirt
pho ying—woman
phor—father
phou chai—man
pla—fish
quai—water buffalo
rue—boat
sue—straw floor mat
thung na—rice field
toi—bowl
wow—kite
yai—big

Additional words and terms may be found in various sections of the unit.

Thai Alphabet

A Thai king invented the decorative alphabet of 44 letters in 1283 A.D. Each Thai word has three to five tones. Each tone of the word has a different meaning. Thais write from left to right as we do in English.

Writing

dek chai—boy   เด็กชาย

dek ying—girl   เด็กหญิง

leg—small   เล็ก

maa—mother   แม่

phor—father   พ่อ

ton mai—tree   ต้นไม้

yai—big   ใหญ่

Thai Words and Phrases

Jah—Hello (used by men or women to inferiors, those who are younger)
Buy rong rein—Go to school.
Laa kon—Goodbye.
Chan rok koon—I love you.

The following sentences show how Ka is used by women at the end of a word and Krap is used by men, according to the rules of politeness.

Sa wat dee ka—Hello (used by women to superiors, elders)
Sa wat dee krap—Hello (used by men to superiors)
Sa bai dee rue ka, Sa bai dee rue krap—How are you?
Kow toad ka, Kow toad krap—Excuse me.
Mai pen rye ka, Mai pen rye krap—That's all right.

Khaup koon mark ka, Khaup koon mark krap—Thank you very much.

Thai Numbers

Nung (nung)—one หนึ่ง

Song (sung)—two สอง

Sam (sam)—three สาม

Si (see)—four สี่

Ha (ha)—five ห้า

Hok (hok)—six หก

Jet (jet)—seven เจ็ด

Pat (pat)—eight แปด

Kau (kau)—nine เก้า

Sip (sip)—ten สิบ

Storytelling—Folktales and Stories

Legends, adventure stories and popular folktales were told in the days before general education began. Storytelling helped people socialize. It was a teaching tool to strengthen Thai identity. Stories were passed from one generation to the next by storytellers.

Village storytellers still hold audiences of all ages spellbound, improving a story with each telling. Stories often deal with how people trick each other.

The folklore of Thailand indicates the people's attitude toward animals that are considered to be almost human. In the stories, each animal represents a specific trait. For example, water buffalo are docile but fierce, and they trust small children; the rabbit is a hero or a trickster; and the parrot is a mimic and not his own person.

Children's Literature

The literature of Thailand and other Southeast Asian countries is based on religion, Confucius' writings, and the Jakarta tales from India.

Thai Stories in America

Few Thai stories for children are available in the United States. Many more stories and folktales are needed to assist children in understanding this culture. Encourage Thais to translate their children's literature into English. Thai-Americans can make a contribution by writing about the Thai-American experience.

Look for these books in your library:
Burmese and Thai Fairy Tales by Eleanor Brockett, (retelling) (1965).
Galong River Boy of Thailand by Judith M. Spiegelman (1970).
Let's Visit Thailand by Frances Wilkins (1985).

Thai Author

M. R. Kukrit Pramoj is described as a Renaissance man. A past prime minister, he is a leading novelist, journalist, and founder of a prominent Thai newspaper, as well as being an economist and a promoter of Thai classical dance.

Poetry

Thais have enjoyed poetry for centuries. Cradle songs are some of the first poetry for children.

Children are taught this poem in school:
When you are young, you should learn and study.
When you are grown
You will use the knowledge you have learned to earn your living.
If something is useful and worth learning
You should pay attention.

Proverbs

Proverbs and folklore are popular with Thais. Proverbs teach children to do good and to be useful to society.

Rural people like to refer to the buffalo when talking about life's wisdom:

If you love your buffalo, tie him up. (If you love your child, protect him.)

You don't force a buffalo to eat grass. (Don't pressure people to follow a certain path)

When eating, don't use the spoon or fork to hit the plate or you will starve in the future. (Don't make loud noises.)

You will be successful and lucky if you wear these colors on these days of the week: Sunday—red, Monday—yellow, Tuesday—pink, Wednesday—green, Thursday—orange, Friday—blue, Saturday—violet.

Reference for Language Development

Esther C. Jenkins and Mary C. Austin, *Literature about Asians and Asian Americans*. New York: Greenwood Press, 1987, pp 174, 175, and 191-2.

MUSIC, DANCE, AND DRAMA

Music (*don tri*), dance (*rum*), and drama (*lakorn*) are difficult to separate in Thai culture because all are used together. Instruments and group singing accompany dance and drama. Words are sung or spoken with music in the background.

More interest in traditional music is evident today. Western music and dance are also popular. Thais enjoy jazz, popular songs, and military music.

So Sam Sai

The *so sam sai* is the most popular classical instrument in Thailand. It has three strings and is played with a bow (usually by women), and sounds like a violin.

Long Drum

A Thai long drum is carried on one shoulder with a strap. The top of the drum may be at waist level; longer ones hang at chest level. It is made of buffalo leather. The long drum, played with the hands, makes a loud, exciting noise. It is used at all types of celebrations and entertainment, especially in the villages.

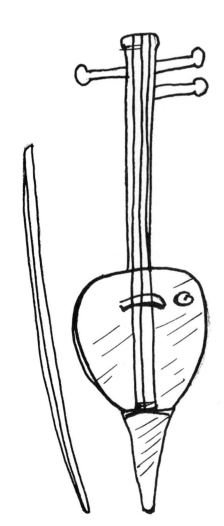

These drums can be made by using a gallon milk jug. Cut the bottom out of the jug. Place a circle cut from a large balloon over the bottom, attaching it with masking tape. Fix a long strip of fabric to the handle of the jug for carrying it over the shoulder.

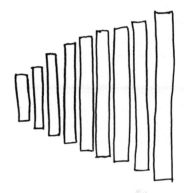

Ranard

The *ranard* is a Thai classical instrument similar to the xylophone. The bars are made of hard wood, usually teakwood, that is shaped with a chisel. The ranard is played using two bamboo sticks with a ball at one end. If the ball is made of cloth, it makes a soft sound; if made of lac, a hard varnish, it makes a hard sound. All music is played from memory since there is no written music for classical instruments.

Provide a xylophone for children to experiment with sounds and to play tones and simple melodies.

A ranard is made from eight 1/2-by-2-inch slats. The longest is 12 inches long and the shortest is 8 inches. Each slat is 1/2 inch shorter than the next. Have the children place these slats on 2-by-16-inch strips of carpet. Strike the slats with a wooden mallet for an unusual musical tone.

Ungalen

All children in school learn to play the *ungalen,* an instrument made of bamboo pieces. A player shakes it to make a sound. It has as many pieces as there are tones in the musical scale.

Music in the Elementary School

Thai children learn to sing classical songs as well as modern ones. The most popular instruments boys and girls learn to play are bamboo flutes, mouth harps, and drums. Popular Western instruments are the piano, violin, and electric organ. Children learn folk dances, especially the ramwong, in which they dance and sing to drum accompaniment.

Ramwong

Ramwong is a traditional Thai circle folk dance. The audience can join the dancers as long as they keep the rhythm and are not too concerned about the way they move their hands. The lively dance is accompanied by instrumental music.

Children can dance in a circle to the rhythm of Thai music. Look for musical tapes at Asian stores.

Classical Thai Dancing

Dressed in highly decorated headdresses and traditional costumes, dancers pantomime a story. The story is told with the hands; every little movement has a meaning. Children begin training in special schools when they are young to perform this art.

Children delight in making these beautiful headdresses. Roll a 12-by-18-inch piece of colored poster board into a cone

shape, making the wide end to fit the child's head. Cut back around the edges. Let each child decorate the headdress by gluing on sequins, glass beads, gold braid and glitter, or old jewelry. Attach metallic gold and silver pipe cleaners with glass beads hung on the ends. Ask parents to donate items for decorations.

Masked Play (Khon)—Traditional Thai Drama

Traditional Thai theater art is a masked play in which a narrator, accompanied by singers in the background, tells a story in verse. The play is based on a well-known story, Ramakian.

The masks are works of art. They are made of papier-mache. Sixteen to twenty layers of tissue paper are used to build the face. These are then smoothed and dried in the sun. The outline of the face is painted black and the features in many colors. It is decorated with gold leaf, ivory, buffalo hide, seashells, pieces of mirror, silver, and gold.

To make a khon mask, inflate a large balloon and tie the opening with a string. Let children tear newspaper into strips, soak the strips in a mixture of one cup of white glue and one quart of water, and then take the strips from the glue mixture and wrap them around the balloon. Tissue paper strips dipped into the glue mixture are used for the last two layers on the balloon. Hang by the string and let dry.

When completely dry, stick a pin into the balloon to burst it. Cut the papier-mache sphere in half, making two masks. Let children paint the masks to resemble the Thai masks, using a mixture of tempera paint and white glue. Provide large shiny sequins, shells, and gold and silver beads for children to decorate the khon masks.

Khon masks are available at import stores. Provide several in the classroom for children to examine.

Shadow Plays *(Nang Talung)*

In these plays, elaborate cutout characters of leather are held against a lighted screen to make the shadows. Some of them have moveable parts. Characters used during the day are painted. The person who manipulates the characters and tells the story is also a singer and comedian. At times, singers and an orchestra accompany the storyteller.

Set up a light bulb behind a sheet or curtain so that children may experiment with this art form. A slide projector or movie screen work very well for this activity.

Li-ke **Folk Theater**

Folk theater, another type of drama, is popular in villages throughout Thailand. It is creative because the players make up the story or drama while on stage. Both men and women, dressed in satin costumes decorated with feathers and sequins, act in these dramas.

Let children volunteer to create a play. Two or more children

engage in a conversation or in a dialogue in a question-and-answer format, responding to each other as they progress. Some children may wish to discuss and practice their drama first and then present it to the group.

Village Entertainment

After the planting or harvesting is finished, Thais living in villages gather in the evening for entertainment. They have rhyming song contests. One person sings a line and another adds the next rhyming line, or one person sings while the others chant in rhythm. Paid

groups of entertainers travel to village and perform indoors or out. Their music and drama are humorous and clever.

Thai Poem

Say this poem while you imitate the elephant:
Elephant! Elephant! Elephant!
Have you ever seen an elephant?
It is very, very big!
It has a long nose called a trunk.
It has two teeth under the trunk called tusks. It has two ears, two eyes, and a long tail.

GAMES (GUN LEN)

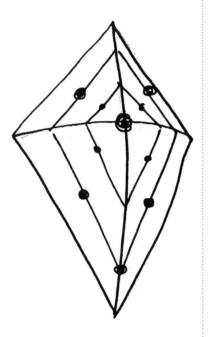

Thais participate in traditional as well as in Western games. Among the traditional games are cycling and go-kart races, takro, and boxing. Basketball, swimming, volleyball, soccer, tennis, badminton, and table tennis (especially popular) are some of the Western games played in Thailand.

A Snake Eats a Tail

Divide the group into two sides—the father's and the mother's sides. At the beginning of the game, the father (the snake) is alone and the mother has all the children. Both sides alternate singing songs. Then the children run in line, like a train. The father tries to catch the last child. When a child is caught, the songs start over again until all the children have been caught by the snake.

Takro

Takro, a wicker-ball game, is one of the most popular Asian games. Takro may be played in various forms, including hoop, net, or circle takro. A takro is a woven rattan ball.

Thais favor hoop takro. A team of seven boys are distributed around a large circle. The team cooperates in trying to gain the highest score during a 30-minute period. The ball must be hit through a high, vertically suspended hoop. Players use their feet, knees, elbows, thighs, chests, and shoulders to pass the ball to one another, trying to keep it in the air and eventually to hit it into the hoop. Hands cannot be used in any forms of takro. If the ball touches a player's hand, the ground, one of the hoops, or any piece of equipment, it immediately becomes "dead."

Children can play an adaptation of this game using a volleyball net or basketball hoop and a whiffle ball.

Kite Fighting

Between February and April, when the southwestern monsoon winds blow from the Gulf of Thailand, Thais enjoy kite fighting, as they have for 700 years.

In late afternoons in the royal field near the Grand Palace in Bangkok, they bring their chairs and gather to watch the kite-fighting teams compete. Men's and women's teams can be formed, or individuals can play against each other. The men have a large kite (chula), while women use a smaller one (pak-pao). (See Creative Art Expression.) The aim of the fight is to entangle and drag the other team's kite down into one's territory. The power of the team depends on its skill in handling the kite, the speed and agility of the players, and the size of the kite's surface.

Martial Arts

Martial arts came from the old style of combat and self-defense.

Thai boxing is not a violent sport. Boxers use feet, elbows, knees, and fists. They may punch, kick, push, and wrestle. Before the boxing bout begins, respect is paid to the kings and coaches. A small band accompanies the ritual and game. The speed of the boxers is matched by the music's tempo.

Physical Education in the Elementary School

Playground equipment at each school varies according to the money available. Many playgrounds have swings, climbers, slides, and tunnels.

Americans recognize games Thai children play—relays, hopscotch, hide-and-seek, and jump rope (or "jump the string") with a group. Girls play jacks with stones. Another game is played by throwing a large rubber band at a target like a coin. Thai children also play "frisbee," basketball, takro, and volleyball. Thai football, similar to soccer, is very popular.

Hoop Game

In a Thai game similar to tennis, a rubber hoop is thrown over a net from side to side. The team on each side tries to catch the hoop. When it is caught, the person who threw it goes to the other team. The winning team is the one with the most players.

SPECIAL EVENTS

Young children learn best through hands-on experiences, provided by many activities in this book. Children gain additional understanding from listening to speakers, taking interest trips, and sharing their learning with their families.

Menu for Family Get-Togethers

Choose from Thai recipes in this unit. Ingredients are sold in Asian stores or supermarkets. Suggest that each family bring to a gathering one dish, such as rice, meat and vegetable dishes (one a curry dish); soup; fruit or tapioca pudding; iced coffee with sugar and water, orange juice, or fruit punch.

Interest Trips

Look for information in your community about Thai restaurants, museum exhibits, and Asian stores that have Thai crafts. Plan to attend Thai programs and festivals.

Guest Speakers

Invite Thai students from local colleges and universities, personnel from airline companies, restaurants, and other Thai businesses, or persons who have traveled in Thailand to come to speak with children.

Teacher Day (*Wai Kru*)

Teachers are highly respected in Thailand. Teacher Day is observed in all schools once a year, from kindergarten through the university level. Students honor teachers for training them.

Children bring pooms, flower arrangements, for their teachers. (See Creative Art Expression.) Each poom must have three symbolic flowers: the eggplant flower, a symbol of intelligence; the needle flower, symbol of a sharp mind; and white grass, symbol of rapid growth. An award is given for the most beautiful poom in each classroom.

A boy and girl represent each class. The girl carries the flowers and the boy the incense sticks and candles. The flowers are presented to the teachers. Scholarships may be awarded to one or two students in each grade. Students promise to study and to respect their teachers and parents.

CELEBRATIONS

Many Thai festivals are joyful, colorful events. Traditional clothing is worn on these days. Many events relate to the rice-growing cycle, ceremonies honoring the king, and religious observances. School children, dressed in their school uniforms, participate in national celebrations.

New Year—January 1 or December 31

This Western holiday is celebrated throughout Thailand. Religious offerings are given. The younger generations exchange gifts and cards. New Year's Eve celebrations are similar to American festivities.

Songkran Festival—April 13 (National Holiday)

The Thai New Year is a very popular holiday. It is a symbol of the Thai love of tradition and of fun. Memorial ceremonies honor the family ancestors. On this traditional day in the midst of the hot season, fish and birds are set free. The king has also designated April 13 as National Fish Release Day to replenish the rivers with fish.

Water throwing is a popular activity. At this time of year, farmers have finished the harvest and can relax, so there is more time for merrymaking.

Royal Plowing Ceremony— Early May

The Royal Plowing Ceremony has been held for 2500 years. The observance is held at the royal field, Sanam Luang, in Bangkok. It marks the beginning of the rice-planting cycle. His Majesty the King presides.

The Lord of the Festival must choose from three *panungs,* the cloth worn around the waist. If he chooses the longest one, little rain will fall during the growing season. If he selects the shortest one, plenty of rain will fall. A procession follows, which includes a red and gold sacred bull that is drawn by other bulls decorated with flowers, drummers in green costumes, drum and umbrella bearers, and four women carrying gold and silver baskets filled with rice seed. The bulls plow a few furrows. The Lord of the Festival scatters rice seed over the plowed furrows. People rush in to gather a few rice grains for good luck after the ceremonies have ended.

H. M. The Queen's Birthday— August 12 (National Holiday)

Nationwide celebration points to Bangkok, where government buildings are decorated and lit at night with colored lights.

Loi Krathong—Full-Moon Night in November

Loi Krathong means "floating the leaf cup." This is Thailand's most beautiful festival. Under the full moon, Thais float their krathongs on the rivers and waterways. These are small, lotus-shaped, banana-leaf boats that contain a lighted candle, glowing incense, a flower, and a small coin to honor the water spirits and to wash away the wrongs of the past year. Thousands of flickering lights float out to sea. It is said that if the candles stay lit, one's wishes will be fulfilled. Thai dancing and fireworks accompany the ceremonies.

Constitution Day— December 10

This day is to commemorate the signing of the constitution in 1932.

H. M. The King's Birthday and Thai National Day—December 5 (National Holiday)

The King's birthday and Thai National Day are celebrated together. Festivities occur throughout Thailand. Government buildings and houses are decorated with spectacular lights at night. One section of Bangkok becomes a fairyland of colored lights.

On Thai National Day, the people renew their determination to maintain the democratic life and look ahead to a happier future. There are religious ceremonies, a reception of the diplomatic corps, and a grand gathering of members of the royal family and high-ranking officials in the Throne Hall.

RESOURCES

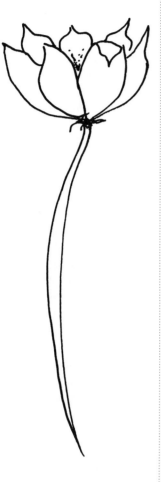

N Nursery
K Kindergarten
P Primary

Books for Children
Ayer, J. *Nu Dang and His Kite*. Harcourt Brace Jovanovich, Inc., 1973. KP
A boy in Bangkok loses his kite. He paddles his canoe on the canal to find it. Colorful illustrations portray the Thai city.

Jacobsen, Peter Otto, and Preben Sejer Kristensen. *A Family in Thailand*. The Bookwright Press, 1986. P
Thai families living in America appreciate a book with photographs about their country. This one has beautiful scenes with a brief text about fishing and living on the river, shopping at the market, and eating favorite Thai foods.

Lye, Keith. *Take a Trip to Thailand*. Franklin Watts, Inc., 1986. P
This is a beautiful book with color photographs of kites, crafts, rice harvesting, houses on stilts, and Bangkok's busy streets.

Thompson, Ruth, and Neil Thompson. *A Family in Thailand*. Lerner Publications Company, 1988. P
Colorful photographs invite children to learn about the games their Thai peers play that are similar to those in America. A look at a Thai school reveals more similarities to American schools than differences.

Books for Adults
Segaller, Denis. *Traditional Thailand—Glimpses of a Nation's Culture*. Illustrated by Yoot-

tachai Kaewdee. Hong Kong Publishing Co., Ltd. (307 Yu Yuet Lai Bldg., 43-55 Wyndham St. Central, Hong Kong), 1982.
This is a collection of twenty-nine selected traditional occupations and skills practiced in Thailand. They range from delicate detailed skills, such as flower arranging, to making palm sugar. This is an excellent source for learning about Thailand's traditional crafts and lifestyles.

Toth, Marian Davis. *Tales from Thailand*. Charles E. Tuttle Company, Inc., 1982.
Older readers and adults learn about Thailand's beginnings, its customs, people, and beliefs through fanciful folktales that reinforce the strength, courage, and faith of this ancient culture.

South East Asia. Ed. by Time-Life Books. Time-Life Books, Inc., 1987.
A brief but explicit study in photographs and text of the six countries of the Association of South East Asian Nations, including Thailand.

Video
Lee's Parasol. Distributed by Coronet Film and Video, 1979.
American children experience Thai lifestyle and learn about the ancient art of making parasols. This exciting craft is vividly illustrated step-by-step, encouraging children to try their creative ideas.

Since 1975 more than three quarters of a million Southeast Asian refugees have settled in the United States. The U.S. has accepted refugees from all social classes, regardless of their job skills.

The first group of refugees were children who were placed in foster homes or adopted by American families. Succeeding groups had lived through traumatic and oppressive experiences, including war, disease, death, separation, and years of waiting for relocation. The purpose of this unit is to assist teachers and administrators in understanding the cultures of these Asian children, whose backgrounds are so different from the U.S. culture. Sensitive teachers can help American children understand Asian values and help Asian children adjust to American life.

SOUTH-EAST ASIAN CULTURES

The information in this unit focuses on Southeast Asian immigrants, but it may be applied to the special needs of any child who is a newcomer to the U.S. Sensitivity to the unique obstacles faced by immigrants will help make their adjustment to their new life smooth and nonthreatening. Activities have not been included in this unit, but you may wish to find out about Indochinese customs and conventions to share with children, or suggest that buddies help their Southeast Asian partners teach the group a song or game together. Folktales, songs, games, pictures, and foods will introduce children to the richness of any culture.

An effort has been made to present accurate information about Southeast Asian children and their families. More detailed background can be found in the references and in Resources.

Barbara Tucker and Janet Brown were valuable consultants in validating the contents of this unit and in interpreting Southeast Asian cultures from the viewpoint of teachers. Ms. Tucker holds a Bachelor of Science degree from Texas Wesleyan, a Master of Science degree in Early Childhood Education from the University of North Texas, and a Master of Arts degree from Southwestern Baptist Theological Seminary. She now teaches ESL in the Birdville Independent School District in Texas. Ms. Brown holds a Bachelor of Science degree from Texas Wesleyan and a Master of Education degree in Early Childhood Education from Texas Woman's University. She now teaches kindergarten and ESL in the Birdville Independent School District in Texas.

SOUTHEAST ASIA DEFINED

Southeast Asia includes many Asian countries. In this unit, the term *Southeast Asia* refers to Cambodia (Kampuchea), Laos, and Vietnam, the three countries under a French protectorate for nearly 100 years until independence in 1953. Most of the refugees since 1975 have come from these countries. The term *Indochina* refers to the three countries collectively.

Cambodia

About 93% of the Cambodians are Khmer, and 7% are Chinese and Vietnamese. The three groups have similar views and lifestyles, stressing respect to others. Socially, the people are reserved and serene, preferring to compromise rather than argue.

Laos

The Laotian culture is similar to the Thai in customs, traditions, lifestyle, and language. They are a hospitable, peace-loving people and have a relaxed attitude toward life.

The Hmong hill tribe lived in the Laotian mountains. This group of farmers has a strong ethnic identity and solidarity. Many of them fled to the United States in the 1970s.

Vietnam

The culture of Vietnam was influenced by the Chinese and the French, who ruled the country in the past. Many Chinese remain in Vietnam today. The upper class adopted the French style of living. Some Vietnamese attended French schools and learned the French language. The Vietnamese work very hard. The children are taught to be polite and respectful to parents, family, and teachers.

In a parent-teacher conference in the U.S., a Vietnamese father told the teacher that his fifth grade son was not allowed to go to bed until he had finished his homework. The younger son in second grade was progressing faster in learning English than his older brother. The teacher reassured the father that his older son would eventually catch up with the other children, but right now a decent night's sleep was more important.

Similarities of the Indochinese Cultures

The three countries are small—the average is similar to Oregon in size. The climate is tropical with mountains and forests. In the rural areas, the people live in villages. They are rice farmers or fishermen. Their food, including rice as the basic staple, is similar to other Asian countries. Family ties are strong. Usually the families are large, and three to four generations may live together.

Indochinese respect authority and age and place a high value on education. Indochinese parents love and respect their children, teaching them to be polite and to obey and respect their elders. Generally, the children are well-behaved.

Their important holiday is the lunar New Year.

Family Life

The Indochinese values are tied to their religious beliefs and the teachings of Confucius. Since many of their values differ from those in America, they are often misunderstood in this country.

The main loyalty of the Indochinese is to the family. The male is the authority and is responsible for enforcing a strict code of behavior. Communication is one-way; the head of the family is not questioned, and discussion is a rarity. The family, the group, is considered to be more important than any one individual. It is not acceptable to call attention to oneself or an individual because it detracts from the loyalty to the family. When a family member has a problem or has made an error, that person must "save face" because each individual's actions reflect on the family. The family must not be shamed or disgraced, even at the risk of overlooking or ignoring unacceptable behavior or an inflammatory situation.

An American teacher wonders if "saving face" causes some families to be hesitant to seek medical care. She had an intelligent Laotian student who suffered from a severe hearing loss. He learned by watching the other children and could do many things. When his uncle came to school for a conference, the teacher mentioned that the child had a problem in learning to talk. She offered to help him find a doctor, but he was reluctant to do so. The uncle responded, "He doesn't speak Laos very well, either"—end of conference. What were the cultural implications of this response?

Infants and toddlers have a great deal of freedom in the home and are reared in a relaxed manner. Parents provide a safe and predictable family environment. From three to five years of age, children learn more responsibility, dressing themselves, being more independent, and doing chores. Strict discipline begins during this period; expected behaviors are not rewarded. Children of all ages are included in adult life. Parents control their children, at times restricting their social interactions to role models deemed acceptable.

ACCULTURATION AND ADAPTATION

Acculturation is the way people adapt to an unfamiliar culture. There are wide differences in the degree to which families adapt to life in a very different culture and in the pace at which the changes take place. The goal of acculturation is to enable people to function in the mainstream of a society. This does not imply that all traditional behaviors must be abandoned. It appears that the older the immigrant, the greater the tendency to adhere to traditions; younger people adapt to a new culture more quickly and completely.

One reason for the rapid acculturation of younger people is school attendance, where children are regularly exposed to new lifestyles and values. In general, the longer an Indochinese family lives in America, the greater the degree of acculturation. People who live in Indochinese communities usually adapt more slowly than those who are located in the mainstream.

Within the Indochinese community, there are differences in degrees of acculturation. Two factors that affect acculturation are English proficiency and socioeconomic status. If American adults, especially teachers, become familiar with each family, they may be able to determine the degree of acculturation and then be able to understand the children's needs.

Most Southeast Asian refugees fled their countries because they lost hope for survival. War, hunger, politics, and other reasons motivated them to look for a better life with hope for freedom and humane treatment. Many family members did not make it to America.

Many Indochinese arrived in the United States confused, afraid, and frustrated. They came from agricultural areas to an industrial and technological society without the support of friends and guidance of family members.

Roles changed in many families. Since it was easier for some women to get work, the role of care-giver became the responsibility of the father. Some men lost their professional status and could find only menial jobs. Conflict in the family resulted when children learned American ways at school.

In America, Indochinese girls are often responsible for the care of the younger children after school and for cooking the evening meal because their mothers, and sometimes fathers, work at night. In their homeland, they were accustomed to having the mother at home full time and to living with their extended families, where adequate help and supervision were always available.

The refugees were shocked by some American behaviors—people in the U.S. are outspoken and assertive, work very hard, and are always in a hurry. Americans have big cars, big homes, and beautiful clothes. It is very different from the easy and simple life they had experienced in Asia.

The children were also affected. Some young children were brain-damaged due to prolonged malnutrition. The life in refugee camps and the harrowing trip to the U.S. caused poor mental health in older children, making them silent and withdrawn.

Children complained about bad dreams, and created harsh drawings of guns and explosions. Many had never attended school. One kindergarten teacher had to teach a Southeast Asian child who had lived in a refugee camp to leave food he didn't like on the plate rather than spitting it out on the cafeteria floor.

A few Southeast Asian children at one school had a tendency to be aggressive and wild. The teachers decided that they may have learned these survival behaviors in the refugee camps, and that they may also have lacked parental supervision after school because the parents were trying to survive economically by working double shifts or multiple jobs.

Considering these experiences, teachers must be sensitive, understanding, and empathetic. Since Indochinese children are reared to control their emotions, it is difficult to determine their emotional health. Teachers may need the help of competent specialists to identify those who need help and to provide it.

EDUCATION

The first generation of Indochinese families in America became acculturated into life in the United States through the schools. Once children made basic adjustments and learned English, they became achievers. Academic achievement is the greatest tribute a child can bring to parents and the entire family. Since their values and behaviors are different from those in America, they may need help to develop social and emotional skills for their well-being here.

Teachers and specialists who are culturally aware probably interpret the behaviors of Indochinese children more accurately than those who are insensitive to cultural differences. For example, in one school a child who was very quiet, an Indochinese virtue, was sent to a speech therapist for "help." Some teachers mistakenly assume that Southeast Asian students are not learning anything because they do not respond verbally. Teachers need to watch and learn to interpret what a child is doing. The interactive environment in an informal classroom is a very good place to observe children without making them uncomfortable.

Indochinese children are surprised by the friendliness of the American teacher and the informality of the classroom. It is unbelievable to them that a teacher would admit an error, sit on a desk, dress informally, and laugh with the children. Teachers, with the help of parents, learn to be sensitive to the anxieties and needs of the children.

Indochinese Schools

School-age children were accustomed to a formal, structured classroom. The lecture method was common. Children learned by rote, reciting a lesson verbatim. There was little interaction between teacher and children. However, the teacher was highly respected. Children would never disagree with a teacher or interrupt a lesson with a question or a comment.

Mathematics and science were emphasized. Books and materials were scarce and children had no opportunity to learn library skills. Only private schools offered kindergarten; play, a learning method for young children, was not considered important.

For the Teacher of Indochinese Children

The following are some guidelines to accommodate Indochinese children in your classroom.
• Introduce the American system of education and life in the U.S. to Indochinese children one step at a time.
• Give children ample time to make adjustments.
• Have other children role-play situations when Indochinese children cannot understand the language.
• Explain appropriate differences between American and Indochinese schools to American classmates as needed.

Your role is crucial in assisting Indochinese children to adjust to school life. The following are four important qualities to keep in mind:
• Present a caring attitude. You are a very significant person to children; they naturally respect

and look up to you. Accept these children as they are, be sensitive to their behaviors and needs, and provide a receptive classroom environment to send a positive message: I care.

• Foster a positive self-concept. Treat the children as worthy individuals who can learn and adapt, offer simple suggestions to them for making academic and emotional adjustments, and tailor learning activities so that the children are successful to encourage the development of a positive self-concept.

• Understand the process of adjustment. Empathize with the adjustments Indochinese families must make and endeavor to understand what it takes to live in American society to develop positive relationships with children and parents.

• Learn about Indochinese culture. Make an effort to learn as much about Indochinese culture as possible and become acquainted with families and Indochinese aides in school to prevent misinterpretations of children's behavior.

Learning the English Language

The ability to understand and speak the English language, and then to write and read it, is basic to success in school. The younger the child and the more standard his native language, the less time is required to learn another language. The experience in one urban school district has been that many Indochinese children who attend an informal kindergarten for one year learn English and are successful in first grade. The informal classroom provides many opportunities for daily interaction among children, who can learn much from each other. The initial emphasis is on oral language.

Development of literacy and the whole language approach, appropriate ways of making the transition from oral language to writing and reading, are excellent methods of learning language for children of all ages. The expectation and hope are that Indochinese children will become bilingual and bicultural citizens, learninging English and the culture of America, while also retaining their native language and traditions.

Language Programs

School districts usually adopt one method of teaching English to non-English-speaking children. Classroom teachers work with ESL teachers in these programs.

In a bilingual program, instruction begins in the native language while children learn English, and gradually the transition is made to teaching in English. An Indochinese aide translates the language as needed. In the ESL program, all instruction is in English. Teaching is done in small groups, with a great deal of interaction between teacher and children. Teachers create many variations of these basic approaches.

For the Teacher

• Enunciate clearly and speak at a moderate rate. Limit the use of slang and idioms; if used, be certain that children understand the expressions. Use simple vocabulary and sentences—basic English.

• Make an effort to have an Indochinese aide or volunteer who can interpret immediately when needed.

• Expect children to have difficulty pronouncing sounds that are not part of their native language.

• Learn some words that express needs—bathroom, illness, hunger, pencil, paper, and so on.

• Phrase questions and directions consistently for children who know very little English. If the form changes, be certain children understand it.

BEHAVIORS AND CUSTOMS OF INDOCHINESE CHILDREN

The selected Indochinese behaviors that follow seem to be the most difficult for teachers to understand. A wide variation of any one behavior is expected. The degree of acculturation and adaptation of the family to American life is an important factor in children's behavior. Some children's behaviors may be traced to their experiences in refugee camps, among other factors. Children born in the U.S. are more likely to adopt American behaviors.

Attempt to know the family well enough to interpret the child's behavior as accurately as possible and secure assistance from specialized consultants in school districts and community agencies.

Names

Cambodians and Vietnamese write their names with the family name first, the middle name (if any) next, and the first name last. Laotians write their names as Americans do.

Find out whether families use the traditional or American style of writing names. First names are used to address others.

Names are important to children and an effort should be made to pronounce them correctly. Americanizing a name is not appropriate unless the family chooses to do so. Some children may wish to use American names.

Birthdays

Vietnamese have two birthdays—one marking their chronological age and one celebrated at the lunar New Year. Prior to the time that births were recorded, everyone's birthday was on the New Year's Day.

Birth records are not always accurate. One teacher suspected that some "five-year-olds" in her kindergarten were younger because of the way they acted.

To determine accurate ages, find out which practice is followed and whether they continue it in America. In any case, it is appropriate to celebrate the child's chronological birthday.

Modesty

Indochinese children are taught to be modest and humble about their achievements. Therefore, they often indicate less than they actually know. They talk about or demonstrate their knowledge only when asked.

At first, expect the children to be modest and do not ask them to change. Allow them gradually to adopt some behaviors of American children.

Praise

It is difficult for Indochinese children to accept praise. Usually they refuse it, saying they do not deserve it. Behaviors that are expected of children in these countries are not given special recognition. Children dismiss compliments by discussing their faults. Acknowledge children's successes with a smile, a quiet "thank you," or similar gesture.

Shyness

For Indochinese children, shyness is a positive trait, a polite way of showing respect to adults and other superiors. Quiet, reserved behavior also maintains harmony in interactions with others, a basic virtue in Indochinese life.

In America, shyness can easily be interpreted as passivity.

Accept shyness in these children. As they become more comfortable in the classroom, they may become less shy in response to the actions and expectations of their peers.

Smile

The smile is a common non-verbal communication in Indochina. People smile in all situations—both when they are happy and unhappy. They smile when reprimanded, when they do not understand a lesson, and when they cannot answer a question.

The smile is a strange habit to American teachers, who often interpret it as smiling at the wrong time. Treat the smile as an acceptable, polite, respectful behavior.

Time

Since most Indochinese came from an agricultural society, punctuality is not important. Time is flexible. Even in urban areas, being on time is far less important than it is in the U.S.

Explain to Indochinese children and parents the importance of punctuality in America. They will cooperate when they understand the idea; parents will begin to pick up their children on time.

Courtesy

One way Indochinese greet each other is the "wai," a non-verbal greeting used for hello and good-bye. The two flat hands are joined and the head is bowed slightly. (See the Thailand unit for an illustration.)

Polite social forms are "thank you," "sorry," "excuse me," and "I beg your pardon." Indochinese say "No, thank you" when offered something; if it is offered twice, they will usually accept it.

Indochinese courtesies need not disrupt the classroom. Explain them to American children and gradually explain American courtesies to Indochinese children.

Self-Control

Indochinese children learn to control their behavior and emotions. They neither show their feelings nor talk about them. They inhibit strong emotions and suppress aggressive behavior.

Learn to observe other behaviors that signal children's emotions. As they gradually interact more freely with you, their feelings may become more evident.

First-generation children from educated families who did not experience war and the camps exhibit traditional self-control. Children who learned to use survival skills in the camps are more aggressive.

School Practices

Indochinese children are not accustomed to speaking in front of a class. Give them time to observe American children.

Indochinese children are not accustomed to asking for help or asking questions. Begin a buddy system, matching an Indochinese child with a compatible American child, and encourage the Indochinese child to depend on the buddy.

Indochinese children have learned to listen carefully. Schedule a daily time to read or tell stories aloud. Use books with a tape of the text and recordings with music, language, and movements.

AMERICAN TEACHERS SPEAK

Some information in this unit comes from teachers of Indochinese children. The following examples are from their experiences.

Young children learn English easily and generally do well in school. Older children often have more difficulty. The American culture confuses them. They cannot speak English, and they hesitate to put forth effort in school because they fear failure.

After teachers began working with Indochinese children, they realized that safety has to be an initial concern, especially for children from rural areas. Children may not be conscious of the hazards of crossing streets, of the need to obey traffic signals, and of the possibility of traffic accidents. In Indochina, many children slept outdoors in hammocks hung across the cool creeks. In America, some have had serious accidents while playing in streams and rivers, especially after heavy rains. Safety should be stressed to parents and children.

An Indochinese child needs to be taught how to use ordinary American conveniences, including the bathroom; Asian-style toilets are very different from American toilets.

ESL teachers discovered that the small class and frequent interaction with the teacher created a safe haven for Indochinese children. As the time approached to ease them into the regular classroom, the teachers instructed them much more formally—similar to the atmosphere in native schools. They were firm, business-like, and very structured. This served to ease the transition.

In the ESL program, Indochinese children made perfect scores in spelling until one teacher changed the order of the words. The children had memorized them in order but did not understand them.

Indochinese children in the ESL program go through a silent phase in which they are very attentive but do not respond. Some teachers assume they are not learning English, but their receptive language is developing.

Since Indochinese children are good listeners, one ESL teacher discovered that a valuable activity is listening to tapes, following the text in the book. She believes it is important for these children to hear a natural speaking voice that models English-language patterns and rhythms. If you do not make the tapes yourself, listen to them before purchasing. The quality of sound varies a great deal in commercial tapes. The stories and information children learn from the tapes and books encourage them to converse and respond orally. The informal classroom, where children interact freely with each other, provides opportunities for Indochinese children to practice oral language when they feel comfortable to do so.

Many teachers took the time to help Indochinese families, especially the first groups of refugees. They taught English to parents or referred them to literacy programs and introduced them to agencies that could provide needed assistance. Former students returned to teachers for help. Some teachers were invited to annual holiday and family celebrations. Today, the new arrivals have a support system from earlier immigrant families. Teachers recommend that the school prepare a list for new arrivals of agencies and people with telephone numbers.

One teacher took a child to the nurse because she suspected an eye problem. She also suspected that the parents, who could not afford medical care, did not know how to find help. If they had lived in refugee camps, medical needs may have been neglected. The child received free glasses and became a high achiever in school.

Donny was in kindergarten. He could speak English and read some words. He was clever enough to make the teacher think that he knew what he was doing, so he was placed in first grade. Soon it became evident that he was not ready for this level. He repeated first grade the next year, a disaster for him. He developed behavior problems. Observant teachers felt that, had he stayed in kindergarten and not been "misplaced," his school life would have been a story of success.

Diagnosing learning levels or disabilities in Indochinese children who speak little English is very difficult. It is hard to find someone who is qualified to assess the child in the native language. Some children need special education in Lao, but since it is not available, teachers do the best they can.

A new Lao family moved into a community. Papone was enrolled in kindergarten, and on his first day there he was fearful about everything. He was terrified during story hour and the children's tea party. When children dressed up during dramat-

ic play, he screamed and held onto the teacher's leg. When asked if he would like a cookie, he cried. The next day, during a thunderstorm and tornado alert when children huddled in the hall, he was almost uncontrollable. After talking to his parents, the teacher began to understand his behavior. Papone had reason to be full of fear because of his experiences in the boat and in the refugee camps. A patient and understanding teacher helped him overcome many fears.

The Indochinese father of two daughters who had lived in refugee camps requested that they be placed in the same classroom at first. Their past experiences had caused them to be fearful of new situations. After a few weeks, they were placed in first and third grade rooms. They adapted easily. The gradual transition into their own level of class had been a wise course of action.

Teachers of Indochinese students became "kid watchers," astute observers of children's behaviors. One girl, when asked if she could read, always shook her head "no." But when she did not know she was being observed, she went to the book center to read. The teacher of another girl who spoke infrequently observed her whispering to other children. Looking at her written work more carefully, the teacher concluded that the girl was learning but was just not ready to speak in class.

Of four boys who were friends, three passed the CAT, but one did not. He spoke English fluently, functioned normally in class, and was well-liked. He had to pass the test to

be eligible to enter junior high school. When the teacher explained the purpose of the test to him—and that if he passed it, he could work on the computer instead of attending ESL class—he took it again and passed with flying colors.

Parents and the School

Learning is very serious to Indochinese parents. They place a high value on education because they believe that it determines the job and position of their children in the future. Parents pressure their children to study and do well in school. They might appear passive, but they are very interested and cooperative. One difficulty may be their inability to understand English. However, some Indochinese adults attend English classes or learn the language from their children or on the job.

Parents respect your authority, believing that you will do what is best for the child. Often they feel that American teachers do not understand the Indochinese culture. Parents will be courteous, listen carefully, and respond positively.

A relationship with parents begins with trust, at times a difficult point to reach. Trust can be established through contacts with friends and relatives who already know you. An Indochinese aide can be a window to the community. Gradually, you will become well acquainted with Indochinese parents. When the parents trust you, they are very cooperative.

Those teaching Indochinese children recommend that you take the initiative in involving parents. It may take some parents several years to become accustomed to attending school conferences and meetings. They may send a relative or older child in their stead because their work schedule may not coincide with the school schedule or they cannot afford the loss of income resulting from their attendance at school functions.

What Teachers Can Do

The following tips will help you interact successfully with parents of Indochinese children:

• Be professional in appearance and behavior.
• Learn to know the parents by making contact with them as often as possible.
• Visit parents, but be aware that they may not be comfortable meeting you in their homes due to their living situation.
• Have an interpreter and translator available as needed. Indochinese from the community may be willing volunteers. Send bilingual memos to the parents.
• Encourage parents to express their views and ask questions. Give them time to develop the courage to do so.
• Learn some expressions in Indochinese languages.
• Attend Indochinese public programs and celebrations.
• Schedule school orientation meetings for parents, using a bilingual aide who can translate.
• Plan a social event for both Indochinese and American parents to share their cultures.
• Establish a school library for Indochinese parents, with books, brochures, recordings, and short information sheets.

Success in America

Southeast Asian children who arrived here in 1975 and soon after generally have done well in school. They learned English quickly and were placed in age-appropriate classes. However, they were acculturated in American families. The Southeast Asians who arrived in more recent years have had more difficulty adjusting to American society. Many come with limited education, years of living in camps, and suffering from many health problems. The incomes of Indochinese families range from poverty levels to upper middle class.

Many Southeast Asians have been very successful. Among them are winners of college scholarships and science fair prizes, high school valedictorians, soccer champions, and a leader of a class at West Point. A high proportion finish high school and graduate from college. Achievement ranges from drop-outs to high academic achievers. In general, academic success in the beginning grades can lead to success throughout life.

HUMAN RIGHTS

Eleanor Roosevelt was a principal author of the Universal Declaration of Human Rights, which was adopted by the United Nations General Assembly in 1948. For the International Year of the Child in 1979, the United Nations adopted a "Declaration of the Rights of the Child." May all children in the world enjoy these rights before the middle of the next century.

UN Declaration of the Rights of the Child

THE RIGHT
• to affection, love, and understanding.
• to adequate nutrition and medical care.
• to free education.
• to full opportunity for play and recreation.
• to a name and nationality.
• to special care, if handicapped.
• to be among the first to receive relief in times of disaster.
• to learn to be a useful member of society and to develop individual abilities.
• to be brought up in a spirit of peace and universal brotherhood.
• to enjoy these rights, regardless of race, color, sex, religion, national or social origin.

International Year of the Child 1979

REFERENCES

Berger, Eugenia H. *Parents as Partners in Education: The school and home working together.* 2nd ed. Merrill Publishing Co., 1987.

Buu, Tri, et al. *Han Hanh Duoc Gap (Happy to Meet You.)* Pennsylvania State Department of Education, Bureau of Curriculum Services, ERIC ED 134 034. Harrisburg, Penn.: 1976.

Dung, Trin H. Ngoc. "Understanding Asian Families: A Vietnamese Perspective." *Children Today,* Vol. 13 (1984), pp. 10-12.

Everingham, John. "One Family's Odyssey to America." (Hmong) *National Geographic,* Vol. 157 (1980), pp.643-661.

Garrett, W.E. "Refuge from Terror." *National Geographic,* Vol. 157 (1980), pp. 633-642.

Hammond, R. E., and G.L. Hendricks (eds.). *Southeast Asian Refugee Youth: An Annotated Bibliography.* Southeast Asian Refugee Studies, Occasional Papers, No. 6, Southeast Asian Refugee Studies Project, Center for Urban and Regional Affairs, University of Minnesota. Minneapolis, Minn.: 1988.

Handbook for Teachers of Vietnamese Students. Intercultural Development Research Association, Office of Education (DHEW), Washington, D.C. ERIC ED 135 881. San Antonio, Texas: June, 1976.

Leung, Esther K. "Cultural and Acculturational Commonalities and Diversities Among Asian Americans. Identification and programming considerations." Paper presented at the Ethnic and Multicultural Symposia. ERIC ED 298 708. Dallas, Texas: 1986.

Los Angeles County Public Ethnic Resource Centers: The American Indian Resource Center, Asian Pacific Resource Center, Black Resource Center, Chicano Resource Center. Los Angeles County Public Library. ERIC ED 298 962. Los Angeles: 1988.

Morrow, Robert D., and H.J. McBride. *Considerations for Educators in Working with Southeast-Asian Children and Their Families.* Proceedings of the Annual ACRES National Rural Special Education Conference, ERIC ED 299 730. February, 1988.

National Association for the Education of Young Children Publications, 1834 Connecticut Ave., N.W., Washington, D.C. 20009-5786. 1-800-424-2460.
Cazden, C., ed. *Language in Early Childhood Education.*
Schickedanz, J. *More Than the ABC's: The Early Stages of Reading and Writing.*
Strickland, D. S., and L. M. Morrow, eds. *Emerging Literacy: Young Children Learn to Read and Write.*

Nguyen, Liem T. *Vietnamese Culture Kit.* Iowa State University of Science and Technology, Research Institute for Studies in Education, ERIC ED 149 602. Ames, Iowa: 1976.

Phap, Dam T. *A Manual for Teachers of Indochinese Students.* Intercultural Development

Research Association., ERIC ED 205 663. San Antonio, Texas: 1981.

"The Social and Psychological Adjustment of Southeast Asians." Urban Education Research Information. *Urban Review,* Vol. 17 (1985), pp. 147-152.

Saylor, Lucinda. *Indochinese Refugees: An Administrator's Handbook.* South Carolina State Department of Education, ERIC ED 266 210, Columbia, S.C.: 1985.

Solheim II, W. G. "New Light on a Forgotten Past." Southeast Asia 2. *National Geographic,* Vol. 139 (1971), pp. 330-339.

Some Hints to Work with Vietnamese Students. Arizona State Department of Education, ERIC ED 133 383. Phoenix, Ariz.: 1976.

Stone, C. Scott, and J. E. McGowan. *Wrapped in the Wind's Shawl.* Refugees of Southeast Asian and the Western World. San Rafael, Calif.: Presidio Press, 1980.

Strand, Paul J., and W. Jones, Jr., *Indochinese Refugees in America.* Problems of adaptation and assimilation. Duke Press Policy Studies. Durham, N.C.: Duke University Press, 1985.

White, P. T. "Mosaic of Cultures." Southeast Asia 1. *National Geographic,* Vol. 139 (1971), pp. 296-329.

RESOURCES

N Nursery
K Kindergarten
P Primary
I Intermediate
A Adult

Books for Children

Diep, Bridgette. *Trip Through Cambodia.* Scroll Press. NKP.

Forney, Inor, and E. H. Forney. *Our Friends in Viet-Nam.* Charles E. Tuttle Co, 1970. P
Simple text and line drawings encourage children to learn about Vietnamese daily life, better enabling them to understand their friends of Vietnamese heritage.

Graham, Gail B. *The Beggar in the Blanket and Other Vietnamese Tales.* Retold by G. B. Graham. Dial Press, 1970. KP
Eight Vietnamese folktales, including an Oriental Cinderella tale and a legend explaining why all crows seem to vanish from Vietnam during the month of Ngau.

Lee, Jeanne M. *Ba Nam.* Henry Holt & Company, 1987. P
The Vietnamese author recalls an adventure in her childhood on Thah-Minh Day. Young children learn that one cannot always judge another by outward appearance.

Mabie, Margot C. *Vietnam There and Here.* Holt, Rinehart, and Winston, Inc., 1985. IA

MacMillan, Dianne, and Dorothy Freeman. *My Best Friend, Duc Tran: Meeting a Vietnamese-American Family.* Julian Messner, 1987. P
This reader introduces children to the Vietnamese culture as dramatized by a boy of Vietnamese ancestry living in California.

Roland, Donna. *Grandfather's Stories from Viet Nam.* Open My World Publishing, 1985. P
The necessity of maintaining cultural values through traditional stories is dramatized by Vinh and Lang in this book. A task card and an activity card suggesting extended experiences are included with the book.

Rutledge, Paul. *The Vietnamese in America.* Lerner Publications Company, 1987. IA

Stanck, Muriel. *We Came from Vietnam.* Albert Whitman and Company, 1985. P
A text for older children with photographs that interest all children. This book describes how a family adjusts to an American way of life, including observing Vietnamese customs.

Surat, Michele Marid. *Angel Child, Dragon Child.* Scholastic, 1983. KP
A courageous Vietnamese-American deals with "the red-beaded bag" and a school where children "wave their hands and say their lessons one by one". The sensitive text is supported by subtle drawings.

Tran Van Dien and Le Tinh Thong. Ngay Kua O Que Hrong Toi. *Once in Vietnam.* National Textbook Company, 1985. P
A series of seven bilingual books that acquaint young readers with folktales of Vietnam. The Vietnamese translation allows American children to become familiar with the Viet-

namese written language. Ask a Vietnamese parent to read these tales to the class.

Tran-Khanh-Tuyet. *The Little Weaver of Thai-Yen Village*. Children's Book Press, 1987.   P
A bilingual literary experience that teaches about the cruelty of war. Consider the age and experience of the children before reading this book to them. The author reminds us of the refugees who came to North America and their struggle to maintain their ethnicity.

Books and Articles for Adults
California's Family Day Care Training Program was designed to recruit and train Lao, Vietnamese, and Chinese refugees to establish their own state-licensed family day care homes in seven weeks. English version.
ED 303 245—Vietnamese Language
ED 303 246—Lao Language
ED 303 247—Southeast Asian Family Day Care Resource Manual

Caplan, Nathan. *The Boat People and Achievement in America: A Study of Family Life, Hard Work and Cultural Values*. University of Michigan Press, 1989.

Carrison, Muriel P. *Cambodian Folk Stories from the Gatiloke*. Charles E. Tuttle, Inc., 1987.
The author has gathered these folktales to foster an awareness of and preserve the Cambodian lifestyle. Delicate drawings enliven the text.

Chen, Lai Nam. *Images of Southeast Asia in Children's Fiction*. Singapore University Press, 1981.

The author analyzes how the West views the East, evaluating 150 children's books about Southeast Asia. The more recent books indicate a more accurate understanding of Southeast Asian countries. Includes annotated bibliography.

Dommen, Arthur J. Laos, *Keystone of Indochina*. Westview Press, 1985.

Hinton, Harold C. East *Asia and the Western Pacific*. Stryker-Post Publications, 1989.
Interesting facts about the history, special days, ethnic background, and population of Thailand, Laos, Vietnam, the Republic of Korea, Japan, the People's Republic of China, Cambodia, and the Republic of China.

Knoll, Tricia. *Becoming Americans: Asian Sojourners, Immigrants, and Refugees in the Western United States*. Coast to Coast Books, 1982.
Histories and cultures of Asian American families—Vietnamese, Laotian, Cambodian and others—are revealed through interviews and accounts of their successes in America. Photographs and bibliography included.

Morrow, Robert D. "What's in a Name? In Particular, a Southeast Asian Name?" *Young Children*, Vol. 44, NAEYC (1989), pp. 20 - 23.
Suggestions for correctly using the names of people of other nationalities. A list of do's and don'ts is included, as well as a list of ideas for caregivers and teachers to help them establish

a rapport with Southeast Asian children and their parents.

Nakatsu, Gail. *Family Day Care Training Curriculum*. Union of Pan Asian Communities, Administration for Children, Youth, and Families (DHHS), ERIC ED 303 244. San Diego (Calif.) County Department of Social Services, 1987.

Proudfoot, Robert. *Even the Birds Don't Sound the Same Here: The Laotians Search for Heart in American Culture*. American University Studies. Lang, Peter Publishers, 1989.

Rigg, P., and V. G.Allen (Eds.) *When They Don't All Speak English: Integrating the ESL Students into the Regular Classroom*. Urbana, Il.: National Council of Teachers of English, 1989.
Request a list of publications: NCTE,1111 Kenyon Rd., Urbana, IL: 61801.
Note: This organization publishes high-quality books and booklets.

Roland, Donna. *More of Grandfather's Stories from Cambodia*. Open My World Publishing, 1984.
Learning from elders is part of the Cambodian way of life. The folktale "How Much for a Shadow" is too abstract for young children, but the story of Cambodia as a country and the family living in America begins to give children insight into the life of refugees and immigrants.

Szymusiak, Molyda. *The Stones Cry Out: A Cambodian Childhood*, 1975-1980. Hill and Wang, 1987.

Tollefson, James W. Alien Winds: *The Reeducation of America's Indochinese Refugees*. Praeger, 1989.

Manipulatives

Language Lotto—Cambodian. Claudia's Caravan.
This game comes complete with a cassette tape containing needed vocabulary. Days of the week, animals, and colors are included for young children to practice; other categories of vocabulary are presented for older children.

Language Lotto—Vietnamese. Claudia's Caravan.
This lotto set, including cards and audiocassette tape, is excellent for ESL.

RESOURCES FOR SOUTH-EAST ASIANS

Action for Children (Publication)
c/o UNICEF
3 UN Plaza
New York, NY 10017

Dainamco
551 West Arden Ave.
Glendale, CA 91203

Department of Health and Human Services
Family Support Administration
Office of Refugee Resettlement
370 L'Enfant Promenade, SW
Washington, DC 20447
Request refugee resource materials.

ERIC Clearinghouse on Languages and Linguistics (ERIC-CLL)
Center for Applied Linguistics
1118 22nd Street, NW
Washington, DC 20037

Intercultural Developmental Research Association
5835 Callaghan Rd., Suite 350
San Antonio, TX 78228

Intercultural Training Resource Center
190 Cummins Highway
Roslindale, MA 02131

Nguyen
P.O. Box 873
Carbondale, IL 62903
Request list of Asia books.

Office of Ethnic and Multicultural Concerns
The Council for Exceptional Children
1920 Association Dr.
Reston, VA 22091-1589

Que-Huong
P.O. Box 156, Station T
Toronto, Ontario
Canada

Southeast Asian Refugees Studies Project
330 Hubert H. Humphrey Center
301 19th Avenue South
Minneapolis, MN 55455

Spoken Language Services, Inc.
P.O. Box 783
Ithaca, NY 14851
Request self-teaching audiocassettes in numerous languages.

UN High Commissioners for Refugees
Palais des Nations
CH-1211
Geneva 10, Switzerland
Publishes Refugee Magazine

UN Publications
c/o UNICEF
3 UN Plaza
Room LX - 2300
New York, NY 10017

MULTI-CULTURAL RESOURCES

N Nursery
K Kindergarten
P Primary

Books for Children

Ada, Alma Flor. *The Gold Coin.* Atheneum, 1991. PI
In a Central American setting, Doria Josefa learns how to care about others.

Agard, John. *The Calypso Alphabet.* Henry Holt & Co., 1989. NK
This Guyana-born author provides a descriptive text, brilliantly illustrated. Caribbean Island words are defined.

Coblence, Jean Michel. *Asian Civilizations.* Silver Burdett, 1988. P
Lavish illustrations and detailed text explore the Asian continent, Japan, and India.

Hoffman, Phyllis. *Meatball.* Harper Collins Publishers, 1991. NK.
A multicultural daycare setting includes many opportunities to experience a blending of diverse languages.

Isadora, Rachel. *City Seen from A to Z.* Greenwillow Books, 1983. NK
Each black-and-white sketch suggests some facet of life in the city. Multi-ethnic emphasis makes this an important inclusion for every library. Children delight in identifying the letters of the alphabet.

Jones, Rebecca C. *Matthew and Tilly.* Dutton Children's Books, 1991. NK
Children identify with a "best friends" theme. A Washington Heights neighborhood is the setting for this clever story.

Kelly, Emily. *Happy New Year.* Carolrhoda Books, 1984. NKP
On New Year's Eve, where in the world do children throw pails of water out their windows at midnight? Or eat twelve grapes at the stroke of midnight? Or set off firecrackers? Included in this brief book are a map, recipes, and descriptions of New Year customs.

Lillie, Patricia. *Jake and Rosie.* Greenwillow Books, 1989. NK
Waiting for a best friend's return can seem interminable.

Lyon, George Ella. *Together.* Orchard Books, 1989. N
Bright illustrations and lilting text encourage cooperation between friends.

Martin, Bill Jr. *I Am Freedom's Child.* DLM Teaching Resources, 1987. NK
"Hooray for Freedom's Child" and hooray for illustrator Symeon Shimin, whose drawings, washed in yellow, brown, and red tones, capture the interest of all. Available as a Big Book.

Marzollo, Jean. *Pretend You're a Cat.* Dial Books for Young Readers, 1990. NK
Jerry Pinkney's glorious pencil and watercolor drawings enliven this clever action poem for children. An amazing book.

McMillan, Bruce. *Dry or Wet?* Lothrop, Lee & Shepard Books, 1988. NK
Fun-filled photographs encourage children to explore the concepts of wet and dry.

Morris, Ann. *Bread Bread Bread*. Lothrop, Lee & Shepard Books, 1989.
"People eat bread all over the world," and here are the beautiful photographs to prove it. Look for *Hats Hats Hats* by the same author to discover that "the world is full of hats."

_____. *Loving*. Lothrop, Lee & Shepard Books, 1990. NK
Poignant photographs from many cultures depict people showing love for one another.

_____. *On the Go*. Lothrop, Lee & Shepard Books, 1990. NK
A photographic glimpse of the means of travel of numerous cultures.

Nunes, Susan. *Coyote Dreams*. Atheneum, 1988. KP
Soft watercolors create a young boy's dream world of coyotes and ancient ones.

Ottos, Svend. *The Giant Fish and Other Stories*. Larousse and Company, Inc., 1981. KP
Three adventures of children and animals introduce children to many lifestyles.

Platz, Helen. *A Week of Lullabies*. Greenwillow Books, 1988. NK
Giovanni and Tennyson head the list of superstars who authored these goodnight poems.

Quinsey, Mary Beth. *Why Does that Man Have Such a Big Nose?* Parenting Press, Inc., 1986. NK
Answers in a matter-of-fact manner the very honest questions that children have about human differences.

Rogow, Zach. *Oranges*. Orchard Books, 1988. NK
This gentle book encourages contemplation of the effort and cooperation it takes to grow and produce an orange.

Sarnoff, Jane, and Reynold Ruffins. *Light the Candles! Beat the Drums! A Book of Holidays*. Charles Scribner's Sons, 1979. PI
An essential resource for teacher's library, this text was written for older children. It is useful when inserting important holidays—such as Martin Luther King, Jr.'s, birthday; Purim; Easter; Cinco de mayo; Thanksgiving day; and many others—into the curriculum plan.

Simon, Norma. *I'm Busy, Too*. Albert Whitman and Company, 1980 NK
Charlie, Sara, and Mikeys prepare for school in separate households. The clever illustrator gives us a bird's-eye view of their busy school life.

Singer, Marilyn. *Nine O'Clock Lullaby*. Harper Collins Publishers, 1991. NK
The difficult concepts of time and distance are explained in an interesting way.

Spier, Peter. *People*. Doubleday, 1980. NKP
In splendid detail, Peter Spier illustrates the differences between peoples of the earth. Through this celebration of human diversity, young children can begin to move from their own familiar world to the whole world.

Tharlet, Eve. *The Little Cooks: Recipes from Around the World for Boys and Girls*. UNICEF. NKP
With the clever illustrations, children find it easy to follow the directions for making baked bananas from Guatemala, empanadas from Chile, shrimp and rice from China, and many other dishes. The colorful format, with children parading about the large bowls of salad or lifting a giant tomato, makes this book a must for every classroom. Laminated pages add to the book's durability.

Books for Adults
Addison-Wesley Big Books Program. Addison-Wesley Publishing Co., Inc., 1989.
Children love this big book collection of eight old favorites that are retold in word pictures and predictable read-along text. The teacher's guides, Whole Language Activities for Early Childhood, include many suggestions for promoting cultural experiences.

The Multicultural Sing-Along Big Book Program (1991) features four original stories set to music, and is also accompanied by a Whole Language Activity Guide.

Banks, James A., and Cherry A. McGee Banks. *Multicultural Education: Issues and Perspectives*. Allyn and Bacon, 1989.
With a textbook format, this scholarly guide includes information for any classroom teacher who seeks to understand the complexities of multicultural education.

Bibliography of Books for Children. Association for Childhood Education International, 1989. From the "Individual Poets" section—with Nikki Giovanni, Arnold Adoff, Lucille Clifton and Eloise Greenfield—to the "Picture Books" section—with Mitsumara Anno and other international writers—this work is extremely helpful when selecting books for your class or school library.

Cech, Maureen. *Globalchild: Multicultural Resources for Young Children*. Addison-Wesley Publishing Company, 1991. Activities organized in a seasonal format heighten children's awareness of other cultures in a sensitive, respectful way. Blackline masters included.

Cohn, Anna, and Lacinda A. Leach, eds. *Generations*. Olive Press, 1987. A splendid publication by the Smithsonian on the occasion of the opening of the International Gallery. The "universal family album" is rich with colorful photographs, quotations, and essays.

Colangelo, Nicholas, Dick Dustin, and Cecelia Foxley, eds. *Multicultural Nonsexist Education: A Human Relations Approach*. Kendall Hunt Publishing Company, 1985. Advocates of multicultural, nonsexist education are challenged by these articles that address the importance of the multicultural approach.

Crary, Elizabeth, et al. *Historical Activity Guide*. Parenting Press, Inc., 1989.
This text was originally written to accompany a text describing Washington's ethnic diversity for the 1989 State Centennial Celebration. The many activities can enrich young school children's experience as they cook sticky rice, play Drop Stick, or fashion an origami crane. Scandinavian, Japanese, Chinese, Latvian, Mexican, and American Indian ideas are shared.

Derman-Sparks, Louise, and the ABC Task Force. *Anti-Bias Curriculum: Tools for Empowering Young Children*. NAEYC, 1989. A guide for beginning "the journey toward anti-bias identity and attitudes." This wealth of ideas for curriculum is a must for every school's library.

Fantini, Mario D., and Rene Cardenos, eds. *Parenting in a Multicultural Society*. Longman, Inc., 1980. Black, Mexican, Asian, Puerto Rican, and American Indian parenting perspectives and family issues are the focus of this anthology.

Frank, Mary, ed. *Newcomers to the United States: Children and Families*. Haworth Press, Inc., 1983. The contributors have addressed the contemporary issues facing immigrants, refugees, and undocumented aliens. Solutions, as well as recommendations for research projects, are suggested in these current, informative essays.

Glover, Mary Kenner. "A Bag of Hair: American First Graders Experience Japan," *Childhood Education*. Association for Childhood Education International, Vol. 66, No. 3, Spring, 1990.
Using the ideas of children, this study included folktales, language, jewelry, plants, insects, and much more! It is a valuable reminder to leave room in your plan book for all the inspirations of the children you teach.

Gollnick, Donna M., and Philip C. Chinn. *Multicultural Education in a Pluralistic Society*. Charles E. Merrill Publishing Co., 1986. Examination of various microcultures and the individual variations of identity precedes sections that describe effective practices for planning multicultural experiences.

Greenfeld, Frederic. *Games of the World*. UNICEF. Plenary Publications International, Inc., 1975. Children learn to play and make games from around the world through colorful photographs and drawings. Learning a bit of history adds to the enjoyment of this experience. Careful selection can provide young children with appropriate games. Suggestions are Piñata, closely associated with the Mexican celebration of Christmas, Tangram, Japanese Kite Flying, Hopi Kickball, and Chinese Rope Kicking.

Guidice, Angela, and Sheli Wortis, eds. *Cultural Links: A Multicultural Resource Guide*. Lamplight Press, 1987. An enormous directory of organizations and individuals who in recent years have promoted a respect for diversity through workshops, consultation assistance, and program and curriculum development on topics covering African Americans, Arabs, Asians, Jews, American Indians, and other groups.

Guidelines for Selecting Bias-Free Textbooks and Storybooks. The Council on Interracial Books for Children (1841 Broadway, New York, 10023), 1980.
Evaluation guidelines for many cultural topics and books, including "Ten Quick Ways to Analyze Children's Books."

Hirsch, E.D., Jr., Joseph F. Kett, and James Trefil. *The Dictionary of Cultural Literacy*. Houghton Mifflin Co., 1987.
Believing that a shared body of knowledge facilitates communication and defines and distinguishes a culture, the authors have compiled a catalogue of "what every American needs to know."

Honey, Elizabeth, et al. *Festivals: Ideas from Around the World.* Delmar Publishers, 1988.
This nifty book from Australia explores festivals and other cultural features of twelve countries.

Jenkins, Esther, and Mary C. Austin. *Literature for Children About Asians and Asian Americans.* Greenwood Press, 1987.
Outstanding information and an annotated bibliography of children's and adult literature from many Asian countries.

Kalman, Bobbie. *We Celebrate the New Year*. Crabtree Publishing Company, 1985.
People around the world celebrate the New Year at different times and in different ways. This informative book's beautiful format and splendid illustrations give the adult ideas for planning this celebration. Facts on food, games, costumes, and parades make this a useful book for any educator planning an enriched environment.

Kendall, Frances E. *Diversity in the Classroom: A Multicultural Approach to the Education of Young Children.* Teachers College Press, 1983.
Teachers of young children will find this book to be an excellent guide for developing a multicultural curriculum. The author's experiences enable her to teach others how to present differences between people as positive qualities.

Kitano, Harry H. L. *Race Relations*. Prentice Hall, Inc., 1980.
Written from the author's viewpoint, this text analyzes racial practices in order to achieve racial equality and justice.

Legg, Phyllida, and Robert Harrold. *Folk Costumes of the World.* Brandford Press, 1978.
To accommodate the growing interest in folk costumes, this book is included. It describes costumes that are used mainly for dancing. These folk garments are also worn in villages in Europe, Asia, and the Americas, and are not considered to be fancy dress. A plea is made to appreciate the authenticity of color and materials.

Lewis, F. N., and Jane Margold. *Children's World View: The Basis for Learning Activities.* Far West Laboratory, 1981.
This is a companion volume to *Responsive Multicultural Basic Skills Handbook for Teachers and Parents: Overview*. Culture-based activities for first through third-graders are further explained using photographs, illustrations of children's work, and sample forms, as well as written directions.

Neugebauer, Bonnie, ed. *Alike and Different: Exploring Our Humanity with Young Children.* Exchange Press, Inc., 1987.
A host of experts on cultural matters voice their beliefs and plans for creating learning environments for young children that facilitate their multicultural awareness.

Pasternak, Michael G. *Helping Kids Learn Multi-Cultural Concepts*. Research Press, 1979.
Parent groups, teachers, and older children gain from these clever ideas that foster appreciation of cultures.

Pytowski, Eva Irena, and Gail Willett. *Theme-Centered Bibliography of Children's Literature: Books with Themes of Personal, Cultural, and Social Empowerment*. Savannah Books, 1987.
This approach to multicultural education suggests that children develop a sense of cultural identity. It includes an outstanding bibliography with suggested thematic content.

Ramsey, Patricia. *Teaching and Learning in a Diverse World: Multicultural Education for Young Children*. Teachers College Press, 1987.

Ramsey, Patricia, Edwina Vold, and Leslie Williams. *Multicultural Education: A Source Book*. Garland Publishing, Inc., 1989.

This book addresses the current dilemma in the area of providing multicultural experiences for children, reviews major issues and changes in our historical understanding, and lists annotated sources.

Reid, William, Jr. *100 Craft Projects from Around the World.* Distributed by OlivePress, 1982.
An excellent resource for teachers planning activities that introduce children to the craftspeople of the world's many cultures. Historical sketches at the start of each craft add to the cultural experience. There are folk arts and crafts from nineteen countries, including Mexico, China, Japan, and Southeast Asia.

Saracho, Olivia N., and Bernard Spodek, eds. *Understanding the Multicultural Experience in Early Childhood Education.* NAEYC, 1983.
A text for sensitizing teachers to the nature of multiculturalism. Some educational methods and materials are suggested.

Seelye, H. Ned. *Teaching Culture.* National Textbook Company, 1984.
A book written for the teacher who needs a text that examines testing, culture shock, and ways to organize cultural instruction.

Shepherd, Mary, and Ray Shepherd. *Vegetable Soup.* Citation Press, 1975.
New and unusual ethnic experiences for children. Some of the ideas are more appropriate for school-age children.

Stanush, Barbara Evans. *Texans: A Story of Texas Cultures for Young People.* University of Texas Institute of Texan Cultures at San Antonio, 1988.
Excellent resource with a multitude of illustrations, colorful photographs, and meaningful information about the resettlement of fifteen diverse groups in Texas.

Texas Department of Human Resources. *Culture and Children,* 1985.
This book presents many useful and interesting cultural experiences and includes a section on how to enrich the environment, which is valuable when introducing children to a curriculum with a cultural focus.

Tiedt, Pamela L., and Iris M. Tiedt. *Multicultural Teaching: A Handbook of Activities, Information and Resources.* Allyn and Bacon, Inc., 1986.
This useful directory for locating materials and information and searching for background on ESL students and bilingualism is suitable for adults working with older children.

Tremblay, Helene. *Families of the World: Family Life at the Close of the 20th Century. The Americas and the Caribbean.* Farrar, Straus, and Giroux, 1988.
Profiles of thirty-seven families are presented. Statistics describe each country's education, health, and housing. Photographs and stories about the families fulfill the author's goal to "help us to get closer to people in distant countries and support the knowledge that "we are one."

Williams, Leslie R., and Yvonne Gaetano with Alerta Staff. *Alerta: A Multicultural Bilingual Approach to Teaching Young Children.* Addison-Wesley Publishing Co., 1985.
This book offers one approach to a multicultural, bilingual curriculum for young children. Alerta was designed to be used with various programs for young children. It is a sourcebook that builds upon the knowledge and experiences children bring to school. For example, one topic is "discovering the cultures in the classroom."

Films, Filmstrips, and Videos
Homes and Neighborhoods. Society for Visual Education, 1988. P
This series of six tapes focuses on home, school, neighborhood, and geographical features of the earth. Teachers can stop frames as needed to accommodate children's level of development and interest and to discuss and extend the material. As children learn to appreciate differences and similarities between various social groups, they learn to accept diversity in themselves and others.

Neighborhoods and Communities. Society for Visual Education, 1987. P
"To help students see how they are linked to others in their homes, schools, communities, and the world" heads the list of objectives for this excellent series of eight filmstrip/audiocassette sets. Presented in an interesting format for older children, the filmstrips can be adapted for younger children.

North America: Land of Many Peoples. Produced and distributed by National Geographic Society, 1983. KP
Children learn that North Americans share traditions begun here and in other lands in this 16-minute filmstrip. Ethnic music, handcrafts, foods, sports, and dances are described.

Someone Special...Me. Society for Visual Education, 1976. KP
To start the great adventure of learning about diversity, importance is placed on beginning to understand how we are like and unlike others. This set of six filmstrips with audiocassettes enables children to learn about values and responsibilities as members of a family and a community.

Supporting Cultural Awareness in Young Children. Produced and distributed by High Scope Educational Research Foundation, 1979.
"Culture is a part of all of our lives." This set explains the importance of knowing the family, the rituals, and the customs that accompany the child to the classroom. Direction is given on how to select cultural props that encourage a child to feel part of the classroom and to understand other cultures.

Understanding Our Families. Society for Visual Education, 1988. KP
This excellent set of four filmstrips with audiocassettes identifies how families are alike and different. The importance of family rules, responsibilities, and needs is presented, and along with the profound influ-ence these have on the development of positive self-esteem.

Materials and Experiences
Ethnic Doll Collection. Educational Teaching Aids, No. 8325-E9
Hispanic, Black, Asian, Indian, and Anglo dolls are sold separately.

Ethnic Dolls. Childcraft.
These dolls foster ethnic pride and role-playing. Hispanic, Asian, American Indian, and Black dolls are included.

Girl and Boy Dolls. Childcraft.
Names that help to identify ethnicity are stereotypical.

Large Block Play Figures. Childcraft, No. 115998.
Eight-inch set consists of seven nonsexist, multi-ethnic career figures.

Multi-Ethnic Dolls. Childcraft.
Hispanic, Asian, and Black vinyl dolls have realistic features.

Standard Block Play Figures. Childcraft, No. 151233.
Wooden play figures, 5 1/2 inches tall, include multi-ethnic characters.

Games and Manipulatives
Friends Around the World: A Game of World Peace. Distributed by Smithsonian Institution, Department 0006, Washington D.C., 20073-0006. KP
Cooperative play features children in traditional clothing in this clever game with the goal of achieving world peace.

Where in the World. Claudia's Caravan, No. 19E.
For older children, this game contains information about geography and culture. Good classroom fun!

All of Us. Judy/Instructo. No. J050024.
Eight-piece puzzle depicts multi-ethnic group.

Career Awareness Puzzles. Educational Teaching Aids, 8215-E9.
Set of eight hardwood puzzles depicts nonsexist and nonracist roles.

Community Friends. Judy/Instructo. No. J050025.
Black policeman and mail carrier in a nine-piece puzzle.

Ethnic Face Puzzles. Educational Teaching Aids, No. 8793-E9.
Wooden puzzles set includes Asian and African faces.

Family Puzzles. Educational Teaching Aids, No. 8402-E9.
Hardwood puzzles that can stand up depict a black family.

Just Like Us People Puzzles. Educational Teaching Aids, No. 8760-E9.
Color prints on wood. Set of nine puzzles with 9-20 pieces each. Multi-ethnic considerations.

Nonsexist Career Puzzles. Childcraft, No. 140954.
Set of eight includes people at work. Both sexes and several racial and ethnic groups are depicted.

People Puzzles. Educational Teaching Aids, No. 8595-99.

Set of eight puzzles, free of sexist, racist stereotypes, focuses on careers.

United States and World Puzzles. Judy/Instructo.
Numerous choices of woodboard and floor map puzzles designed for older children.

Woodboard Inlay Puzzles. Judy/Instructo.
Many puzzles to choose from with nonsexist, nonracist intentions, focusing on occupations.

Musical Instruments. Childcraft.
Maracas, wood blocks, castanets, tub drums, tom-toms, and koko drums with authentic African sound are available.

Rhythm Band Instruments. Kaplan.
This company offers bongos, tom-toms, maracas, and the slit log.

Rhythm Instruments. Oscar Schmidt.
Numerous instruments include some used in programs fostering cultural awareness—maracas, castanets, wood blocks, sticks, and others.

Rhythm Instruments. ABC Supply Co.
Bongos, tom-toms, maracas, and the Ella Jenkins' rhythm set are listed in the catalog.

Children of the World Posters. Childcraft, No. 154443.
Sixteen 14 1/2-by-19 1/4-inch multicultural posters describe the clothing, homes, and lifestyles of children "from Africa to Mexico."

Children's Book Council Order Center. 350 Scotland Rd., Orange, NJ 07050.
Individual posters and poster sets with "International Literacy Year," "Families Reading Together," and "Posters for Peace" themes feature the work of Mitsumasa Anno (Japanese), Felipe Davalos (Mexican), John Steptoe (African-American), and other famous illustrators and may be used to enrich your school environment.

Human Relationship Study Prints. Educational Teaching Aids.
Study prints include "Living Together in America" and "Children Around the World."

NAEYC Posters.
The National Association for the Education of Young Children offers award-winning posters for the classroom for $4.00 each. Discounts are available.

Records and Audiocassettes
Earthmother Lullabies 1 and 2. Distributed by Music for Little People.
Iroquois, Latin American, and African-American cradle songs head the list of songs on this tape of lullabies from around the world.

Fink, Cathy. *When the Rain Comes Down.* Distributed by Smithsonian/Folkways.
Ethnic styles are explored in these children's selections.

Glass, Henry, and Rosemary Hallum. *Around the World in Dance.* Educational Activities, Inc., 1972. PI
"Mowrah Cawkak" (Nigerian folk song) and "Rabbit and the

Fox" (American Indian) can easily be learned by children. Old favorites "Bingo" and "Hokey Pokey" are good for warm-up. Children are introduced to a rich new vocabulary and rhythms.

Hello, Everybody. Distributed by Kaplan School Supply Co. LP album, 1X16479.
Music and lyrics for Puerto Rican, Chinese, and African-American folk songs.

Jenkins, Ella. *I Know the Colors of the Rainbow.* Kaplan. No. KAC595.
This tape for young children has some of the favorites.

_____. *Seasons for Singing.* Distributed by Smithsonian/Folkways.
Songs from around the world are presented for children.

_____. *We Are America's Children.* Distributed by Smithsonian/Folkways.
"We Are Native American Tribes," "Black Children Was Born," and "This Land Is Your Land" head the list of favorites that encourage singing and playing along.

Language 30. Claudia's Caravan, No. 39H.
Choose the Chinese (Mandarin), Japanese, Korean, Spanish, or Vietnamese language to learn with the help of these tapes. A dictionary and audiocassettes are provided.

Moore, Thomas. *Thomas Moore Sings Our Community.* Produced and distributed by Thomas Moore records.

Mr. Moore's rich baritone leads a spunky group of young voices and reminds all to "love together, people who are dark and people who are light." Other records distributed by the same company and with the aim of cultural awareness include *I Am Special Just Because I'm Me and Celebrate Children,* with Thomas Moore.

Palmer, Hap. *Holiday Songs and Rhythms.* Kaplan, No. KAC538. "Cinco de mayo" is included on this tape with a holiday emphasis.

Raffi. *One Light, One Sun.* Educational Teaching Aids, No. 9253H-E9. Shoreline Records, 6043 Yonge St., Willowdale, Ontario, Canada M2M 3W3 Songs dealing with feelings about oneness.

Slonecki, Catherine. *Children's Songs Around the World.* Educational Activities, Inc., LP record ARS6, 1989.
Such favorites as "Flower Drum Song" from China, "Shalom Alecheim" from Israel, and Mexico's "Cielito lindo" are included in this collection. Children learn the songs as they hear the rhythms, instrumental sounds, and other children's voices. The snappy tune of Australia's "Waltzing Matilda" encourages all ages to chime in. This tape can also be used as background music. Children join in the musical experience in a very natural way.

Catalogs and Supply Houses
ABC School Supply, Inc., P.O. Box 4750, Norcross, GA 30091-4750.
A nice selection of ethnic dolls, puppets, puzzles, and Lego people.

Childcraft, 20 Kilmer Rd., P.O. Box 3081, Edison, NJ 08818. Large block play figures, wooden family figures, animals from the "wilds of Africa and jungles of China," doll families, pliable people, ethnic dolls, puzzles, instruments, and globes are described with color pictures and annotations.

Claudia's Caravan (Multicultural/Multilingual Materials), P. O. Box 1582, Alameda, CA 94501. Selected materials for providing a multicultural approach. Claudia lists books for adults and children, bilingual books, games, records, tapes, puppets, and dolls. The Caravan distributes all the Count Your Way Through... Series. Includes Africa, China, Japan, Korea, Mexico, and others.

Educational Teaching Aids, 199 Carpenter Ave., Wheeling, IL 60090.